# On the Titanic in a Delicate Condition

# On the Titanic in a Delicate Condition

by

Ned W. Schillow

and

Dru T. Schillow

Cover design by Kate Howell Design

Front cover photo credits:
Left: Eloise Smith holding Lucian Smith II (Source: Downtown Morgantown Walking Tours, The Clio)
Right: Madeleine Astor holding John Jacob "Jakey" Astor VI (Source: Encyclopedia Titanica)

Back cover photo credit:
The *Titanic* immediately after being launched on May 31, 1991, in Belfast (Source: Titanic Belfast)

ISBN-13: 9781072472643

Printed by Kindle Direct Publishing

10 9 8 7 6 5 4 3

# *Dedication*

*This book is dedicated to our baby brother*
GUY JAMES SCHILLOW
*Born with a delicate condition*
*August 31, 1952*
*Died*
*Nov. 25, 1952*

*and it is also dedicated to the women on the Titanic who were carrying life as they struggled to save their own*

# Table of Contents

# Preface

*Having children just puts the whole world into perspective.*
*Everything else just disappears.*

*--Kate Winslet*

It had been eleven years since we, as brothers, worked as co-authors on our two short novels, *Titanic Hearts* and *Titanic Tears.* Dru was clearly the guiding force for both of those books, which were intended for a juvenile audience. Then, starting five years ago, Ned tackled four works of non-fiction, with Dru providing solid back-up in terms of his *Titanic* knowledge-base, resources, and willingness to do a great deal of proof-reading. At long last our schedules have finally worked out for the two of us to work together once again as co-authors, but first we needed to settle on a topic.

Our interest in the *Titanic* runs deeps, so it was not difficult to come up with ideas. We quickly turned our thoughts to the parents and children aboard the *Titanic,* particularly focusing on the mothers. This offered a real possibility. Mothers in 1912 were clearly in charge of the upbringing of their children. Even in the cases where both parents were aboard the ship, it would be the mothers who needed to look after their sons and daughters, to keep them occupied, and to tend to all their needs, while the fathers were far freer to come and go as they pleased. Very few of the women were traveling with a nursemaid, tutor, or other caregiver to help with their children, so the mothers were often alone with their offspring, much as they would have been back home. Of course, little has been written about how the women and children spent their time on the *Titanic,* and we were not about to create novel-like descriptions out of whole cloth. We began to focus our preliminary thoughts on whether we could learn enough about the backgrounds of these women and their loving, protective roles as they attempted to save their children when the crisis occurred. Then we started mulling over some of the stories that we already knew about these mothers, and things took a decidedly dreadful turn.

We recalled Augusta Goodwin, who was aboard the ship with her husband, Frederick, and their six children. The offspring ranged in age from 16-year-old Lillian down to their toddler, Sidney, only one year and seven months old. What kind of frantic feelings must have filled Augusta's soul as she and Frederick tried to gather their entire family together in the confusing corridors of third-class and negotiate their way to whatever escape might be available on the Boat Deck? In the end, all eight members of the family died that night, leaving the reason for their failure to reach the lifeboats completely unknown.

Certainly we could write about Maria Panula and her five children, who were on their way to Coal Center, near Pittsburgh Pennsylvania, where her husband already lived. When Maria had come aboard the *Titanic* with the children, she may have been assisted by her former neighbor in Finland, Susanna Riihivuori, who possibly was acting as a family maid.

Maria's protective love for her children was unquestionable. Her care for them was intensified by the fact that she had already lost three children over the years, including Emma, who died at the age of nine by drowning. Now Maria found herself on a sinking ship, water rushing in, completely separated from her oldest two boys. Despite the fact that they were only fifteen and sixteen years old, they had been housed with the single men at the opposite end of the *Titanic*. Driven by a mother's need to protect her children and refusing to have any more of her children drown, she was determined to gather everybody together and move them to safety. Unfortunately, having her family spread out over the entire ship and dealing with the confusion that overwhelmed the steerage corridors, she failed in her effort. Like the Goodwin family, none of them escaped the sinking.

It is all too easy to be critical of Maria's fatal choice to not lead the younger children to the Boat Deck that could have at least saved some of them. Realistically, decisions that needed to be made while the *Titanic* was foundering were impacted by a situation unlike anything the mothers had ever faced. Certainly, the conditions did not provide the opportunity for carefully honed arguments, and we knew that the first-class Allison family would be a perfect case in point. Initially, Hudson Allison felt no major concern when the early news about the *Titanic's* plight came to his attention, and apparently his wife, Bess, at least tacitly agreed. The family nurse, Alice Cleaver, was not so casual in her reaction. She bundled up Hudson Jr., better known as Trevor, and headed up to the lifeboats. By the time the Allisons accepted the danger of the situation, the nurse and their infant son were nowhere to be found.

Up they went to the lifeboats, and Hudson saw to it that Bess and their two-year-old daughter, Loraine, were safely seated in one of the boats. Overcome with grief and giving into her maternal instinct regarding her missing son, Bess struggled her way out of the lifeboat, pulling Loraine along with her, and back they went onto the deck. Bess was mentally and emotionally unwilling to leave the ship without baby Trevor, nor could she relinquish Loraine into somebody else's care, which would have allowed her little girl to be saved. Mother and daughter stood hand-in-hand, looking about, hoping beyond hope that Trevor would suddenly appear. What was motivated by a misbegotten act of love meant that only the Allison baby would survive and that Loraine would become the only child in all of first- and second-class to die that night.

Tragic story upon tragic story began to pile up. Dru recalled the Danboms from Sweden. Anna was traveling with her husband, sister, brother-in-law, a family friend, and her baby son Gilbert, who was just two days shy of his five-month birthday. They never managed to gain access to a lifeboat, and the image of Anna tightly holding on to her baby as the *Titanic* went down seems inescapable. The horrible combination of love, fear, and resignation had to play with her emotions as fate took the life of the youngest *Titanic* victim along with his mother.

This was not necessarily the end of the Danbom story. Five days later, the SS *Bremen* entered the waters where the *Titanic* sank, and onlookers aboard the ship looked soberly at a scene that included all kinds of flotsam and jetsam with chairs, doors, tables, pillows, and icebergs peppering the sea. Suddenly, a cry rang out and fingers pointed. Bodies were spotted, scattered amidst the debris. Leoni Hermann was only eleven at the time, but she remained forever haunted by a sight that drew her attention. "The first one was a lady with a baby. We ran downstairs and told them [the crew], everybody came up.... Everybody was crying." While there is no way to know if this was Anna and her baby, Gilbert, such is a haunting possibility.

The two of us pondered the negative, heart-wrenching direction our discussion had taken. To be sure, there were some wonderful survival stories among the third-class passengers involving the mothers and their children. We were both well aware of the tales involving Leah Aks and her ten-month-old son Filly and Thelma Thomas and her five-month-old son Assad.

In both situations mother and son ended up in different lifeboats as a result of the growing confusion on the ship. In Leah's case, her child was ripped from her arms and thrown into a lifeboat that departed before she could get in. In contrast, Thelma had been hustled into a lifeboat first, but almost immediately the sailors started to lower the boat before her brother-in-law, Charles, was able to hand the baby to her. Both mothers were panicked and nothing could be done to ease their fear. The tearful hours they endured as the lifeboats bobbed about on the frigid water seemed endless, especially for Thelma who had no idea whether Charles had been able to get her son into another boat. Fortunately, those hours of fearful uncertainty at sea were followed by joyful reunions on the *Carpathia*.

But then our thoughts turned to the Asplunds, and we were back to tragedy once again. Selma Asplund threaded her way to the Boat Deck, clenching the hands of two of her young children, Lilian and Felix. The three of them boarded one of the lifeboats together. Unlike the Goodwins, Panulas, and Allisons, Selma's maternal instincts were sufficiently intact during the growing frenzy, and she understood that she needed to save the children who were with her rather than waiting for her husband and her other three children to arrive. Sadly, the rest of the family never made it to the lifeboats. We could not fully imagine the tearful difficulty Selma faced with the surviving children once they reached the *Carpathia*, where the fates of the rest of the family became clear. The loss must have been overwhelming, made especially unbearable by the reality that five-year-old Lilian's twin brother, Carl, was among the family members who died.

By this time, we were beginning to question whether a book focused on the mothers and children aboard the *Titanic* was too sorrowful a topic to pursue. Of course, with the exception of Loraine Allison, the survival of all the other first- and second-class children and their mothers would be full of positive stories. In a few cases there were moments of contention when the sailors tried to bar the older boys from boarding the lifeboats, but in the end the mothers prevailed in protecting their offspring. The ongoing cry of "mothers and children first" ultimately worked in their favor, and for these women it was almost as simple as just appearing at the lifeboats with their children in hand. But third-class realities created a startlingly different story. Only 34% of these children survived with a corresponding rate for their mothers. Frantic crowds, confusion in lower deck corridors, conflicting instructions, and frightened inaction overwhelmed far too many of them.

We figured we could effectively deal with this disparity between the classes, but the germ of our idea regarding the joys, love, and protective instincts of the *Titanic* mothers was turning into a treatise on the sociological mores of the day. We were compromising our initial idea of writing a book that would capture motherhood at its finest among the women on the fated ship.

Then another thought bubbled to the surface. There was a group of mothers-to-be whose unborn children constituted the youngest survivors of all, even though their names did not appear on any manifest. Of course, some of the women were so early in their pregnancies that they did not yet know they were with child. But those who knew they had newborns on the way had already experienced that initial rush of joy and excitement and love when they imagined what the future held. We decided that it would be fascinating to research the mothers aboard the *Titanic* who are known or suspected to have been pregnant at the time that they sailed. Only a few of these women were already familiar to us, so we would have a lot to learn on our journey, and their personal stories would provide a good mix of both joy and sorrow. We had our topic; our minds were made up. We could finally get our research underway.

In memory of these 17 women, we, the authors, will donate 17% of our royalties from the sales of this book to the Maternity Care Coalition, serving families across southeastern Pennsylvania. The goal of this organization is a noble one, and they clearly state that "the mission of Maternity Care

Coalition is to improve the health and well-being of pregnant women and parenting families, and enhance school readiness for children 0-3."

Maternity Care Coalition

*Strengthening families, inspiring change*

# A Note to the Reader

*There are two lasting bequests we can give our children. One is roots. The other is wings.*

*--Hodding Carter Jr.*

When we set out to write this book, we hoped to capture a true sense of the lives and vitality of the seventeen women aboard the *Titanic* who were awaiting the births of their children. Naturally, the story of the ill-fated ship bears a heavy burden of tragedy, and some of these women were included among those whose lives were lost when the ship went down. But in the days that preceded the disaster, these women would have been enjoying the adventure of being at sea, amazed by what the ship had to offer regardless of what class they were in, and eagerly looking forward to reaching America. For those who already knew that they were with child, there was the added bonus of joy and wondrous anticipation of what the future had to offer.

The major problem we faced was that historical evidence rarely addresses such emotional issues. Home towns, siblings' names, marriage records, reasons for being aboard the *Titanic,* stateroom assignments, and even the number of the lifeboat in which someone was rescued might be available, but these are little more than a litany of facts. We wanted to be sure that our stories about these women were filled with a sense of life that would serve as a welcomed reflection of the lives they carried within. Our goal was to provide more than a listing of facts that would seem like little more than bland summaries of cardboard characters.

Part of this was easy to accomplish. Even though there is little or no direct evidence of how these future mothers spent their time on the ship, certain activities could readily be assumed. Naturally, there was the excitement of being on a new ship on its maiden voyage. This certainly would prompt every person who boarded with the temptation to roam whatever portion of the ship they were entitled to be in, to explore its corridors and public rooms, and to acquaint themselves with their new surroundings. It seemed safe to assume that every individual on the ship stood by the railing at some point, peering at the ocean or looking up to the night sky. With the incredible restaurants that White Star had created for the *Titanic,* surely each of the women must have enjoyed and commented on the wonderful dining experiences and the delicious meals that were offered. Describing these future mothers engaged in such simple shipboard realities would bring a sense of life into their stories.

That said, we also decided to introduce each chapter with a scenario that was not backed by well-supported evidence, but which we hope the reader finds feasible and believable, if not necessarily accurate. It is hard to imagine Ada Doling leaving for a month to visit her mother in New York without some sort of special goodbye to her four sons. It seems reasonable that the Wests searched for ways to entertain their four-year-old daughter during the long voyage beyond merely staying in their cabin and walking the decks. Knowing that the Marvins were 18-year-old newlyweds with a motion picture camera on hand made it natural to imagine them laughing and pointing and racing from one location to the next as they photographed the ship's departure from Southampton. And so the listing of scenarios continued to grow.

We encourage the reader to not worry about the historical record as they read the beginning of each chapter. The facts will follow. Instead, enjoy the possibility of being swept up in the moment with these mothers-to-be and their loved ones. Be embraced by the fact that these were real individuals who were themselves caught up in amazing surroundings and experiences. Understand that every one of them was buoyed up by the hopes and dreams of what lay ahead. Join them on their journey.

# Introduction

*I think that I see something deeper, more infinite, more eternal than the ocean in the expression of the eyes of a little baby when it wakes in the morning and coos or laughs because it sees the sun shining on its cradle.*

*--Vincent Van Gogh*

Under normal circumstances it should have been a simple, uneventful crossing. Of course, the room stewards would be kept busy with the 743 passengers who were aboard the *Carpathia*, but that total was nowhere near the ship's full capacity. Most of the 128 first-class passengers were looking forward to their upcoming holidays along the Mediterranean coast, and the New York to Trieste run would conveniently transport them to Italy. Many of the passengers were elderly couples, but a small number of starry-eyed honeymooners were also aboard. All of them would welcome the warm climate that they were heading toward. Twice during the winter the temperature had dipped below zero in New York City, the upper Midwest had been unusually frigid, and snows in New England and the mid-Atlantic states had grown tiresome. Spring weather would soon be arriving, but in the meantime the Mediterranean warmth would provide a most welcome change.

So far, however, the honeymoon couples had not found much opportunity to linger on the decks whispering sweet nothings to one another, given the annoyingly cold conditions during their first three days at sea. At least the 14th had been sunny and warm, but by early evening the temperature grew quite chilly again. This was certainly not the sort of weather to enjoy outdoors, and the passengers turned in for the night rather than spending time gazing over the ship's railings. Meanwhile, Captain

Arthur Rostron was forced to decrease the speed of the ship due to reports of icebergs. This would definitely delay their progress towards warmer weather, but safety was what mattered.

Another 50 second-class passengers were aboard the *Carpathia* anticipating their own vacations. The 565 in third-class were mostly immigrants who had settled in America but were now heading back to their former homelands, looking forward to visits with family and friends. Some already planned to accompany their relatives or former fellow-villagers to the "Land of Promise" when it was time to return to the United States.

To be sure, the room and deck stewards as well as the kitchen staff knew that the 743 passengers would keep them busy, but they never anticipated that more than 700 additional passengers would board the ship in mid-ocean. During the early morning hours of April 15, 1912, the *Carpathia* sped to the area of the Atlantic where the *Titanic* had sunk during the night. The passengers on the *Carpathia* had no idea that anything unusual had occurred until they began to pick up subtle signs that something was amiss. Some of them had their sleep disturbed by the unusual sounds emanating from the outer decks. The vibrations of the ship created by its higher-than-normal speed roused others. A bit later the *Carpathia* stopped moving entirely, and that seemed equally odd.

Some of the passengers finally threw on their robes or heavy coats and headed out from their cabins, only to discover that stewards were piling blankets in the corridors and that a few of the lifeboats were swung out. The crew members assured the inquisitive passengers that all was well and that the *Carpathia* was not sinking, but all this extraordinary activity was enough to keep them on deck, peering into the darkness.

Dawn finally arrived, and eventually twenty lifeboats appeared, bobbing about in the icy waters. The crew of the *Carpathia* took the survivors aboard with impressive efficiency. Faced with the task of meeting the needs of a passenger tally that had suddenly doubled, the victualling crew members performed admirably, taxing their own fortitude and resolve, providing meals, rounding up spare blankets, and setting up dormitory-like quarters in every spare inch of public space the ship had to offer.

The women who could not be accommodated in private quarters were generally moved into the dining saloons, the women's writing room, or the library. Many of the men ended up in the smoking rooms or were provided space somewhere along the corridors. A small number settled down on the outer decks, wrapping themselves in heavy blankets. The survivors endured the discomfort of sleeping on hard table tops or floors, perhaps cushioned by a few towels or old blankets, with a few fortunate enough to have been provided with straw mats. A room full of snoring men and the general bustle of dozens of people nearby did not provide easy sleeping conditions over the coming days and nights, but exhaustion eventually provided the rest they so desperately needed.

The closest port of call was Halifax, Nova Scotia, but heading there would entail sailing through heavy ice conditions. Such would have been a questionable idea in any event, and to subject the *Titanic* survivors to such a passage would have been mentally tortuous for them. The most cost-effective route for the Cunard liner would have been to continue eastward to the Azores, still moving the ship in the general direction of its final destination, but food supplies for the expanded number on hand would not last that long. Captain Rostron also eliminated Boston as a possibility when he came to realize that the best option was to return to New York. This decision would inconvenience the *Carpathia* and its regular passengers, but it would best meet the needs of the *Titanic* survivors who were originally heading to that city as their ultimate destination.

Many of the passengers and upper-level crew members aboard the *Carpathia* contributed personal assistance to the sudden influx of individuals. Some gave up their cabins, or at least offered the unoccupied berths in their own rooms. In other cases, *Carpathia* passengers moved into cabins with one another, freeing up additional space that provided true privacy for some of the *Titanic* survivors. As a result, many of the first-class women and a few of the more well-connected men from the *Titanic* ended up in quarters appropriate for their status.

Among the women provided with her own quarters was Madeleine Astor. She was not yet 19 years old, and she suddenly found herself widowed as a result of her husband's death when the *Titanic* went down. Colonel John Jacob Astor IV had been the richest man aboard the ship, but that money meant little to Madeleine now as she dealt with her sorrow.

Overall, the *Carpathia* had become a ship of widows. The tragic deaths of their husbands left many women grieving throughout the four days it would take them to reach New York. Some remained virtually silent; some stifled their tears and sobs until they could cry no more; some simply withdrew as much as possible; some were inconsolable and mentally overwrought as evidenced by their uncontrollable wails.

Making the effort to provide whatever support they could, passengers aboard the *Carpathia* provided spare clothing, toiletries, or even simple access to their cabins during the daytime so that the survivors could fix their hair or lie down for a brief bit of comfort. Unfortunately, their generosity was no match for the hundreds of persons who only had the clothes on their backs, including those who were wearing only the skimpiest of nightclothes or kimonos when they escaped the sinking ship.

Of course, some of the widows, as well as those couples fortunate enough to survive together, had to rise to the task of comforting their own children and meeting their needs. The older teenagers could fend for themselves, at least to some extent. Jack Thayer was a 17-year-old who miraculously survived the night as one of the group of men who balanced upon overturned collapsible B. He also was one of the fortunate first-class males provided with private quarters on the *Carpathia*. His mother, Marian, also survived, but his father, John, Second Vice President of the Pennsylvania Railroad, had gone to his death. One of the *Carpathia* passengers provided Jack with a bunk and some warm, dry pajamas so he could recover from his ordeal. Jack certainly appreciated this and soon fell asleep, but found himself strangely intrigued by the fact that after he was taken aboard he had accepted some brandy to offset the cold which had chilled him to the bone. He had never partaken of hard liquor before, and this added an odd recollection to his memorably horrible experience.

The younger teens and the older children tended to stay close to their mothers, at least at first. Sadness and confusion made this a comforting routine, but four more days at sea was too long to maintain such ongoing proximity. Ruth Becker was only twelve and fully realized how fortunate she had been. How grateful she was that her father remained safe in India, completing his service as a missionary. The rest of her family were present with her on the *Carpathia*. Her mother, Nellie, and the two younger children were rescued in lifeboat 11, and Ruth would have been there as well had her mother not asked her to run back to their cabin to gather some additional blankets. Ruth did not return in time to make it into the same lifeboat with the rest of her family, and only after their joyful reunion on the *Carpathia* did Nellie learn that her daughter was rescued in lifeboat 13.

However, Ruth now found herself completely bored. She had done her best to entertain her siblings in this peculiar circumstance and helped her mother as needed. But she also wanted to discover another way to pass the time other than just walking the decks. Sneaking sugar cubes from the tables provided just the sort of diversion she craved.

The first few hours aboard the *Carpathia* had not been boring for Ruth, of course. Not only was her reunion with the rest of her family a highlight, she also was involved in trying to locate Leah Aks's son. Leah had also been rescued in lifeboat 13 and sat near Ruth during that long night. In a reversal of the Becker family's situation, Leah's son Philip was on his own in lifeboat 11, but the circumstance was startlingly different. Little Filly (also known as Frank), was only ten months old and had been torn from his mother's arms during the confusion of the *Titanic* evacuation. At least Leah had some comfort in seeing her baby tossed into lifeboat 11, so she knew he was probably safe. But the night in the lifeboat was a long one as she frantically awaited their reunion on the rescue ship.

Once they reached the *Carpathia,* Ruth and a few other passengers worked diligently to help Leah find her son. At last Leah heard the sound of her baby's cry and found her boy in the arms of an Italian woman. Unfortunately, this other woman insisted the baby was hers, and only through the intervention of Captain Rostron was the mystery solved. Leah provided an unarguable bit of identification when she described the small birthmark on Filly's chest. Perhaps the baby was still wrapped in the shawl that Madeleine Astor had loaned to Leah while they were still on the *Titanic,* but that detail was of no real consequence. At that point, all Leah focused upon was that she and her son would soon be in New York and on their way to Norfolk, Virginia, where her husband Sam resided.

Of course, the babies and toddlers had particular needs that the rescue ship were not prepared for. Three French-speaking women, Mathilde Weisz and her new acquaintances, Juliette Laroche and Antonine Mallet, worked together in this regard. All three women had lost their husbands when the *Titanic* when down, but the latter two were still faced with caring for the needs of their children. Three-year-old Simonne Laroche would occasionally toddle off on her own, with Juliette quickly springing into action to get her daughter back. But that was a problem far more easily solved than the lack of diapers. Only through a clever ruse to round up a sufficient supply of napkins and towels were they able to accumulate their much-needed supply.

Included among the eleven toddlers and nine infants who had been rescued was the youngest survivor of all. Tiny Millvina Dean was only two months and thirteen days old at the time of the sinking. Eva Dean was grieving the loss of her husband, Bertram, but she still needed to attend to her baby Millvina and her son, also named Bertram, who was not yet two years old. Of course, with two such young children to watch after and suddenly being on her own to care for them, it is likely that Eva was glad to accept some assistance while she was aboard the *Carpathia*.

Perhaps she did not realize while she was aboard the *Carpathia* that Millvina was the youngest survivor of the disaster, and certainly she had no interest in hunting her way through the ship to determine such a fact. However, this was something the press jumped on as a human-interest story, and things would get out of hand when the Dean family returned to England aboard the *Adriatic.* Thoroughly intrigued that such a tiny infant like Millvina could have survived the sinking, many of the women aboard the ship were more than willing to stand in a long line for the opportunity to hold the child. One of the officers finally issued an order that a strict ten-minute time limit would be enforced as the maximum time each woman could cradle the baby.

In a very real sense, however, there were survivors aboard even younger than Millvina, which returns us to Madeleine Astor. She had stayed shut away in her room, rarely leaving it other than for meals. Madeleine reflected on all that had occurred, mindlessly resting her hand on her slightly protruding abdomen. She was already five months pregnant, a reality that had led her and the Colonel to cut their European trip short. This unborn child was truly a survivor of the *Titanic* disaster, obviously younger than Millvina Dean, and Madeleine's pregnancy was not unique among the *Titanic* passengers. At least sixteen other women can be counted among those who were with child at the time the *Titanic* sailed, and thirteen of them, including Madeleine, were now scattered about the *Carpathia.* This is their story, as well as the story of the conception and delivery of the *Titanic* itself.

# The Birth of the *Titanic*

*Whatever the mind can conceive and believe it can achieve.*
*--Napoleon Hill*

## Conception (1907)

Florence Ismay carefully set the Chinese porcelain teacup on its matching saucer and turned towards Lady Pirrie. "Margaret, you have outdone yourself. This meal was incredibly delicious."

J. Bruce Ismay immediately chimed in with a hearty "Hear, hear!"

Lady Pirrie graciously acknowledged the compliment while admitting to herself that the cook clearly had risen to the task that evening. The two of them had planned tonight's menu together, and the end result was successful in every way.

When the Ismays had headed to Lord and Lady Pirrie's home in London's Belgrave Square earlier that day, they already knew that the meal would be a fine one. However, the main purpose of dinner at Downshire House that evening was, as usual, for the men to discuss business. At least Lord William Pirrie and Bruce kept their discussion reasonably generic during the meal itself, although it was still focused on joint ventures which had been undertaken between Lord Pirrie's Harland & Wolff Shipyards and Ismay's White Star Line.

The women were quite familiar with the so-called Big Four ships and could easily join the dinner talk about the *Celtic, Cedric, Baltic,* and *Adriatic.* Constructed between 1901 and 1906, each of the first three successively took on the title of the world's largest ship. Moreover, the *Adriatic,* was the largest of them all at 24,451 tons, but by the time it took to the sea it had already been surpassed by the Hamburg Amerika's *Kaiserin Auguste Victoria* at 24,581 tons and which began its runs four months earlier. It was true that the *Adriatic* was still Britain's largest passenger ship, but two Cunard liners were only months away from stealing both the national and the world titles. The *Lusitania,* at 31,550 tons, and *Mauritania,* at 31,928 tons, would give Cunard bragging rights by the end of 1907, and they also would each achieve the Blue Riband status as the world's fastest ship, supplanting the German records of the last decade, and further obscuring White Star's claim on that title from thirty years ago.

*Downshire House, home of Lord William Pirrie, where the* Titanic *and its sister ships were conceived. (Source: History Hub Ulster)*

Now, with dessert and hot beverages completed, Margaret knew it was time to let the men really get down to business. She invited Florence to join her in the parlor, and the women excused themselves from the dining table. William looked at Bruce in anticipation of whatever grand design the latter would suggest as the next major White Star initiative. The emphasis would not be on speed, but rather would focus on size, luxury, and comfort. Just as the *Adriatic* had become the world's first ocean liner with an indoor pool and Turkish bath, Ismay certainly would introduce new innovations that would continue to distinguish White Star from its north-Atlantic competition.

J. P. Morgan, owner of the International Mercantile Marine for which Ismay served as Chairman, had made it clear that he wanted the finest ships afloat under the IMM's umbrella. Now it was time to make White Star shine all the brighter, and Bruce's starting point seemed unexpectedly grand. He was envisioning a new class of ships, the *Olympic* class, and its trio of ships would all be in excess of 45,000 gross tons, a major leap forward in size which would vastly eclipse the Cunard liners. William was immediately excited by the prospect, but he cautiously pointed out that ships that large could not match the *Lusitania* or the *Mauritania* in terms of speed. "That will not matter," came Ismay's reply. "The pure luxury we will offer will make passengers perfectly happy to spend a few additional hours aboard. The experience for those traveling the Atlantic on these ships will be unsurpassed in the industry, and word of mouth alone will supersede Cunard's emphasis on the speed which won them the Blue Riband." Speed was still a consideration, but Ismay re-emphasized that the ocean-going-experience on the White Star liners would be far more noteworthy.

Building such huge vessels, well over 800 feet on length, would be an incredible undertaking, but Lord Pirrie was confident that Harland & Wolff would be up to the task. As the discussion with Ismay continued, additional ideas bubbled to the surface and the two men grew more excited by the prospect. The germ of Ismay's vision and quickly drawn sketches at the dinner table would eventually give way to more precise drawings and planning under an order signed on April 30, 1907. As Lord Pirrie and Bruce Ismay left the dining room to rejoin the women, they had no doubt that their vision could be achieved. The triplet ships, in general, and the *Titanic,* in particular, had been conceived.

## Phase One – The First Trimester (1907-1909)

Conception is one thing, but bringing the vision of the world's largest movable objects to full term would be a challenge. Even before construction could begin, thousands of carefully drawn sketches had to be completed by the Harland & Wolff draftsmen.

A young man, nattily dressed in his black suit and vest, pushed himself back from the table. Somewhat absent-mindedly, he tapped his pencil several times against his forehead, trying to understand how he was to proceed with the sketch of the second class cabin before him. As one of the younger Harland & Wolff draftsmen, it would not be out of line for him to ask one of his colleagues for some advice, but he avoided rushing into doing so. He certainly did not want to risk being known as the new guy who could not even figure out the easiest of instructions.

*Harland and Wolff Drawing Office (Harland & Wolff photograph, converted into a large mural at a special* Titanic *exhibition, Mystic Aquarium, Connecticut, photographed by author on September 25, 2014)*

He looked upward at the sunshine pouring in through the windows in the high arched ceiling of the Drafting Office. "You would think that this would be enough to shed some light on the matter," he mumbled to himself, somewhat bemused by his own wordplay. Who knew that these similar cabins could be so different, with those structural curves, internal pipes and beams, and the supporting skeleton of the ship? Suddenly he realized what needed to be done, and he went back to work, manipulating his drafting tools across the paper with confidence.

Full funding for the *Olympic* class of ships was estimated at £3 million, an immense fortune for the times, and it fell to Bruce Ismay to secure the finances. A combination of making new shares of stock available and redirecting profits realized by the White Star Line would be achieved by July of 1908, and the formal paperwork with Harland & Wolff was signed on the 31st. In the meantime, the majority of the draft sketches needed to be completed. Drafting would continue even after construction began, but sufficient plans had to be in place in order to help refine cost estimates, dictate materials to be requisitioned, and envision what would soon be under physical development. Final planning for the *Gigantic* could wait, but because the *Olympic* and the *Titanic* would be built side-by-side, officials for both the White Star Line and Harland & Wolff needed to fully visualize the task before them.

Lord Pirrie set to work, locating the steel supply needed for these simultaneous projects and securing the manufacturing of the gigantic turbines which would propel such large ships. Lord Pirrie's brother-in-law, Alexander Montgomery Carlisle, assumed the general responsibility for the design of the ship. As General Manager he took on this challenge with a feeling of exhilaration. There was nothing routine about designing ships that were far larger than any others at sea, and the challenge involved far more than simply enlarging an existing model. As he would later explain at the British *Titanic* Inquiry, the ships "were entirely designed practically by Lord Pirrie. The details, the decorations, the equipment, and the general arrangements all came under me."

In many respects, the easiest task involved creating a plan that would accommodate more cabins and suites than had ever been previously imagined, but Bruce Ismay's vision for these new luxury liners also included the challenge of many of the finest amenities. White Star had always been an innovator, introducing dining saloons that spanned the full breadth of the ship nearly forty years ago when the original *Baltic* was commissioned. More recently, Harland & Wolff had incorporated the interior swimming pool and Turkish Bath for the *Adriatic*. But this new class of ships would be incredible, with many two- and even three-room suites in first class, specialized cafés, generously sized lounges for all three classes, and a visually impressive grand staircase. All these features only began to indicate what would be intriguing and incredibly demanding to fit into the overall design.

Carlisle and his team embraced the challenge. Initial decisions were incorporated and then modified as the need arose. Much needed to be learned about the realities in constructing such huge vessels. Double hulls and watertight compartments had to be incorporated into the plans. Structural engineers needed to calculate stress patterns and determine where additional support would be needed.

Crucial to formulating the initial drafts was Thomas Andrews, an architectural specialist and nephew to both Lord Pirrie and Alexander Carlisle. As a Managing Director and head of the drafting department at Harland & Wolff, Andrews helped oversee much of this early work. His responsibilities expanded accordingly when Carlisle unexpectedly retired in 1910 at the relatively young age of 55. By then, the *Olympic* and the *Titanic* were both under construction, although neither ship had yet been launched, and it was Andrews who would handle the leadership for fitting out the twin ships as well as overseeing much of the décor.

On September 17, 1908, orders were delivered to the Harland & Wolff Shipyard for construction to formally begin, although preparation had already been underway. As was true for all such ships, the initial work on the twins' construction had to be handled in slipways. However, the *Olympic* and the *Titanic*, ships numbered 400 and 401 by Harland & Wolff, would be nearly 900 feet in length, and no shipyard in the world had such large facilities in existence. The work to create these new slipways, adjacent to one another, had been grueling. Three existing slipways were reconfigured into two and then reinforced with concrete to support the ships that were to be cradled there. A casual observer might have been impressed by the huge dimensions, but for the workers at the facility, these slipways clearly foreshadowed the construction of ships unlike anything they had ever worked on. Excitement rippled through Harland & Wolff, and many of the men hoped that they would become part of the construction team.

*Slipway preparation for the* Olympic *and the* Titanic, *1907 (Source: Harland & Wolff photograph, National Museums Northern Ireland)*

Actual work on the *Olympic* began in slipway 2 on December 16, followed by the laying of the *Titanic*'s keel in slipway 3 on March 31, 1909. At long last, what had been merely a dream was now becoming a physical reality. The keel – the backbone of the *Titanic* – was a visible indication of what lay ahead.

*Keel of the* Titanic *(Source: Titanic Belfast)*

Olympic *hull in the foreground;* Titanic *keel in the background (Source: David Goran on Vintagenews.com)*

## Phase 2 – The Second Trimester (1909-1910)

The muffled sound of men's heavy work shoes striking cobblestones steadily increased in volume, a clear indicator that it was 5:30 p.m. and the workday had ended for thousands of employees at Harland & Wolff. More and more men poured out of the shipyard, grimy from a long day which had begun at 6:00 a.m. Their pace gave no indication of their exhaustion, however, as these were hard-working laborers, accustomed to the demands of their jobs, and they wanted to return to their homes in the nearby Belfast neighborhoods as soon as possible.

*Workers leaving the Harland & Wolff Dockyards, 1911 (Source: Harland & Wolff Photograph, History Extra)*

But an observant individual might have noticed that something seemed different that day, April 20, 1910. There were far fewer raucous yells and less open laughter than would normally be expected. Word had travelled quickly that afternoon that one of their counterparts had lost his life while working on the *Titanic*. By then only a few of the men had learned the identity of the man who had died, and in hushed tones they asked one another for details about what had occurred and who was involved, wondering if he had been an old friend or a former co-worker whom they had known for years. Quite the opposite. The victim was Sam Scott, a 15-year-old catch boy.

Nobody had actually seen the accident occur, but it was easy to figure out that he had somehow lost his balance while trying to catch a red-hot rivet that was headed his way. Riveters often worked in teams of four, with the additional assistance of the heater boy (also known as the bellow boy) who would heat the rivet to the proper level. He would then use tongs to propel the rivet down a chute or through the air or across the deck. Once the catch boy caught the rivet, he would pass it to the holder-on, who in turn inserted it through a hole, holding it in place with a heavy sledge hammer. Two other men worked on the other side of the plate, alternating their strikes to secure the rivet. A few moments of inattention or an overly aggressive reach on Sam's part had caused him to fall 23 feet from the ladder on the staging where he had been standing. His death was a somber reminder that the birth of the *Titanic* was dramatically intertwined with the specter of death, a reality that all the men laboring in ship-building realized was an ongoing possibility.

While Sam's death was the first, it would not be the last as the *Titanic* continued to grow, with seven more workers losing their lives during the process. It seemed harsh to label this an acceptable risk, but the men and the company essentially considered it as such. In some respects, it is amazing that the toll did not rise even higher given the dimensions of the ship.

Harold & Wolff had to erect the world's largest gantry above the slipways where the *Olympic* and *Titanic* were being built, an amazing 840 feet long, 270 feet wide, and 228 feet high. Its network of lifts, cranes, and towers were able to move huge beams and expansive plates of steel into place, requiring more than three million rivets to attach them. The vast majority of these rivets were driven in by hand rather than by hydraulic means, and the resulting noise could be overwhelming.

Steel beams extended up from the keel, serving as the ribs for the hull and a framework that defined the outer dimensions of the ship. The *Titanic* also boasted a double bottom as a safety feature in the unlikely event of damage when it would go to sea. The framing was completed by April 6,

1910, and finally the steel plating could begin. As the steel plates were attached, careful inspection was a high priority to make sure they formed a water-tight skin for the ship.

*Postcard of the Great Gantry under which the* Titanic *and* Olympic *were built, possibly photographed in 1911 after both ships had been launched (Source: Titanicitems.com)*

Decks were installed one at a time, with a sufficient skeletal system of beams, pillars, and crossbars to support the weight of the flooring and whatever equipment, furnishings, and human occupants would eventually be situated at each level. Twenty-four double-ended Scotch class boilers had to be fitted in, each one 20 feet long and 15 feet 9 inches in diameter, holding six coal-burning furnaces apiece. In addition, five single-ended boilers were also included in the six boiler rooms, and sufficient space for coal bunkers to hold 6000 tons of coal had to be figured into the ship's design.

The structure of the ship became ever-more apparent as the ship grew during this phase, and many times the workers themselves were overwhelmed by the immensity of the *Titanic* and the *Olympic*. The challenge of interweaving ductwork and an extensive plumbing system throughout the ship was daunting. Exhaust smoke and waste gases from the boilers would eventually be breathed out through three of the four funnels, but these would not be added to the ship until after it was launched. The network of plumbing had to carry hot and cold water to the galleys, cabins, and bathroom facilities throughout the ship, essentially a massive circulatory system to meet the needs of the passengers and crew.

Titanic *(left) and* Olympic *(right) under the Arrol Gantry, shortly before the freshly painted* Olympic *was launched (Source: The Vintage News)*

It was on October 20, 1910, when the *Olympic* was launched, one day after the *Titanic's* plating was completed. For the first time in its existence the *Titanic* was alone under the "Great Gantry." Growth would continue, much of it in the interior, and the ship was clearly moving towards its own delivery date.

## Phase 3 – The Third Trimester (1910-1911)

William Parr had eagerly anticipated the launching of the *Titanic* for days. He arose earlier than normal on May 31, 1911, so he could secure an advantageous location from which to watch the big event. As the crowd continued to gather behind him, he was glad he would not have to peer through a sea of heads to observe the launch. His status as an assistant manager in Harland & Wolff's electrician's department had helped him gain access to such a good location, but specific viewpoints were not guaranteed except for the specially invited guests and the high-level officials who were provided with seating closest to the launch itself. There were also a number of persons who purchased tickets to sit in the grandstands, with the proceeds going to the support of two nearby hospitals, the Children's Hospital on Queen Street and the Ulster Hospital for Children and Women.

The crowd was enormous, with an estimated 100,000 persons jostling for position. For ninety minutes before noon, full-to-overflowing tram cars carried excited onlookers along either Queen's Road or Corporation Street to the drop-off point, from which they would walk the rest of the way. Because of all the activity on the grounds, the Harland & Wolff employees had the day off, without pay of course, yet many of them were present for the launching as well. Roughly 15,000 individuals worked at Harland & Wolff and many were directly involved in the planning or physical construction of the *Titanic*. Thousands of them felt a closeness to the ship, and they wanted to be part of the day's festivities.

William turned to the man next to him, another Harland & Wolff employee but one he did not know, and the two of them struck up a conversation about their respective roles with the company. Parr explained that he had only been working there since the spring of 1910 and had been involved most of the time until then with the outfitting of the *Olympic*. He helped oversee the crew of electricians who wired the ship, including the specialty lines that ran from the crow's nest to the bridge and from the bridge to the engine room, crucial for communication should an emergency occur. He would soon be engaged in the same sort of responsibility with the outfitting of the *Titanic*.

*The* Titanic *under the Great Gantry, shortly before launching (Source: Vintage Archives)*

Parr had been amazed by the beehive of activity that outfitting involved, running the gamut from boiler installation and attaching the propellers to lining the walls with exquisite wood paneling and furnishing the galleys and dining saloons. William then mentioned how impressed he was with the Grand Staircase which he described as the heart of the ship, at least for the first class passengers.

The worker next to William listened politely, and then took his turn to explain what his role had been during the past several months once the plating of the *Titanic* had been completed. A multitude of tasks related to the structure of the ship had to be completed during those seven months before it could be launched. Much of this internal steelwork was permanently put in to place during this time, including machine casings, hatchways, and ladders. In many locations, steel decks and beams had to be designed, fitted, and then temporarily removed to allow the passage of machinery that would be installed later. William clearly recognized how physical this labor was and complimented the other man on his contributions to the *Titanic*.

William glanced at his pocket watch, noting that the 12:15 p.m. launching of the ship was still thirty minutes away. He chuckled a bit when he overhead a father somewhere behind him describing to his children what they were about to see. Clearly, the man must have been a member of the community with no direct connection to the shipyard, because he told his offspring to keep their eyes open for the high smokestacks at the top of the ship. Perhaps the father had spotted the *Olympic* two days earlier when it underwent its sea trials and assumed the *Titanic* would look the same. Naturally, the sister ship was fully built, whereas the *Titanic* still needed to grow after today's delivery into the harbor. Even the bridge and most upper deck structures had not yet been built on the *Titanic*, and the four funnels still needed to be installed. Indeed, the *Titanic* had to mature before it could head out into the world under its own power.

While the future of the *Titanic* seemed certain in William's mind, it was only natural that his own destiny remained a mystery. How surprised he would have been had he known that the following April he would actually be aboard the *Titanic* as part of the Guarantee Group. In that capacity he would be called upon to use his expertise regarding the electrical system should the need for troubleshooting arise during the maiden voyage. By then his wife, Gertrude, would have given birth to their first child, Dorothea Kathleen, on January 5, 1912. How tragic that such exciting times would end for him when he would go down with the *Titanic*.

William looked at his pocket watch again, surprised that only five minutes had passed. He stared hard at the Great Gantry, but he was too far away to really see what was going on underneath. Bruce Ismay and Lord Pirrie had taken their final walk along the ship while it was still cradled in the slipway, and the men reminisced a bit about how they had conceived this incredible class of ships four years ago.

What an exciting week this was for both White Star and for Harland & Wolff, with *Olympic's* sea trials on Monday and *Titanic*'s launch today. As they joined the dignitaries in the principal viewing area, many reached out with congratulatory handshakes and pats on the back. And there stood J. P.

Morgan, owner of the International Mercantile Marine, with his normally imposing countenance betraying his own excitement.

*Lord William Pirrie and J. Bruce Ismay inspecting the* Titanic *before its launch (Source: Wikimedia Commons)*

Robert Keith, Head Foreman Shipwright, had been busy all morning, as it was his responsibility to oversee the entire launch. The transition from the *Titanic*'s position on its building blocks to the launchway below was technically quite involved. After all, the ship weighed an estimated 24,360 tons at this point, well below its eventual gross register weight of 46,328 tons, but still an enormous size to transfer to the water below. The delicate condition involved in this changeover of positioning required great expertise and cooperation. Teams of men stood nearby, ready to move the bilge and keel blocks out of the way, calling for all the brute force they could muster. Twenty-three tons of tallow, train oil, and soft soap had been slathered onto the standing and permanent ways, so that the ship could slide down the channel and into the water. The only other thing holding the ship in place was a hydraulic launching trigger which would finally get things underway.

A hush fell over the crowd shortly after noon, and while quiet chatter persisted, the people wanted to make sure that they did not miss the signal rockets. The rising tide finally reached the point where it would be safe to launch the ship, and the rockets were sent up at 12:05. Teams of shipwrights knocked the final timbers out of the way, and at 12:13 Robert Keith released the trigger which allowed the huge ship to begin moving.

Unbeknownst to the crowd, and probably even to Keith himself at that point in time, James Dobbin had been crushed under one of the huge support timbers that he and his squad had hammered out of the way. His pelvis was crushed, his injuries severe, and after fighting an additional battle with pneumonia he would die two days later. As he lay there, writhing in pain, the *Titanic* gradually started it descent, picked up speed, and finally reached an estimated speed of 12 knots, nearly 14 miles per hour, as it slid down the launchway.

The air was filled with shouts and cheers of celebration during the 62 seconds that it took the ship to reach its resting spot in the River Lagan. Its movement was purely controlled by gravity. The ship was as helpless as a newborn at this point, and only the restricting interaction with the water and the special anchors attached to the ship by sturdy hawsers would bring it to a halt.

Excited shouts continued all around as the crowd got its first look at the amazing ship, 882 feet 9 inches long, the world's largest. She was beautiful, her fresh coat of paint gleaming in the bright light of midday. Handkerchiefs and hats were waved in the air, hands clapped, and ongoing cheers lasted for a few more minutes, but eventually the excited clamor settled down. Fifteen minutes later, the crowd was heading back to the city proper.

Over in the grandstand, Bruce Ismay and Lord Pirrie were beaming, proud fathers of the second born of the eventual set of triplet ships. In the midst of the excitement, Bruce debated whether he should lean over and address both Lord and Lady Pirrie with a cheerful "Happy Birthday" wish. He could leave this as an open-ended remark as to whether he was referring to the ship or to both of the Pirries. Coincidentally they were celebrating their own birthdays that day, and what a fine gift the successful launch had been.

At last the *Titanic* was in the river, with tugboats guiding it to its new home. The ship would be housed at a 16-acre berth, 40 feet deep even at low tide, making it a safe location for the outfitting to begin. The launching had been a success. The *Titanic* was born.

*The* Titanic *shortly after being launched (Source: Titanic Belfast)*

Slightly more than eleven months later, the *Titanic* was ready to begin its maiden voyage with 2224 persons aboard. Among them were seventeen women who were in a delicate condition.

# Conception

The moment of conception is nothing short of miraculous, as cells from both parents unite into a single cell and bear the promise of a future child. Clinical descriptions of zygotes, blastocysts, mitosis, and undifferentiated cellular material meet the needs of the scientific and medical communities, but the reality for the future parents still remains a mysterious secret.

# Ada Julia Elizabeth Bone Doling

## Less Than Two Weeks Pregnant

*The jewel of the sky is the sun, the jewel of the house is the child.*
*--Chinese Saying*

For the third time that morning Ada Doling hit her knee against the kitchen cupboard. "Slow down," she muttered to herself, and for a few minutes she actually did. But then she started to pick up speed once more until a spoon dropped from her hand, clattering its way across the floor. A smile crossed her lips in amusement this time, and she thought about her actions over the last three days.

Getting prepared for her extended trip to America left Ada overly stressed about things that were actually falling nicely into place. The house was clean and her baggage was packed. She had lined up several persons to help take care of her family while she was gone, knowing full well that her husband, John Thomas Doling, would watch after the children when he was home, but he really was useless in the kitchen. He was just like every other Edwardian male in that regard. Besides, his role as manager of the nearby Atlantic Hotel in Southampton often meant last minute emergencies and somewhat irregular hours. Now that the coal strike had ended, the opportunities for immigrants to travel to North America would be on the increase once again, and this would mean plenty of business for the hotel, which particularly catered to these individuals on their final days before embarkment.

Ada had fretted over this last breakfast she would serve the boys before heading down to the pier. Porridge seemed too ordinary. Thick slabs of brown bread generously sprinkled with sugar and cinnamon would be tasty but not special enough. Fresh eggs with ham from the butcher shop seemed too extravagant. Finally, she realized that what she served for breakfast was not the issue. The important thing was just to sit down with her family on her final morning at home.

Oh, how Ada loved her sons. John Jr.'s thirteenth birthday in 1912 meant he was old enough to help watch over the other boys, including ten-year-old William, nine-year-old Reginald, and little Victor, whose sixth birthday was that year. As excited as she was about taking this trip to America, she was concerned about how much she was going to miss them while she was away. She also had to wonder how well the children really grasped the length of time she would be gone.

"Boys! Breakfast!" Ada called all, and they came running in. Certainly this was not a day to dawdle. They sat down together at the table, enjoying the meal and peppering Ada with the same questions that they had been asking her for days. She was more than happy to repeat her replies one more time.

"Yes, the *Titanic* is the largest ship ever built."

"Yes, we'll be leaving at noon, and I'll be away for a bit longer than a month."

"Yes, boys, I'll be visiting your grandmother and our other relatives in New York."

"No, I don't know exactly what the room will be like on the ship, but I hear that even our second-class accommodations will be nicer than what other ships have in first-class."

"Yes, your Aunt Elsie and I will be sharing the room together."

In this final response Ada was referring to her sister-in-law, Elsie Doling, only 18 and slightly older than half of Ada's 34 years. In fact, it was Elsie's father who built the hotel where John worked. Elsie was only four years old when Ada and John married, and it was wonderful watching her grow up. This trip on the *Titanic* would be a fine opportunity to get to know Elsie as the fine woman she had become as a young adult.

Ada's sons were done eating, but she was not quite ready to dismiss them yet. She carefully looked from one boy to the next, almost as if she were memorizing their faces for the long trip ahead. Her normally stern countenance softened as her eyes moved from one to the next. Suddenly her mind performed a mental flip-flop, and her thoughts turned to her own mother, Julia Bone. How grand it would be to visit her in New York. Julia had moved there five years ago, a rather brave move given that she did so at the age of 55. Their reunion would be quite special, and because Ada had never traveled to America before, she was confident that the experience would be incredibly memorable.

*Ada Doling (Source: Encyclopedia Titanica)*

One of the boys stirred slightly, and she immediately realized that they were becoming a bit restless. Ada dismissed them from the table and then tended to the last few tasks she needed to do before heading to the White Star dock. At least it was a short trip from her home on Canute Road to the *Titanic*, only about a mile away.

When Ada and Elsie reached berth 44, the area bustled with activity. The boat trains from London had already arrived, and passengers were waiting their turn to board the huge ocean liner. Many stood there with their mouths agape, but not Ada. Living so close to the port, she had seen the impressively large *Olympic* depart from there in the past, and the *Titanic* was only a few inches longer. Still, how could anybody not be impressed by the sheer size and beauty of White Star's newest ship? Excitedly, they made their way to their cabin. Oak paneling, a gleaming white linoleum floor, a handsome wardrobe, a dressing table with a washbasin complete with fresh running water, and even a comfortable sofa greeted them. No wonder the line could assign these rooms to first-class passengers if demand warranted it. And the bathroom facilities just down the corridor would be quite convenient.

As the two women unpacked their luggage, they burst into laughter several times in the process of tripping over one another. As nice as the room was, it was still on the smaller side as one would expect on a passenger liner, but this did not matter to Ada. She planned on spending as little time in the room as possible. Strolling the decks would be invigorating if the weather permitted, and the fine public spaces like the library lounge would provide a pleasant change of pace. She had even heard that the ship's small orchestra was scheduled to perform in the second-class areas on occasion, and that would be splendid.

Ada remained true to her decision to spend time out on the second-class promenade deck. She and Elsie were especially interested in observing the activities as they left Southampton, and they were aghast when a near collision with the SS *New York* could have scuttled the entire trip. This made her realize that as excited as she was to see her mother, she could not prevent her thoughts from turning back to her family. Obviously, she would miss her husband, but she found her love for her sons to be the overpowering emotion at the moment.

As the *Titanic* turned into the Solent, the tricky passageway riddled with its shifting sand bars, Ada repositioned herself along the railing for a clear view of the Isle of Wight. This was where she grew up, and she was eager to try to spot locations along the coastline that were familiar to her. Many times Ada had joined her parents on the ferry traveling between the

Isle of Wight and Southampton, but with her mother now living in New York, her own sons had no compelling reason to experience this crossing. But life moves on, and Ada found herself reflecting on the parent and child relationship, going back and forth mentally between her link to her mother and her ties to her sons.

When the *Titanic* reached Cherbourg that evening and Queenstown the next day, Ada and Elsie watched the hubbub of activity as the tenders carried passengers to the ship, as baggage was unloaded, and as final provisions for the ship were brought aboard. As luck would have it, a newspaper photographer happened to take a picture of the second-class portion of the Boat Deck that showed Ada and Elsie strolling along, passing by the lifeboats on the starboard side. In the days that followed, this photograph would appear in a number of newspapers.

*Elsie and Ada Doling strolling along the deck of the* Titanic *while anchored at Queenstown (Source: Titanic.superforum.fr)*

To Ada's left was a man whose identity in the coming years would be uncertain. The most likely possibilities are Edwin Wheeler or Henry Price Hodges. The former was George Washington Vanderbilt's valet, who worked with Ada's brother, Edward; the latter was a piano dealer from Southampton who was said to be a friend of the Dolings. Either individual would be a reasonable alternative, recognizing that it would be unseemly for ladies of this era to appear unaccompanied in public. Their presence along with Ada and Elsie, arranged for in advance, would bring comfort to the Doling families, knowing that the women were being taken care of.

As the voyage continued over the next few days, the weather was pleasantly cooperative for mid-April, and spending time walking along the second-class decks was a pleasant diversion. Ada would often stop along the way, gaze at the ocean, and think of her husband and sons back in England or her mother in New York. Perhaps more than any other time in her life, the benefits of having such warm and loving family ties became crystal clear.

Unfortunately, the air temperature grew much colder by late afternoon on April 14, and Ada was not so inclined to linger on the outside decks. What she did not realize, of course, is that the *Titanic* was on a collision course with an iceberg that night. The gentle calm of turning in for the evening was shattered, and the intensity of the situation grew ever more urgent when the room stewards instructed everybody to don their lifejackets and report to the lifeboats. The will to live is a powerful force, and Ada took steps to make sure that she and Elsie would be as safe as the situation could warrant. With all the assertiveness that her five-foot, five-inch frame could muster, she led her sister-in-law to the lifeboats. But it was not merely a sense of self-preservation that drove her. She needed to survive so she would be able to return home to the children she so loved.

What Ada did not know was that she might have already been pregnant with her fifth child, who would be born the following January. If she had become pregnant just before she left England, that would mean that the child would be born nearly 42 weeks later, two weeks longer than the average gestation period. Of course, if she did not become pregnant until after her return to Southampton aboard the *Philadelphia* in May 11, she would have been with child for only 38 weeks at most. Certainly two weeks either way from what is considered average would not be at all unusual, and the possibility is quite real that Ada's future baby might indeed be, technically, the youngest survivor of the *Titanic*.

The Doling women were fortunate. They managed to secure seats in a lifeboat, and for the next several hours they floated about in the icy Atlantic. Ada's emotions ran from relief that she had gotten off of the ill-fated ship to fearful anxiety that no ship would ever locate them in the middle of the huge ocean. Finally around 4:00 a.m. the distant lights of the *Carpathia* came into view, and the survivors in the lifeboats were saved.

Ada needed to get word to her family, unaware that the list of survivors was already being telegraphed from the rescue ship. She made arrangements to have a marconigram sent back home to Southampton, to let her husband and sons know she was alive and well. What she could not have known is that Harold Cottam, the *Carpathia* telegrapher, was so overworked that he could not keep up with the deluge of reports and messages that needed to be sent out. Even with the assistance of Harold Bride, the only surviving signaler from the *Titanic*, Ada's message never was sent.

When Ada stepped off the *Carpathia* in New York City on April 18, the weather was dank and wet. But she did not care, for at last she was reunited with her own mother. An emotional roller coaster took over: tears, laughter, sobs, and sullen reflection played out regarding all she and Elsie had been through. In the days that followed, Ada thoroughly enjoyed her visit with her mother, but as the return date drew closer, she could hardly wait to once again hug her husband and beloved children.

It was quite a scene back in Southampton when she got home, and again the barrage of inquiries from the boys seemed endless. As they excitedly questioned their mother, she could not stop herself from lovingly looking at them over and over, filled with relief that she had returned home safely and overcome with the tender affection she felt for each of them.

For weeks afterwards, family and friends prodded Ada with questions about the *Titanic*, and she wavered between feeling compelled to answer their inquiries and not wanting to mentally relive that terrifying night. Fortunately, a new reality shifted everybody's attention. When it became obvious that Ada was pregnant, joyful anticipation was considerably more satisfying than rehashing the past. On January 30, 1913, she gave birth to her last child and only daughter. The Dolings called the little girl Ida Julia Augusta, choosing her middle name in honor of Ada's mother, which was

Ada's middle name as well. Fate clearly smiled on the Dolings, and Ada quickly discovered that the love she had felt for her sons immediately expanded to include one more. While it remains forever uncertain whether Ada was already pregnant with her daughter when she was on the *Titanic,* Ida's 68-year-long life stood as a testament of her mother's survival.

# Ethel Louisa Clarke Beane

## Less Than Two Weeks Pregnant

*Life is a flame that is always burning itself out, but it catches fire again every time a child is born.*

*--George Bernard Shaw*

The nurse jotted down Ethel Beane's vital signs, specifically noting that her pulse was thready and that her blood pressure was disturbingly low. This was not entirely surprising for a nursing home resident who was 90 years old, but the indicators did not bode well for the elderly woman. If Ethel could have read the nurse's mind, she would have been pleasantly amused – not at the medical assessment, of course, but rather that the nurse thought she was only 90 years old. In actuality, Ethel was getting close to her 94$^{th}$ birthday. Many years before she shaved some years off her actual age to make herself sound younger than she actually was, a ruse which mattered to her at the time, and this little deception had remained with her to the present day. Ethel never felt that the white lie mattered much, although at this point in her life she realized that her true age might have given her some extra bragging rights.

In the last few years Ethel discovered her thoughts repeatedly reviewing her life. In the big picture of things it had been a fine one, but a few personal tragedies had intervened. At least her childhood recollections were reasonably positive. Oh, sure, only five of the eleven children born to her parents had survived, but her own birth in 1889 placed her in the middle range of the offspring, so she had no personal memory of many of the ones who had not survived. Ethel was a bit surprised when she finally realized what a struggle it must have been for her parents, Boaz and Louisa Clarke, to meet the needs of the family on her father's income as a boot factory warehouseman. They never had money to spare, but Ethel did not remember any sense of growing up in abject poverty.

Being raised in Norwich, Ethel was surrounded by solid, working-class people. The city of 100,000 people took great pride in the beautiful cathedral in town, but the structure merely represented a legacy from an earlier age. The current, ongoing concern was making ends meet. When Ethel was old enough, she held several different positions, including a brief stint as a personal maid. However, it was her time as a dressmaker and furrier that defined her. Ethel still remembered those days as being a bit frustrating. Her dressmaking skills were often limited to making somewhat simple frocks and following routine patterns, which really did not excite her. Those women desiring fancier dresses would generally travel into London instead. On the other hand, her role as a furrier was far more intriguing, especially when she needed to meet the challenge of restyling or repairing an older piece.

Ethel had no intention of remaining in the clothing industry, however. She was in love, and had been for years. Edward Beane lived down Northumberland Street from the Clarkes, and he had become acquainted with Ethel when she was only 17. Of course, because Ted was ten years older than she was, Ethel was too self-conscious to express her feelings, but the crush she felt was surprisingly strong. Or at least that was what she told herself many, many years later in the nursing home.

Ted, a laborer by trade, went to New York along with two of his brothers in 1907, but he returned to Norwich three years later. By then Ted was a man of the world, full of stories about the success he had found in America, where he found great success as a bricklayer. The primary reason Ted had returned was to visit his friends and find a wife, clearly desiring to wed a woman from England. By then Ethel had entered her twenties, and Ted found himself unquestionably attracted to her. Words of marriage were soon in the wind, and their 1912 wedding fulfilled her long-felt dream. As a young bride, all she could see was a starry-eyed future.

Naturally, Ethel and her husband talked at great length about their plans together as a married couple, although Ted made one decision abundantly clear. They would be moving to New York soon after their wedding. Like any good wife of that era, Ethel had little say in the matter, but to be honest about it she was looking forward to the change. Surely, life in America would open wonderful opportunities beyond the life she had experienced in Norwich, and Ted made it clear that he would have far more financial success as a bricklayer on the other side of the Atlantic. With their minds made up, they decided that their honeymoon could be delayed for a while after their wedding, waiting until they were actually aboard the steamship that would carry them across the sea.

*Ethel Beane (Source: Norfalktalesmyths.com)*

And, oh, what a steamship it was! Ted purchased second class tickets on the *Titanic,* which simply added to the fabled life that Ethel suddenly felt she was living. The news and advertising about White Star's latest vessel were nearly unbelievable. It was the largest ship ever built, the accommodations were the finest available, and the line was well known for providing incredible meals for its passengers. Ethel could hardly wait.

Packing, unfortunately, became a somewhat difficult chore. Ted took care of his own baggage, of course, but Ethel nearly felt overwhelmed by the decisions that she needed to make. She thinned her wardrobe, not that she had an overabundance of clothing to begin with, and she knew there was little point in transporting her older, somewhat worn garments. Personal items needed to be carefully sorted out, and Ethel made sure to include her precious pieces of jewelry. She did not own very many necklaces or dress pins, but some had been gifts and would serve as special remembrances of friends and family once she left England. Besides, jewelry would not take up much room among her belongings.

However, there was no compromising when it came to their wedding gifts. There was simply no way that Ethel could leave any of those behind. They had just been given to them in the recent weeks around the time they got married. Besides, if her pieces of jewelry were going to remind her of individuals back home, their 65 wedding gifts would trump those memories in spades. Sure enough, when they boarded the *Titanic* on April 10, 1912, all of these presents traveled with them, carefully packed, with the more fragile pieces cushioned appropriately so they would survive the journey.

Slowly the ship left the pier at Southampton, and Ethel could barely contain her excitement. While Ted had crossed the Atlantic before, this was her first voyage, and it carried with it all kinds of unknowns and grandeur. They stood at the railing, waving goodbye at the crowd of strangers below and gazing out at the busy port, when a loud noise reached their ears. Although they could not identify the sound of the hawsers snapping as the SS *New York* was torn from its docking place due to the *Titanic*'s undercurrent, they could certainly see the suddenly freed ship moving toward them.

Ethel shot a quick glance at her husband, and then turned her eyes once again to the wayward ship. Closer and closer it came. They could hear the shouts of some of the *Titanic*'s officials and were relieved to see a tugboat closing in on the *New York*, but it was not clear if it could intervene in time. Relief finally flooded over the Beanes as they watched the scene play out, for the tug managed to stop the runaway ship just four feet away from colliding with their own ship. Of course, this meant that their departure would be somewhat delayed, but that was far better than being on a damaged ship and having their trip canceled.

However, Ethel could not quell her emotions, finding it impossible to shake the feeling that this near-collision was an omen of doom. Ted had to admit he was a bit rattled as well. As they continued to talk, they both realized how good their fortune had actually been, and gradually the excitement of their voyage and their new home in America re-entered their thoughts. When they finally got underway once again, all seemed to be going smoothly, and they could really begin to enjoy their experience at sea. Besides, Ethel was wildly in love with her new husband. Over the coming days she repeatedly placed her hand into the crook of his arm any time they walked along the outer decks or headed to the dining saloon. Being in love and finally on their honeymoon was certainly grand.

The couple had bedded down for the night on April 14th when a slight shudder tremored through the ship at 11:40 p.m. The Beanes were not particularly aware that anything serious had happened, although the growing din in the corridors was becoming quite evident. Passengers were making a surprising amount of noise as they walked about, talking about the warning they received from the room stewards, and heading on their way to the Boat Deck. When the woman from the cabin next to Beanes came banging on the door informing them about what was going on, Ethel found comfort in Ted's words that this was just a boat drill. Of course, this seemed a bit unusual considering the fact that it was now past midnight, but Ethel trusted her husband. He had been at sea before and had a frame of reference that he could draw from.

But then the woman from the neighboring cabin pounded on their door once again, and this time Beanes traded their nonchalance for a reaction of true concern. They finally acted on the instructions to get into their lifebelts and head to the lifeboats. Ethel followed her husband's lead, and they made their way up from the second class decks. She made no effort to even tuck away any of her favorite pieces of jewelry, and naturally the wedding gifts remained behind. Such seemed to be the right thing to do, given that she and Ted were still assuming that nothing was seriously amiss.

By the time the newlyweds reached the upper decks, Ethel could hardly believe her eyes. The picture that presented itself was startling. The ship's officers and crew members were struggling to fill the lifeboats while keeping the growing crowd under control. Ted and Ethel made their way over to lifeboat 13, and she was quickly seated in one of the ever-decreasing number of spots that still remained. By then, Ethel felt a curious mix of exhaustion and fear, and she could not believe it when First Officer Murdoch yelled out, "No! Women only," instructing her husband to step back. For the time being only women and children were being loaded.

Ted followed the order as he was instructed, and Ethel did not give his action much thought. She simply was too tired to think clearly, and besides, he would surely get into another lifeboat. Once the women waiting nearby had been loaded into the lifeboat, Murdoch opened up the last few spots to a few of the men in the vicinity. Among them was Lawrence Beesley, a British schoolteacher who would later write about the events of the night. Then the crew started lowering the lifeboat to the dark Atlantic below.

What happened next as far as the Beanes were concerned would forever remain their own secret, a far bigger one than the one that Ethel would later tell about her own age. In fact, Ted would eventually give two entirely different versions of what occurred, and Ethel certainly did not contradict him. In one version, Ted described how he kept his eyes glued to his wife's lifeboat once it reached the sea, and, when the opportunity presented itself, he dove into the ice-cold ocean. He explained how he swam for hours (an unlikely possibility, given the realities of hypothermia) until he reached a lifeboat. Amazingly it was lifeboat 13, meaning that his earlier efforts to visually follow the boat's course had paid off. In the meantime, Ethel had become hypnotically fixated on the lights of the sinking ship, which somehow had an almost beautiful appearance despite the horror of what was playing out. Suddenly she became aware of the splashing and shouting of a man approaching the lifeboat, and she helped pull him aboard. What a joyful reunion that was when she discovered it was Ted who had made his way there. As thrilling as all of this was, Lawrence Beesley never wrote about this rather significant rescue in his thorough coverage of the night's events. Such an omission seems curious.

Ted and Ethel's second story stood in sharp contrast. Ted put forth the claim that after he leaped into the ocean, he was picked up by a completely different lifeboat and therefore was not immediately reunited with his wife. Not only that, even after the two Beanes were taken aboard the rescue ship, the *Carpathia*, they still did not manage to locate one another. Of course, this seems incredible as well. Oh sure, there was confusion as the rescued passengers milled around trying to find their loved ones once they reached the *Carpathia*, but the ship really was not so large that the young couple would be unlikely to meet up. Yet they maintained that it was not until they reached New York that they would reunite, more than three full days later.

Maybe Ted was simply one of the lucky men who stepped in along with Beesley, or maybe he managed to leap in as the lifeboat was being lowered from the next deck down, securing one of the few remaining seats. In any event, Ethel was never going to definitively state what had really occurred. With so many men perishing that night, all the surviving males came under a certain amount of social scrutiny as to how they survived, and the stories they told to others had to satisfy their inquisitors.

Of course, when they reached New York they were destitute. Ethel remembered that about $300 to $500 had been left behind in their cabin, and it now lay at the bottom of the Atlantic along with her jewelry, their wedding gifts, and all their other belongings. She accepted, with gratitude, a box of clothing that the Women's Relief Committee had provided to the couple. And she could hardly believe the efforts of Mrs. George Stott, a resident of the nearby Chelsea Hotel, who tirelessly intervened on the behalf of the *Titanic* survivors. The White Star office was willing to give $20 to Ted so the Beanes could make their way to Rochester, but Mrs. Stott remained adamant that the newlyweds deserved more, and she promised to help file a claim on their behalf. She even paid their fare to Rochester. Ethel truly felt blessed by this stranger's generosity and efforts.

Starting out a new life in a strange land, surrounded by individuals they had never met before, was a challenge for Ethel and Ted, but their new neighbors welcomed them with open arms, especially after learning about their experience aboard the *Titanic*. Then, as the months passed, Ethel discovered she was pregnant, and this served as a new joy to share with her neighbors. It became clear that she must have been pregnant while she was aboard the *Titanic,* given the timing of the impending birth of their child. Probably she was in this condition even before they boarded the fated ship, but it was a bit intriguing to imagine that she had become pregnant while they were in transit. Maybe some good really did come of that sea of blackness.

Sadly, tragic fate was to lift its head one more time. When January 13, 1913, arrived, Ethel delivered a still-born baby. She and Ted were devastated. While time is said to heal all wounds, Ethel would forever carry the loss of this child as an emptiness in her very being. In the years that followed, the Beanes were blessed with two sons, Edward who was born in 1913 and George who followed in 1916. She was forever grateful with each of their births, but never for a moment did she consider them compensation for the loss of her firstborn.

*Ethel and Edward Beane, with sons George and Ted (Source: Eveningnews24.co.uk)*

Ethel and Ted rarely spoke of the disaster throughout their lives, but their two sons were proud of their parents' story. On one of those rare occasions when the Beanes agreed to give an interview to a newspaper reporter, the boys remained nearby, offering reminders to their parents in order to help them deliver their tale. In this particular interview in 1931, the reporter included Ethel's word that she was only a 17-year-old bride at the time the *Titanic* sailed. So there it was, part of the public record, that Ethel was actually a few years younger than reality would support. Surely, she thought, there was no harm in this little bit of deception!

# Kate Florence Phillips

## Less Than One Month Pregnant

*Motherhood: All love begins and ends there.*
*--Robert Browning*

Kate Phillips had already finished restocking the supply of small, white paper bags which lay hidden away behind the counter. Now she turned her attention to the oversized glass jar waiting to be refilled with gobstoppers, always in high demand by the school boys on their way home from classes. Frankly, she found these candies to be rather vile, both cloyingly sweet and awkwardly large. She much preferred the brightly-colored barley sugar candies, but the older boys shunned them because they were molded into the shapes of toys. They felt they were too old for such treats.

As Kate turned her attention to the wine gums, the bell above the entrance door jingled. In walked Henry Morley, the owner of the shop, and she headed to the far corner of the store where the hand-crafted chocolates were on display. The shop manager greeted Mr. Morley, and he lingered for a few minutes to talk to her. Kate grew a bit agitated at the long delay; she could not continue rearranging the chocolates forever. Eventually, Mr. Morley made his way over to the display case and quietly whispered two words to Kate. "Three weeks."

What in the world was that supposed to mean? Kate tilted her head inquisitively and looked at Henry with readily apparent confusion. Henry reached in his pocket, pulled out a note, and slipped it to her in a motion subtle enough for the manager to overlook. Then he turned, cheerily said his goodbyes to the others in the store, and headed out the door while Kate slid the note into the pocket of her smock. She could hardly restrain herself from reading it, but she knew she needed to wait until a more private time.

Finally, the opportunity presented itself. Kate pulled the note out of her pocket and clutched it to her chest. How was it possible that she, a 19-year-old assistant clerk for Morley Brothers Confectionery Shop, could now be so seriously in love with her 38-year-old boss? Her hands trembled as she unfolded the note and scanned its content. Three weeks! They would be leaving Worcester in just three weeks, heading to a new life together in California.

When she finally met up with Henry she asked him, "How can we afford to do this?" Her real focus was on making sure their departure was really going to happen, but she certainly did not want them to end up in America without sufficient funds to survive. Henry's answer was simple. He had withdrawn nearly £700 from his Worcester shop accounts, which would provide them ample cash.

Kate found it difficult to tell her parents that she was leaving home, and she provided them with just enough information to satisfy their concerns. But if her own story was this complicated, how would Henry cover his own tracks? It was unlikely that he would just tell his wife that he was leaving her and never returning, even though they had fallen out of love long ago. On the other hand, it clearly would be difficult for him to desert his nine-year-old daughter, Doris. Then there was the more widespread issue that Henry was known throughout Worcester thanks to his business contacts, and something believable needed to be stated. He offered up a simple story to his acquaintances that he was on his way to California for the sake of recent health problems. While the stated destination was Los Angeles, he hoped to end up in San Francisco where he would open a new confectionery shop of his own.

Time passed almost too quickly in terms of packing and saying goodbye to friends and family. Kate remained fairly cagey in terms of not providing too many details, but she could hardly wait until they left the city on March 3rd. She could finally be seen with Henry and not worry about being spotted. Their clandestine affair had been frustrating at times, as they needed to avoid being seen in public by people who knew one or both of them. The only convenient aspect was that Henry's wife, Louisa, ran the confectionery store in Malvern, so her whereabouts were well enough defined for the lovers to avoid being detected by her. What Kate did not realize was that their supposedly stealthy moves had not fully succeeded, and gossip about her and Henry was already circulating.

One especially difficult task still remained. The couple traveled up to Birmingham, where additional confectionery shops were owned by the family. These stores were under the careful watch of Arthur Morley, Henry's brother. Together they explained their plans to Arthur, who would now be faced with Henry's share of running the business. Arthur was not pleased with what was being thrust upon him, but he was still willing to transport Kate and Henry to the Southampton docks. Besides, Arthur had had an affair of his own three years earlier, so he really was not in a position to take the moral high ground. Also traveling with them to the pier were Thomas and Mary Phillips, Kate's parents, now fully informed as to what was taking place.

Southampton was bustling with activity when Kate and Henry reached the White Star pier. Kate's mouth fell open at the incredible sight of the *Titanic,* and she quickly pointed out, "It's huge! How can it possibly stay afloat?" Arthur burst out in laughter, both at her naïve remark as well as wondering, once again, why Henry was so fascinated by her. True, she was a beautiful young woman, but she certainly did not possess a mature sense of culture or a solid understanding of the ways of the world. But this was his brother's decision, and he was not about to argue the point, especially not here at the pier.

The couple quickly joined the line of second class passengers waiting to board the ship. As they drew near the front, Kate overheard the brief exchanges of information that were taking place ahead of them, and her heart started racing. Of course, they had to give their names! How could she have not thought of that? A White Star official approached them, and asked them to identify themselves. Morley quickly replied, "Mr. and Mrs. Henry Marshall." Kate suppressed a giggle, and a sense of relief washed over her. At last, the two lovers were safe to truly appear together as a couple, with no fear of being spotted by anybody who could cause them any trouble, and their assumed identities would sufficiently mask their reality. So what if Henry gave their home address as 73 New Street, Birmingham, the location of Arthur's second floor home above one of his confectionery shops? Surely that would not be a problem.

As the *Titanic* pulled away from Southampton, Kate and Henry kept waving for quite a while, convinced that they were still able to see Arthur and the Phillipses, standing in the slowly receding crowd. When they headed to their cabin, Kate's eyes were riveted on every detail she could absorb. Awestruck by everything she saw, she leaned over to Henry and whispered, "This is so amazing." The rest of the day was glorious, and they passed their time exploring the ship, enjoying a wonderful dinner, and then heading back to the privacy of their cabin once again.

After eating breakfast the next morning, the couple made their way outdoors, and Kate took hold of Henry's arm as they gazed out across the water. The ship still had one more stop to make around noon in Queenstown, and then they would finally be on the open Atlantic. "Let's head to the back of the boat to see what it's like there," Kate requested, still not familiar with the terminology that most passengers would fall into while on a voyage of this nature.

They slowly strolled along the second class promenade to the farthest point on the stern. Kate looked down at the swirling eddies of water, fascinated by their blue-grey hue and the frothy white caps that formed along the surface. She finally tore her eyes away, gazed lovingly at Henry's profile, and said, simply, "I love you, Mr. Marshall." Henry replied, "I love you too, Mrs. Marshall," chuckling at their use of the assumed names they had registered under the previous day.

It was glorious! Each time they left their cabin Kate would hold firmly onto Henry's arm. To be seen publicly, strolling the decks and not worrying about being identified was so freeing. At twice her age, Henry found her behavior a bit clingy at times, but he was also very much in love. Besides, having this beautiful woman at his side was most flattering. Only on those rare occasions when Henry wanted to head to the men's smoking lounge would they be separated, and Kate generally would ask him, "You'll take me to the library first, won't you, darling?" She was confident that he would return to her more quickly, rather than if she were left alone in the cabin.

What a stark contrast these strolls were in comparison to their final walk together on the *Titanic*. Kate clenched Henry's arm with both of her hands as they nervously trekked to the Boat Deck. Her life vest seemed too tight, the night air was too cold, and the steady hum of noise reverberated too loudly. Her eyes darted left and right, trying to make sense of the scene before them. Meanwhile, she was still sorting out the messages they had heard about icebergs and damage. Sailors and officers were steadily filling the lifeboats, but Kate could not imagine getting into any of them. "No,

Henry, I can't go. I won't leave you," she sobbed. The more Henry urged her to climb in, the stronger she held onto him. "How can this be happening?" she worded with silent lips. After all this time wanting to be together, he was now insisting that they be apart, and she would not give in.

As it turned out, Kate had no choice in the matter. She winced as the sailors pulled her loose from Henry's arms and tossed her into lifeboat 11. Kate let out a quiet wail, and the tears started to flow. As the boat was lowered, she took one last look as Henry's face, praying that somehow he would be permitted into another lifeboat. She knew he did not know how to swim, so his hopes of survival were limited. Desperately she held on to her purse. Their room key was inside and that would soon be rendered meaningless, but her purse also held the beautiful blue sapphire necklace that had been a gift from Henry. She was not about to lose this treasured piece of jewelry.

Once aboard the *Carpathia,* Kate's greatest fear was confirmed. Henry had not survived. When she reached New York, she had no choice but to return to her parents' home, although it would be several weeks before she would do so. Obviously, there was no way she could continue the trip to California, nor was there any point in doing so. At least assistance from the Red Cross helped her meet her immediate financial needs.

By the time she reached Worcester, Kate learned that a reporter, Silas Smith, and his young assistant, Norman Pegg, had figured out the true identities of Mr. and Mrs. Marshall. In the process of poring over the list of passengers' names and addresses the reporters discovered that 73 New Street in Birmingham was the location of Morley's Confectionery in Birmingham, and details continued to fall into place from there. Kate slowly read the April 20th clipping from *Berrow's Journal* which referred to Henry and herself, allowing the readers to infer the relationship between them.

FORMER RESIDENTS OF WORCESTER DROWN

> It has been rumoured for several days past that Mr. Henry Morley, who formally carried on business in Worcester as a confectioner, was on board the *Titanic,* and that his name was

> not among the list of those reported to have been saved. The latest telegrams to hand indicate that he went down with the ship. It is understood that he sailed in the name of Marshall, and that although persons of that name are among the survivors, Mr. Morley is not one of them. It is, however, known, that a young Worcester woman, who had booked in the name of Kate Marshall, was saved. The widow, Mrs. Morley is the proprietress of a business in Malvern.
>
> There now is no longer any hope that Mr. H. J. Spinner who was on his way to Gloversville has survived, and much sympathy is felt by his widow, who like Mrs. Morley, is left with one child.

The Worcester newspapers did not take the opportunity to actually list Kate's last name, but the *Birmingham Evening Dispatch* was not so discreet. Kate was mortified. Their secret was out, and acquaintances averted their eyes when they saw her in public. Her parents, Thomas and Mary Phillips, were faced with the embarrassing reality of their unmarried daughter who had run away with a married man. And Louisa Morley now found herself as a widow with a daughter to raise on her own, while suffering the shameful abandonment perpetrated by her husband.

But the worst was yet to come. How difficult it was in the coming weeks to utter the words, "Mama, I'm pregnant." The possibility that the scuttlebutt surrounding her affair would fade away as time passed would instead be forever on display through her own child. A daughter, Ellen, was born on January 11, 1913, underscoring the strong possibility that Kate was already pregnant before she boarded the *Titanic.*

When it came time to fill out the information on the birth certificate, Kate hesitated at the line on which the name of the father was to be indicated. "I can't do it. I won't." She was adamant, and the entry remained blank, a reality that would haunt both mother and daughter.

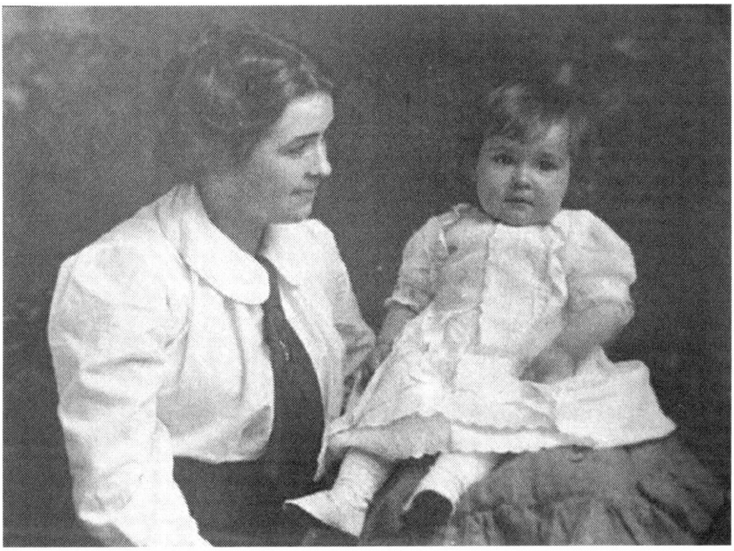

*Kate Phillips with daughter Ellen (Source:* The Sun*)*

# First Trimester

Early in the first trimester, the former ball of undifferentiated cells that formed the zygote develops into an embryo, with cells showing characteristics of their specialized functions. At the one month point, the embryo is about a quarter of an inch long with evidence of a pumping heart as well as arm and leg buds. Two months later the fetus will have grown to a three- to four- inch length. By then, arms and legs are distinct, including fingers and toes and nails. Ears, teeth, organs, the central nervous system, and the spinal cord are well underway by the end of the first trimester.

# Juliette Marie Louise Lafargue Laroche

## One Month Pregnant

*We never know the love of a parent until we become parents ourselves.*

*--Henry Ward Beecher*

Juliette gestured to her older daughter, quietly requesting, "Simonne. Come here." The three-year-old hopped off her chair and approached her mother, who used a napkin to wipe off a streak of errant jam that trickled down the front of her little girl's dress. "There. That's better. We certainly don't want a stain to set in."

With that, Juliette glanced down at her other daughter. "Oh, I've got to stop thinking about Louise as a baby. She's less than three months away from her second birthday. How can that be?" At least Louise had escaped any dribbles of jam, but the front of her dress was littered with crumbs from the slice of toast she had been attacking. Juliette brushed off the debris and then looked up at her husband. "See, Joseph. This is why we needed to travel on the *Titanic*!"

Joseph smiled back at his wife, amused that jam and bread crumbs had served as proof that they had made the right decision. They were thrilled when they originally received tickets aboard *La France* as a gift from his mother in Haiti, but then they learned about the restrictions that the Compagnie Générale Transatlantique line put on young children. Had they actually crossed the Atlantic aboard *La France*, the children would not have been permitted to eat meals in the dining saloon. Such a policy would have been an annoying restriction even under the best of circumstances, but the Laroches agreed that Louise's health problems made this an impossible demand. Louise had been born prematurely, and Juliette felt compelled to be with the toddler as much as possible, including meal time. Switching to second class tickets aboard the *Titanic* allowed them to meet their family needs, making their change in booking arrangements a wise decision.

When the Laroches headed back to their cabin after breakfast, Juliette turned to her husband with a simple request. "Would you mind watching the girls so I can write a letter home to father?" Joseph readily agreed, having discovered how much he was enjoying the time he was now able to spend with his daughters. What a sharp contrast this was to the limited time he had with his wife and children when he was working as an engineer for the Paris Underground.

Juliette wished she had started her letter yesterday, but April 10th had been exhausting. They had arisen quite early to take care of last-minute preparations, saying a tearful goodbye to their French relatives and closest friends, and then journeying to the boat train at Gare Saint-Lazare. How fortunate they had been when M. Renard agreed to transport them to the station. He even bought each of the girls a balloon while they waited to board the train. When Louise suddenly burst into tears, the adults quickly spotted her balloon escaping to the clouds. M. Renard replaced it with no hesitation whatsoever.

The train ride seemed to take longer than Juliette expected, especially since the girls were too excited to fall asleep. Then, when they reached Cherbourg they learned that the ship had been delayed. Rumor had it that the *Titanic* nearly had an accident when it left Southampton, but Juliette was too busy watching her daughters to pay much attention to those stories. Besides, most of the ongoing discussion regarding the incident took place among the English-speaking passengers. Joseph could understand the chatter, but she could not. What difference did that make, anyway?

At least last night's sleep had offset her exhaustion. The ship was now well underway and would make one more stop in Queenstown in just a few hours. She needed to get this letter written by then so it could be posted in time. The family left the cabin, first heading to the library on Deck C where Juliette could concentrate on her writing. Joseph headed out with Louise in her stroller and Simonne pushing it from behind. Because the family had not fully explored the ship as yet, Juliette knew they would be well-occupied, although her own descriptions in the letter might be a bit limited. "Why am I so worried about describing the ship? I know father would be glad to hear from us no matter what I write."

Certainly, he would be interested in their sleeping arrangements. Making sure her pen was properly inked, Juliette continued her writing. "We have two bunks in our cabin, and the two babies sleep on a sofa that converts into a bed. One is at the head, the other at the bottom. A board put before them prevents them from falling. They're as well, if not better, than in their beds."

*Juliette and Joseph Laroche, with daughters Simonne (left) and Louise (Source: New York Amsterdam News)*

What else should she write about? One thing Juliette had fretted over was whether they would encounter much overt prejudice while aboard the ship, and Father knew about her concern. After all, she was a white woman married to a black Haitian. To be sure, Juliette and Joseph had noticed some disapproving glances, but overall their earliest impressions were that the voyage would be fine and that their family would not be reduced to being the social pariahs of the ship. Juliette was delighted that her daughters were already accepted so warmly, quite a relief for the young mother. The good news she could pass on to her father was that Simonne "was playing with a young English girl who had lent her her doll. My Simonne was having a great conversation with her, but the girl did not understand a single word. People on board are very nice. Yesterday, they both were running after a gentleman who had given them chocolates."

Prejudice was the very reason the Laroches were heading to Haiti. Joseph had arrived in France when he was only 15, a common way for talented young Haitians to receive a higher education at that time. With a degree in engineering under his belt, Joseph was fairly quickly hired to work for the French subway system, only to discover that any opportunities for his own advancement were being throttled. His handled his professional duties with great expertise but was told he would not yet be given any raises nor would his responsibilities be extended, supposedly because he was still too new. Yet younger men with less experience were granted promotions and even hired at salaries greater than his own. The only thing that helped offset Joseph's frustrations was meeting Juliette. The two quickly fell in love, and her father readily agreed to allow his only child to marry this talented young man.

Juliette paused from her letter writing to think back to the wonderful wedding celebration they had enjoyed four years earlier. And how blessed she felt by the birth of their daughters since then. Motherhood suited her well, and she loved the two little ones so much. However, as Joseph's professional opportunities stagnated, something needed to be done. They started talking about the possibility of moving to Haiti, where he would begin a position as a mathematics teacher.

Juliette's concern regarding daughter Louisa's health issues was the major issue which had delayed their final decision to move. Knowing that

Haiti was a poor country, she had to make sure that the medical support to meet her little girl's needs was available. Joseph assured her that Cap-Haïtien boasted some fine doctors, and that their family would have access to their expertise. After all, the Laroche family took pride in their 17th century ancestor, a French nobleman and military man who married a local Haitian. Since then they were among the most important individuals in the country. Their social status alone would be sufficient to get the best health care, and it certainly did not hurt that Joseph's uncle was Cincinnatus Laconte, the governor of Haiti. Such connections would guarantee them with the finest the country had to offer. Finally, her mind was put to rest.

Juliette shook her head to return her thoughts to the present and she got back to her letter writing. Still concerned by the prospect of keeping the girls occupied during the remaining days of the crossing, Juliette was pleased by the number of children she spotted. "This morning I tried to count all the children on the boat. In second class only, I am sure that there are more than twenty. There is a small family with four children, they remind me of my Uncle's. The youngest looks very much like fat Marcelle. I am writing from the reading room: there is a concert in there, near me, one violin, two cellos, one piano." As much as the concert was a pleasant diversion right now, her focus would naturally be on Simonne and Louisa for the entire voyage.

There was a bit of relief in the next piece of news Juliette added to the notepaper. "Up to now, I have not felt seasick. I hope it will go on this way. The sea is very smooth, the weather is wonderful." Of course, nobody wants to put up with a queasy attack of mal de mer, but that was not the only thing on her mind. She believed that she was in the very early weeks of yet another pregnancy, and sea sickness coupled with morning sickness sounded like a horrible combination. It was too soon to raise such a possibility in this letter, so she shifted directions once again, penning, "If you could see how big this ship is! One can hardly find the way back to one's cabin in the number of corridors."

With that, Juliette dashed off a few lines about their approach to Queenstown, the limited time to get her letter finalized for mailing, and a variety of greetings to other family members back in France. Just as she finished, she glanced up to see Joseph and the girls returning to the library.

Sealing the letter, she rushed out to greet them, lovingly planting kisses on the forehead of each of her daughters. Off they went, making sure that the letter was posted and then entertaining themselves with the activities involved in loading one more set of passengers. All the while Juliette reminded the children about their own boarding the previous evening, asking them questions and pointing out whatever she could to keep them entertained. As much as she cared for the girls, it seemed like a mother's work was never done. With those long days at sea ahead of them, Juliette wondered how well she would cope with it all.

Juliette's concerns about keeping Simonne and Louise occupied during their journey proved to be unfounded. The few playthings that the Laroches had kept handy in their cabin had turned out to be more than sufficient, and besides that Joseph had taken full advantage of showering his attention on the girls. Juliette smiled at her husband each time she found him on his hands and knees playing with the children, and the few times she warned him about getting his trousers dirty were met with a hand-motioned response of leave-us-alone-I'm-having-fun. Juliette's thoughts then turned back to the possibility that she was pregnant. How nice it would be to have a boy this time. Joseph would love to have a son, but as long as it was healthy was the only thing that really mattered.

The girls found a wonderful friend in André Mallet. Because he was only a couple of weeks older than Louise, they were ideal playmates, and it was clear that Simonne was delighted to direct many of their activities as the big girl in charge. The Laroches first met the Albert Mallet family on the boat train in France, and Juliette especially enjoyed the opportunity of chatting with Antonine Mallet in their native tongue. Being surrounded by so many English-speaking passengers, it was so comforting to have somebody else to talk with besides their husbands.

The days passed quickly, but unfortunately the temperature started dropping noticeably late on Sunday afternoon. Juliette's concern about Louise's health meant that play time on the promenade deck was no longer an option. At least dinner was not that far off, and soon afterwards she put the girls to bed. Once they were settled, Juliette and Joseph decided to get into their bunks as well. The warm blankets felt good, and the gentle motion of the ship quickly put them to sleep.

The quiet calm was replaced with increasing commotion sometime around midnight. Joseph went out to investigate and came back with the news that the *Titanic* had experienced some kind of accident, apparently having hit an iceberg. Juliette awakened the girls and somehow managed to dress them in warmer clothing, despite their sleep-deprived protests. Then the family of four made their way to the Boat Deck. All the while Juliette asked her husband what was going on. With the orders being shouted out in English, she had never felt more excluded in her life. The only thing she was convinced of was that she had to make sure her girls were safe.

Suddenly, Simonne was torn from Juliette's arms and tossed into a nearby lifeboat that was dangling high above the water. "Mon enfant, criai-je, mon enfant! ... C'est mon enfant qu'on vient de m'enlever!" the frantic mother remembered calling out. *My little girl, I cried out, my little girl! ... They've taken my little girl away.* Suddenly Juliette felt herself being picked up and hustled into the boat as well.

There in the crowd stood Joseph, with Louise in his arms. He held the toddler as high as he could so she would not be hurt by the surging throng. Juliette knew she had no way to communicate with the crew members, her French at odds with their English. Whether it was Joseph's strong command of English or a sailor's insightful assessment of the situation that finally resolved the situation was not clear to Juliette, but what relief she felt when Louise was taken from her husband's arms and lifted into the lifeboat. But then horror washed over her when it became clear that Joseph was about to be left behind.

"A bientôt, ma chérie," Joseph shouted out. "Il y aura de la place pour tout le monde, va, dans les embarcations ... Veile sur nos fillettes ... A bientôt!" *I'll see you soon, my darling...They'll be room for everyone, go with the lifeboats ... Look after our little girls ... See you soon!* Tears filled Juliette's eyes as the boat she sat in started its long descent to the ocean.

All through the night Juliette clutched her daughters, especially trying to keep Louise sufficiently protected from the frigid night air. The girls slept for the most part, but the concerned mother remained fully awake, playing the horrifying scene over and over in her mind and wondering what would happen next. There was not a great deal of chatter in the boat, not that it would have mattered anyway. She had no way of understanding what was being said, and as a result did even not know whether any sort of rescue ship was on its way.

Several hours later the *Carpathia* came into sight, and one by one the lifeboats drew close to its side so that the survivors could be lifted aboard. Juliette experienced a curious mix of relief and concern as she watched her daughters being hauled up in large burlap bags. Then Juliette was hoisted up in a bosun's chair, not that she had any idea of what it was called, nor did she care. More than anything else, she knew she now needed to find Joseph, hoping that he had made his way to safety in another lifeboat.

Juliette' search was in vain. Her husband had not survived, and she suddenly found herself a 22-year-old widow, with two little girls to watch over and no clear-cut plan as to what she should do next. Then she spotted a familiar face among the other survivors. Antonine Mallet was standing nearby with André in her arms, tears staining her cheeks. The two French women surged toward one another, joining together in their shared sense of loss. They found strength in each other's company, and once they achieved some sense of composure, they began to discuss what steps they now needed to take.

One surprising concern was something they had not anticipated just hours earlier. Both Louise and André needed diapers, and the mothers' struggle to communicate this need to the stewards on the *Carpathia* produced no solution. As the two women continued to discuss their dilemma, Mathilde Weisz overheard their words. The French-speaking Belgian was dealing with the loss of her own husband, but her strong-willed personality drew her to Juliette and Antonine. Surprisingly quickly, Mathilde hatched a plan. The women could surreptitiously carry some of the linen napkins out of the dining saloon, and these could be fashioned into diapers. "But what if we are caught?" asked Juliette. Mathilde had already thought this through. If a steward or other crew member should happen to spot them, the women could simply sit down atop the napkins. A barrage of words would undoubtedly tumble forth from the stewards, and the woman could meet the challenge with blank stares and protestations that they only spoke French. Eventually the officials would give up. The plan worked, and the babies' needs were met.

*Simonne and Louise Laroche being held by a passenger aboard the* Chicago *during their return to France. Insets show Juliette and Joseph Laroche (Source: L'Union Suite)*

Once the *Carpathia* reached New York, Juliette found her next decision was an easy one. Because she had never lived in Haiti and only her deceased husband's family resided there, she knew it would not be practical to continue on the Cap-Haïtien. Instead, she made arrangements to return to France aboard the *Chicago*. She and her daughters moved back home with her father in Villejuif, safely comforted by familiar surroundings. She never remarried, remaining true to the love of her life and practically smothering her daughters by being overly protective. Fortunately, one reality brought her some comfort. On December 17, 1912, Juliette gave birth to her only son, and naming him was a simple task. When she gazed lovingly down at the boy's face for the first time, there was no doubt that he would be called Joseph Lemercier Laroche, Jr.

# Adele Hakim Nasser (Adāl Hakīm Naṣr Allāh)

## One Month Pregnant

*Sometimes the smallest things take up the most room in your heart.*

*--A. A. Milne*

As usual, Adele Nasser's wideset eyes disclosed her emotions. This time they reflected emptiness and isolation. She had survived the sinking of the *Titanic,* but she had no idea what was now in store for her. As a result, it was simpler to just keep to herself, suffering in confusion and silence. When the *Carpathia*'s purser spotted her tucked away in the corner at the far end of the room, he headed over and asked, "Is your name on the roster of survivors?" She gave no response. She had no idea what he said, and it was only with the greatest effort that he was finally able to record some sort of listing for her. Unfortunately, he was unsure how closely his written words represented her actual identity.

At least the steward's efforts met with more success. When asked, "Would you like a blanket madam?" Adele could see the heavy swaths of cloth under his arms and could nod or shake her head accordingly. And while she had no real desire to eat as the *Carpathia* continued its westward trek, she sometimes accepted a cup of coffee or tea, and occasionally she would even nibble on a small cake or piece of bread.

As the *Carpathia* slowly approached the New York Harbor docks, she could hardly have felt more alone, even though thousands had shown up to greet the *Titanic* survivors. She looked around once again. She figured there were slightly more than 100 second class survivors gathered nearby, counting the children. A few were chatting loudly, eager to finally be reaching America. Most, however, spoke in hushed tones; and a few sat alone, like Adele, silently trying to figure out what would happen next.

Almost mindlessly she searched out the men, thirteen in all, and reconfirmed once more that her husband, Niqūlā, was not among them. "How foolish I am to hold such a hope," she sighed. Tears filled her eyes.

A sailor started shouting out orders, and the room full of survivors took their turn to exit the ship. When Adele reached the start of the gangway, she had her first glimpse of New York City. So large, with such tall buildings, and so brightly lit even at night. Unable to process the reality in front of her, she shifted her thoughts to her home back in Lebanon. "Oh, Zahlah, how much I miss you," she muttered to herself. How naïve she had been, growing up in that wonderful town whose red-roofed houses spilled down the rolling foothills near Mount Lebanon. Life was simple there, and farming fruits, vegetables, and vine crops helped sustain their Orthodox Catholic community, with the railroad providing the means of shipping excess crops to other parts of the country. But now, looking at the overwhelming city before her, she realized how primitive Zahlah actually was. Of course, she understood this back in Paris where she and Niqūlā traveled before boarding the *Titanic,* but she was not alone then and her husband made it seem so exciting.

"Why did my mother agree to let me marry Niqūlā in January? And why did we have to sail for America?" she wondered to herself. She was only 14 and he was 29, an age difference that really was not particularly unusual for Lebanese couples. Still, she had some reason to believe he was actually three additional years older and had lied about his age when he had returned to Zahlah in search of a wife. Of course, the immigration record keepers believed that she was 17, age being such a slippery thing to nail down. The only thing that was definite was his intent to take his new wife to America, which he made abundantly clear when they decided to marry.

Niqūlā had lived in the United States since 1908 and Adele was fascinated by his stories about his other family members who had lived in America for many years even before he did. Of course, her mother had received letters from Cleveland, Ohio, over the years after some of her own children settled there, but Niqūlā's accounts sounded much more exciting. The opportunities were endless – uncles and cousins operated the very first nickelodeons in San Francisco, other relatives opened numerous confectionary stores, and he even had his own shop on Sanchez Street. He also was a carpet dealer and had found the means to sell exported rugs from Syria, which were shipped on a regular basis to New York. What a catch Niqūlā was for Adele. No wonder her mother approved of their marriage.

"But what will I do now?" The thought overwhelmed her as she reached the bottom of the gangway, and she was exhausted even by this short descent. It made no sense to continue on to San Francisco, for she really did not know Niqūlā's extended family at all. Staying in New York certainly was not reasonable, as she knew nobody here. She had no money to get back to Lebanon. The wisest choice was to tell the officials about her relatives in Cleveland, although she had no idea if there was any way to contact them. All seemed hopeless.

Suddenly a woman came out of the crowd and tenderly led Adele to a group of other survivors who were to be taken to a nearby hospital. Adele did not fully grasp what was happening until they got there, but she was certainly grateful that somebody was watching after her. Gradually she came to understand that the Red Cross and many other volunteers were doing what they could to assist the survivors who were so frighteningly isolated in New York.

As she recuperated, Adele had plenty of time to reflect on the terrible events of April 15. Although Zahlah had its share of freezing nights, nothing could compare to the intensely frigid conditions while they floated on the inky black Atlantic in that crowded lifeboat. The only warmth she experienced during the long wait for the *Carpathia* came from huddling together with the well-dressed lady next to her in the boat. Only later did she learn that this woman was Madeleine Astor, the young wife of the richest man aboard the *Titanic,* and both of them were destined to learn later that horrible night that they had become widows. She winced at the memories, and suddenly she was aware once again of the lingering remnants of pain that the cold had caused to her extremities.

Later, Adele decided to write a letter to Madeleine Astor, clearly referring to the financial strife she was facing. Adele fully realized how destitute she was, and she carefully alluded to the particulars of her plight. She also masked her age once again, trying to make herself sound more mature.

"Dear Mrs. Astor,

"I sat in the same boat which saved you when the Titanic went down. I also will soon have a baby. My husband, Nicholas, was drowned. All our money and things went down with him.....I am twenty-one. I married Nicholas nearly three years ago. He used to have a tannery in Brazil. We were returning to the old country and had got as far as France when we learned that Turkey and Italy were fighting. We started back for New York on the Titanic. Alas, that we did. This is all that is necessary to let you know. Hoping you will live forever in my [illegible]. Adele Nasrallah"

*Adele Nasser (Source: Department of Vital Statistics, El Paso, Texas)*

The thought of sending this letter lay in the future, however. For now, Adele could only continue her recuperation, still uncertain about what her feasible options might be. What relief she felt when familiar faces finally appeared. Her brother, Ilyās, and others from the family had arrived from Cleveland. It was a bittersweet but most welcome reunion.

"I am not alone!" Indecision and confusion came to a quick end, and Adele gladly traveled to Ohio with them. Once they arrived, she threw her arms around her sister, Mahībā Anter, who was waiting at her home for their arrival. Never had family felt so reassuring, and as her recovery continued over the next few weeks, she appreciated their protective care.

Her new home in America was not at all like Zahlah. Cleveland sat on a polluted river, smoke pouring into the air from the many factories in the area. And she could hardly believe how flat it was, with nothing resembling the rugged foothills back home. But she had to adjust, not only to her new surroundings but also to the fact that she was pregnant. Spring gave way to intense summer heat and then crisp autumn winds blew in. All the while Adele's belly grew, and by the time December arrived, the air became bitter cold, reminding her once again of that tragic night at sea. Although her world had been turned upside down with the loss of her husband, at least there was some excitement in her heart with the thought that she soon would be a mother. There was hope and meaning to life once again.

Fate was not finished with Adele. On December 9 she gave birth to a son, who died within just a few hours. The tears would not stop flowing at first, and her eyes clearly reflected her inner sorrow and pain during the weeks that followed. Despite the love and support of her family in America, once again Adele felt very alone.

# Helen Margaret Walton Bishop

## One-and-a-half Months Pregnant

*A mother's joy begins when new life is stirring inside…when a tiny heartbeat is heard for the very first time, and a playful kick reminds her that she is never alone.*

*--Unknown*

"I now pronounce you man and wife. You may kiss the bride." The former Helen Walton turned her face upward and looked lovingly into Dickinson Bishop's eyes. He leaned forward, and muffled murmurs punctuated with polite chuckling rippled among their family and friends as the bride and groom enjoyed their first kiss as a married couple. They then turned toward their guests, and 19-year-old Helen beamed with delight. She was very social by nature and was enjoying every minute of the wedding.

Gerald Walton spared no expense for the dinner that followed. He and his wife wanted to make sure that the wedding of their only child would be a memorable one, both for the newlyweds and for all the family and friends gathered there. Thanks to his role as president of the Royal Easy Chair Company, Gerald could certainly afford to make a lasting impression.

As the newlyweds greeted their guests, Helen chatted pleasantly and with sincere warmth. Dick was a bit more reserved by nature, but he seemed energized whenever somebody asked about their upcoming travel plans. "We're heading to the Mediterranean in January for a whirlwind honeymoon." he replied, and then coyly added, "Well, not exactly a whirlwind. We'll be there for the entire winter and will head home in the spring, probably by mid-April." His listeners recognized the expense associated with such an extended stay, but they also knew that Dick could well afford it. When his first wife passed away, he inherited a share of her family's Round Oak Stove Company, making him a man of sizable wealth.

Time seemed to drag between the Bishops' November 7, 1911, wedding and their January 12, 1912, departure, but at last the day arrived and Helen could barely contain herself. The voyage to Europe aboard the *Adriatic* of the White Star Line was everything she hoped it would be. Their cabin was well-outfitted, the food was amazing, and just standing at her husband's side while gazing at the ocean was so romantic. Even shuffleboard turned out to be a delight. And how exciting it was to talk with the other first class passengers on the ship. Helen never had any problem striking up a conversation with total strangers on the promenade deck, and she enjoyed the friendly banter during the meals in the dining saloon.

*Helen Bishop (Source: Titanic Faces Blogspot)*

Their first stop in the Azores was magical, and as the ship drew close to the Strait of Gibraltar, Helen made sure that the two of them were on deck to enjoy the view of the well-known site. "Oh, Dick, how magnificent it is." They lingered by the railing for quite some time, comfortable in the pleasant Mediterranean warmth. Once again they reviewed all the sights they would see in the coming months: the Vatican, the Colosseum, the Duomo in Florence, the Casbah of Algiers, Egypt's pyramids, the Sphinx, and the Eiffel Tower among others. Of course, Helen made sure there would be plenty of time for shopping, and both of them looked forward to viewing some of the world's greatest pieces of art.

As grand as these destinations were, Helen and Dick also sought out the local culture and whatever unique experiences might come their way. While in Egypt they heard about a local fortune teller, and Helen was insistent. "Dick! We have to go! Wouldn't it be exciting to learn what is in our future?" He was skeptical, but he knew it would make for an interesting story later on. Helen would revel in telling about it and besides, it would be scandalous fun just listening to whatever would be prophesied.

Much to her surprise, Helen gave her heart to another in Florence, Italy – a small dog, which she promptly named Freu-Freu. Dick never expected that their honeymoon trip would end up as a party of three, including the dog. Four, actually! During their extended honeymoon, Helen learned she was with child, and the couple could not have been happier. While their date to return to Michigan had been open-ended, this news put their final travel plans into action. They would head back to Dowagiac, set up their new home, and prepare for the arrival of their first-born.

England's recent coal strike had played havoc with trans-Atlantic travel, and the Bishops really wanted to return aboard one of the White Star liners, given their earlier experience with the *Adriatic*. To their delight, they learned that White Star's grand new ship, the *Titanic*, would be stopping in Cherbourg on April 10, well-suited for their needs. Details about its finery made it apparent that it would be noticeably grander than what they had experienced during their eastbound crossing. Besides that, this was the world's largest ship to ever sail. What an adventure it would be, and what stories Helen could share when they got back home. In poring over the alternatives for their room, they opted for B-49, an outside cabin located on the Bridge Deck. They both were pleased with its location, situated at the end of a short corridor that led out to a bank of elevators that stood just behind the Grand Staircase.

Like so many other couples aboard the *Titanic*, Helen and Dick strolled arm in arm as they explored its labyrinth of decks and corridors. Their first views of the Library, the Palm Court, and the Veranda Café reconfirmed how much more luxurious this ship was than the one they had fallen in love with just months earlier. As they passed by other first class passengers, the Bishops nodded and smiled, and Helen wondered whether any of them would become shipboard friends. Suddenly, she tightened her hand about Dick's arm and subtly moved her head in the direction of a couple standing several dozen feet away.

"Dickinson! Are those the Astors? We must go over an introduce ourselves." Photographs of Colonel John Jacob and Madeleine Astor had peppered the newspapers for many months, with readers intrigued by the latest chapter in his life. Astor had divorced his first wife two years ago, and now he was married to this beautiful woman who was even younger than his son Vincent. While Helen was savvy enough socially to avoid making a pest of herself, she also realized that the swirl of gossip surrounding the Astor marriage had left the couple ignored by some members of the upper class. "We'd have so much to talk about!" Helen continued. "She and I are just about the same age, and we are both expecting babies. Oh, Dick, we have to meet them." Dick was hesitant, but he also knew it was probably useless to argue with Helen.

As it turned out, Helen was right. The two women seemed to enjoy each other's company and indeed they had enough common interests to fuel their discussions. Madeleine and Helen chatted many times when they encountered one another in the coming days. However, neither of the women could have anticipated that fate would bring them together for a far more somber conversation after midnight on April 15. A minor shudder had passed through the ship a bit earlier, engines were stopped and restarted, and the middle-of-the-night noise in the corridors brought many of the first class passengers to A-deck to find out what exactly was going on.

Details were sketchy at first, and Helen was glad to spot the Astors once they arrived. Helen was confident that if anybody would really know what was happening, certainly the Colonel would. Not surprisingly, others reached the same conclusion, and throughout the night many of the most important passengers aboard the ship clustered together with the Astors to discuss the unfolding events. But the freezing night air was taking its toll. "Would you mind heading back to our cabin, and bring me my muff?" she asked her husband, and he immediately headed down.

Meanwhile, the Colonel briefly left the group to speak with Captain Smith. He came back with the definitive news that they indeed had hit an iceberg and then added an alarming warning. He advised Madeleine and the other persons standing with her, including Helen, to return to their cabins and retrieve their lifebelts. Astor made it clear that he was convinced that the damage was not serious, but Helen was rattled by everything that was unfolding. She headed downstairs, and back in their room she nervously told Dick, "We need to get our lifebelts and head back upstairs." They quickly did so, and as they prepared to return to A-deck, Freu-Freu caught hold of Helen's dress with its teeth. "No, dear one, you cannot go with us," chuckled Helen, despite her concern about what might lay ahead.

Gradually a small group of first class passengers once again formed, this time with lifebelts tucked under their arms. Certainly they did not want the somewhat cumbersome vests to cover up their outfits. Discussions resumed, which became more intense when they were told to actually put on their lifebelts. As they continued to talk, Helen kept glancing over at the activity of the sailors and officers. She could readily see how serious they were in meeting the task at hand. They removed covers from the lifeboats and started hoisting them into position for loading.

Helen had trouble believing this precaution was necessary, and the others took that stance as well. Madeleine firmly proclaimed that she was not about to leave her husband's side to get into one of those boats, convinced that the idea of doing so was silly. Most of the women sounded just as adamant, wondering how it could possibly make any sense to leave the solid safety of the *Titanic* in exchange for the flimsy wooden boats which were about to be lowered to the icy cold ocean where they would bob about erratically. But Helen's resolve was wavering. She became less sure that their conclusion was right, although she had to admit that nobody seemed to be heading over to the boats when the call for "women and children first" rang out. It was a standoff.

Then a voice pierced the night air. "How about letting the newlyweds get into the lifeboats together?" It was not clear whether it was the officer who stood by lifeboat 7 who had spoken up, or Captain Smith, or just somebody in the crowd, but Helen's mind was instantly made up. "Let's go, Dickinson," she said while pulling firmly on his arm, and they quickly crossed the slightly sloping deck to get to the boat. Helen climbed in, although it would be more descriptive to say that she was pushed in. Her entry was not at all elegant, but she took a certain amount of pride ever afterwards in claiming that she was literally the first passenger on the entire ship to enter a lifeboat. Dick got in next to her, and over the next few minutes they watched the other passengers board, including one more newlywed couple.

Helen felt her throat catch when Margaret Hays got in, clutching her Pomeranian, Lady. Helen clearly felt it would have been improper to return to their cabin for Freu-Freu and have the dog take up space in the lifeboat. But now she had to second guess herself, especially when the crew started lowering the boat, making it the first to leave the *Titanic*. There was so much space available. A formal headcount revealed only 28 were seated there, even though the lifeboat could have held 65. Only three crew members were among them, which struck Helen as being far too few.

The Bishops could do little more than watch the steady progression of lifeboats leaving the ship over the next hundred minutes, but it was a different sight that caught Helen's eyes. She leaned over to her husband and whispered, "Look at the lights. They're disappearing into the water." When their lifeboat was about one hundred yards away the lowest row had vanished from sight, and by the time they reached a position that Helen was convinced was a mile away, the second row was also gone.

Helen tried to focus on everything that occurred, especially noticing how calm things seemed until the very final minutes when the slant of the *Titanic* became quite severe. Later, when she had the opportunity to describe this at the United States Senate Hearing, her words were vividly clear. "Indeed, everything seemed to be quiet on the ship until her stern was raised out of the water by the list forward. Then a veritable wave of humanity surged up out of steerage and shut the lights from our view.... we could see the black masses of human forms and hear their death cries and groans."

With the *Titanic* gone, Helen said a silent prayer, thankful that she, Dickinson, and their unborn baby were safe. However, her mind kept turning back to the little dog they had left behind. She had grown to love Freu-Freu so intensely in those past few weeks.

Watching the sailors in the boat struggling with the oars, Helen and Dick decided they would help them row, and other passengers also joined the effort. With only three crew members aboard, it was obvious how understaffed they were. Helen felt some relief when they joined up with lifeboat 5. An awkward at-sea exchange of passengers and crew members took place, causing the boat to rock frighteningly in the icy water and forcing Helen to ignore any queasiness that she felt. At least they now had more assistance, and the valiant efforts of the sailors did not escape her attention.

On the other hand, Helen was particularly disturbed by the lack of action on the part of one of the other passengers. "Dick, have you noticed that man over there?" she asked, referring to a man who falsely claimed to be a German baron. "All he does is sit there and smoke." Alfred Nourney, the self-proclaimed Baron von Drachstad, never even offered to row at any point during the night, and Helen was not impressed. But Pierre Maréchal was another story, as he handled the oars with resolute intensity. "How does he manage to keep that monocle in place the entire time he is rowing?" she wondered.

One of the dining room stewards had brought along some green flares, which at least provided a bit of comfort throughout the pitch black, moonless night, although Helen noticed that "they cast a ghastly light over the boat." She looked at the others, their faces drawn. A few sobbed quietly, and hushed whispers were still loud enough to be heard by others. The overriding concern at this point was whether they would ever be found in such a huge ocean. Nobody had any idea whether any messages had gone out to potential rescue ships.

Suddenly, Helen's head snapped up. "Everybody, listen to me. We definitely will be saved," she excitedly assured them. "When my husband

and I were in Egypt, we had the chance to go to a fortune teller. Now that fortune teller predicted all kinds of things, including that we would be in a ship wreck and an earthquake, and that I would die in a car crash. We can't argue about the ship wreck – here we are. But I've never been in an earthquake so far, and I certainly cannot die in a car crash out here. We have to survive or else the rest of my prophecy can never come true." Whether anybody else accepted her argument was immaterial; Helen was convinced. While the session with the fortune teller had been a bit of a lark, the dead-on reference to a ship wreck had made things surreally correct. She could worry about the earthquake and car crash later on.

The rescue ship came in the form of a Cunard liner, the *Carpathia,* and the Bishops discussed what they would do once they reached New York now that they were rescued. It would be such a relief to see Helen's parents, who were already in the city. They had been in Florida for the winter months and the plan had been in place for the Waltons to return to Michigan with the Bishops once they docked. With all that had occurred in the interim, Helen was so grateful to head to the Waldorf-Astoria where her parents were staying.

The Bishops toyed with the idea of taking the train home to Michigan, but then decided to send a telegram to Dickinson's parents to the effect that they would stay with their original plans, subject to one modification. The Bishops' chauffeur, Earl Patterson, would still drive them home in the Lozier from New York to Michigan, but they would delay their return for at least another week.

The extended time in New York provided a bit of extra time to recuperate, but Helen had another idea in mind. "We have nothing to wear, Dickinson," she said, pointing out the obvious. "All of our clothing except for what we are wearing is now at the bottom of the Atlantic, and I'm not about to go home in this tiresome outfit." Of course, she was right about this, and the opportunity to purchase a new wardrobe would be great fun. She enjoyed shopping at various New York City establishments which offered a finer assortment of dresses and suits than what they could get at home in Dowagiac or even in Detroit, for that matter. Replacing the rest of their personal property, valued at $20,000 and including some incredible pieces of jewelry, would take more time, and that could wait for the future.

Their delay in New York also provided them with the time to be questioned during the United States Senate *Titanic* Hearings, an opportunity that Helen was not about to miss. On April 30, Helen raised her right hand, a slight tremble betraying her nervousness, and she was sworn in. It was day 11 of the hearings, and she nervously wondered what the Senators might ask her, now that so many individuals had already told their stories. To her relief, the first question of any substance centered on what she did after learning about the accident. Helen thought back to that night, knowing that she had turned in earlier after returning from the lounge, while Dickinson stayed up a bit longer to catch up on some reading. "My husband awakened me at about a quarter of 12 and told me that the boat had struck something. We both dressed and went up on deck, looked around, and could find nothing. We noticed the intense cold; in fact we noticed that about 11 o'clock that night. It was uncomfortably cold in the lounge. We looked all over the deck; walked up and down a couple of times, and one of the stewards looked at us and laughed at us. He said, 'You go back downstairs. There is nothing to be afraid of. We have only struck a little piece of ice and passed it.'"

Helen explained that they followed the steward's advice and returned to their cabin for about fifteen minutes, only to be alerted by Albert Stewart, a neighboring passenger, to return upstairs. Her testimony continued, sometimes animated and sometimes intense. She was struck by the realization that not only had she been a part of history, but now her words were also being recorded for all eternity. Carefully she described their long wait, the behavior of other passengers around them, the lifeboat, and the arrival of the *Carpathia*. Her testimony did not take long, but she made every effort to respond honestly to the questions and to include information that she thought would be helpful.

All the while Dickinson listened to his wife's testimony, and when the Senators turned to him for more details, he made it clear that she had done a superb job. Helen always had a flair for words, and she had explained things well, as he knew she would. Initially, he had no further details to add, but then he recalled some comments he heard about the closing of the watertight compartments. After that, the Senators followed up with some additional questions regarding orders being called out while they were still on the ship and about the passengers in the lifeboat. All the while, Helen smiled encouragingly at her husband until his testimony ended. Finally it was over, and it was time to return to Michigan. Unfortunately, the springtime road conditions were not ideal, and the chauffeur only drove the Bishops as far as Buffalo. From there they took the train the rest of the way home.

Not surprisingly, the Bishops were the center of attention when they reached Dowagiac, and Helen especially reveled in the opportunity to release her statement to the press. Only when the excitement settled down could they really turn their attention to setting up their new home and preparing for the arrival of the baby. What fun it was gathering together furniture for their unborn child and putting together a modest collection of infant clothing. Naturally, they would not know the gender of the child until he or she was born, and only then could they really start to purchase clothes that would be specifically appropriate for their future son or daughter.

Thoughts about the *Titanic* never fully disappeared, but the feelings grew less intense as the months rolled by. Helen felt it was odd that the Egyptian fortune teller never said anything about the birth of their child, but did that really matter? The prediction about a boat-wreck was almost certainly just an unexpectedly accurate shot in the dark, and with Michigan being an unlikely place for the predicted earthquake to occur, Helen did not dwell at all on the possibility of a life-ending car accident. Her attention was clearly focused on the arrival of their first born.

December in Michigan can be bitterly cold, even before winter formally arrives. Fortunately, as December 8 drew near the weather conditions were not extreme. Helen was glad about this when her labor pains started, for she certainly did not want help to be hindered from arriving should the delivery be a difficult one. Little Randall Walton Bishop was born that day, but something was not right. The situation was grim as the baby struggled to survive, and two days later Helen and Dick lost their baby. That they had survived the sinking of the *Titanic* less than eight months earlier only to have this tragic ending seemed completely unfair. No other word but "devastated" could describe Helen, as eager anticipation and dreams of the joys of motherhood were replaced by overwhelming loss.

# Mary Eloise Hughes Smith

## One-and-a-half Months Pregnant

*Every child begins the world again.*
*--Henry David Thoreau*

It was New Year's Eve, and Eloise Smith could hardly wait for 1912 to arrive...not that she was focused on that night's events, which she knew would be great fun. What she was really thinking about was her society debut, just nine days away. She carefully spread her gown across the bedspread to look at it once again, and her mind danced with images of what the formal tea would be like at the venerable Willard Hotel. Among the guests would be some of Washington D.C.'s most socially connected individuals; and naturally her father, Congressman James Hughes of West Virginia, had also invited the full array of his closest political colleagues. The venue was only two blocks away from the White House, but of course President Taft would not be in attendance. Eloise laughed at the thought, even though a little bit of youthful naivete toyed in her head with such a scenario. This would be an afternoon of incredible memories, and she was looking forward to returning home to Huntington, West Virginia, to tell her Sunday school class all about it.

As always, coming back to Huntington offered Eloise a bit of breathing room and relaxation from the intensity of the capital, but this trip also presented a surprise. Lucian Smith seemed to come out of nowhere. Friends of his had encouraged him to seek out Eloise, and he had to admit that the photograph they showed him of the young woman was quite enticing. They met, and Eloise was smitten. Lucian was a handsome 24-year-old. He was sociable, easy to talk to, and everything she ever dreamed of.

Eloise tried to quash the feeling of love at first sight, but clearly love was winning. She knew that at the age of 18 there was still plenty of time to find a beau, but she could hardly imagine anybody who would be finer than Lucian. Besides, he came from a family of some wealth. The Smiths of

Dawson, Pennsylvania, had made a small fortune in the coal industry, and this would certainly meet with her parents' approval. How fortunate she was that Lucian had moved to nearby Morgantown to attend and graduate from the University of West Virginia, and afterward he remained in the city while living with his sister's family.

Eloise's decisive and somewhat impetuous nature made it easy for her to say "Yes" when Lucian asked her to marry him. Wasting no time at all, they set their wedding date for February 8, just one day shy of a month since her society debut. Eloise insisted that the ceremony be held at Central Huntington Church, which her family had supported for years. Her mother, Ida, was a charter member there since 1894, so she was easily able to arrange for their Thursday wedding, even under such short notice. Eloise's excitement continued to grow, almost as if she had stepped inside a fairy tale.

Eloise and her father made their way toward the entrance to the church's main aisle. She glanced down at her lovely white satin gown one more time, her eyes twinkling. There was no mirror nearby, of course, but just the sight of orange blossom lace and her orchid bouquet was enough to put a small smile on her face. The processional music pealed forth from the organ, and Eloise felt her father's firm hand gently leading her toward the aisle that had been strewn with pink rosebuds. At the opposite end stood Lucian, a loving smile on his face. The rest of the wedding party watched her approach with visible joy, and the attending guests stood in respectful silence as the bride headed toward the altar. Normally, Eloise was clear-headed and mindful of her surroundings, but now she found herself overcome by the wonderment of the ceremony. Everything seemed to be a blur of pure emotionality, and she decided that was a good thing. Her love of Lucian was unmistakable.

Less than two weeks later the newlyweds were in New York, and Eloise felt her heart beat with excitement as they walked up the gangway to board the *Olympic*. Not only were the White Star liners known for their glamor and highest of standards, but this was also the largest ship afloat in the entire world. How thrilling 1912 had been so far!

A nattily-dressed member of the crew led the Smiths to their cabin, and Eloise realized that she would have trouble finding her way back there again. She had been so busy looking around that she paid little attention to how they reached their room. The porter bid them goodbye, and she smiled when he referred to them as "Mr. and Mrs. Smith." She was still adjusting to that.

Unpacking could certainly wait, so the newlyweds headed out to explore the ship and wave farewell as the *Olympic* left its New York dock. The ship was magnificent! Lucian and Eloise made the rounds, intrigued by the gymnasium, indoor pool, lounge areas, and even an a la carte restaurant, although they anticipated that they would usually be eating in the main dining saloon. The wood paneling was exquisite, and Eloise could tell that White Star had spent generous amounts of money on fine upholstering, handsome light fixtures, and other artistic touches. The Smiths were truly impressed.

The one feature the Smiths immediately fell in love with was the A-deck promenade. The view of the ocean was unhindered, the fresh air was invigorating, and the opportunity to stroll or linger as the mood struck was inviting. Day after day they spent part of their time here, although there was a bit of a downside. When the ship was steaming ahead at full speed, and the wind and sea conditions were perfectly in tune, sea water could spray high enough to reach the forward section of the promenade. Eloise wanted no part of being sprinkled by the icy cold February water, so she steered Lucian away from the railing any time she spotted puddles reflecting upon the floorboards. Just the thought of being sprayed made Eloise uncomfortable, and it was fodder for both laughter and annoyed outbursts among the first class passengers who happened to be there at the most inopportune times.

Unfortunately, their high-speed progress came to a distinct end when the ship somehow lost a propeller blade. The ship's speed was reduced accordingly, and therefore Eloise did not have to worry about getting soaked again. This also provided her with the opportunity to recognize how efficiently the ship's officers handled the crisis. In particular, she was especially impressed with Captain Edward J. Smith, whose reassuring words and confidence were most comforting.

When Eloise and Lucian reached Europe, their grand tour could begin. The couple's plan included some of the continent's most famous sights and museums, but they also planned to relax, shop, and benefit as much as they could along the warm Mediterranean coastline. Not for a second, however, did Eloise envision one very special opportunity that would arise.

The Smiths made their way to Egypt, a newly popular destination for many travelers, and near the pyramids and the Sphinx were camel handlers. "Lucian! We have to ride the camels!" Eloise blurted out, and her husband immediately agreed. This was an opportunity too good to miss and would be so much fun to describe when they returned home. Eloise climbed aboard while the camel was still kneeling on the ground, and as it stood, she could hardly believe how high she was. Once underway, the ride was certainly not comfortable, as the animal's loping walk created an odd instability as the hump swayed back and forth, but that did not matter to Eloise. Her delighted laughter filled the air as the short ride continued.

Like most other wealthy travelers of the day, Lucian and Eloise left their return date open-ended, figuring they would continue their tour until they wearied of being away from home. It seemed that day would never come, but then came the unexpected. "Lucian," she said softly one night. "We're going to have a baby." Her husband could hardly believe the good news, and the two of them started discussing their future with great excitement. After all, they had only known one another for a few weeks before they married and they had been traveling most of the time after the wedding. Now they needed to return to West Virginia, set up their new home, and prepare for the arrival of their son or daughter.

Almost immediately they started planning their trip from Egypt back to West Virginia. Eloise wrote home saying, "Lucian is getting so anxious to get home and drive the car and fool around on the farm....We leave here on Sunday....By boat to Brindisi [Italy], by rail to Nice and Monte Carlo, then to Paris and via Cherbourg either on the *Lusitania* or the new *Titanic*....I will love so much to tell my Sunday School class when I get home..." However, she decided not to mention her pregnancy in any of her letters; that would be a wonderful surprise for later.

In the meantime, Lucian sent messages to the Ritz-Carlton in New York, making arrangements for the same rooms where the couple had stayed before their cruise over to Europe. He also made sure that a taxi and porters would be waiting for them when they reached the docks. As to which passenger ship to take home, he and Eloise finally settled on the *Titanic*. They had been thoroughly impressed with the service they had aboard its sister ship, and besides, now that the *Titanic* had surpassed the *Olympic* in size, the opportunity to sail on the newly-designated largest ship in the world seemed preordained. As a bonus, they learned that Edward J. Smith would be Captain, and they were confident that his leadership and expertise would again make the choice of a White Star liner a wise one. They adjusted their pace through Europe accordingly to reach Cherbourg by April 10.

Because the *Olympic* and *Titanic* were virtually identical in their floor plans, Lucian and Eloise found it easy to select cabin C31, located in the forward part of the ship, for their return trip. This outside cabin was one of the smaller first-class rooms, but its relative proximity to the Grand Staircase made Eloise quite happy. Once aboard, they again delayed unpacking so they could look about, but this time they clearly were not exploring an unfamiliar layout. Quite simply it was fun to look for what differences they could locate in comparison to their earlier vessel. Eloise approved of Café Parisien, beautifully set up with white wicker furnishings and decorated with an ivy-covered French trellis, the overall effect looking very much like a casually elegant sidewalk café. They also agreed that the reception area for the Dining Saloon near the Grand Staircase was a nice addition, and they found themselves debating whether some of the décor had been trimmed in different colors.

When they reached A-deck. Eloise's mouth dropped open, and she burst out laughing. No longer would they need to joke about getting soaked on the promenade. Apparently, there must have been complaints about the occasional spray of water which reached that great height on the *Olympic*. White Star wisely had installed sliding windows along a new steel screen for the *Titanic* that could be opened or closed as the weather necessitated.

The Smiths quickly fell into their routine at sea, strolling, reading, sitting on the deck chairs and chatting, playing a bit of shuffleboard, and savoring the incredibly fine meals. They made a point to enjoy the concerts provided by the small orchestra that was aboard, with the music making for a very pleasant diversion.

Sunday, April 14th, was a more subdued day, of course. Captain Smith led the first class worship service, and once again Eloise added this to the list of stories to tell her Sunday school class. It seemed that everybody aboard had slowed down their pace in observing the Sabbath, but part of this might also have been due to the air temperature dropping in the afternoon, which made passengers far more inclined to remain indoors.

After dinner, the Smiths found it quite comforting to slowly sip their coffee and listen to the band playing in the reception room, but other forms of entertainment were also beginning to surface. Card playing was normally frowned upon on Sunday, but by then it had grown quite dark on that moonless night, and somehow this seemed to draw the Sabbath to a close. Lucian decided he would enjoy a bit of card-playing diversion, so Eloise excused herself. It was growing late, the cold air outdoors had made her more tired than normal, and she felt that a bit of extra rest would be good for both her and the baby. Eloise returned to the cabin and was soon asleep, while Lucian headed to Café Parisien where he joined three Frenchmen, Paul Chevré, Alfred Omont, and Pierre Maréchal, for a few rubbers of bridge. The games were lively and well-played, and the company was clearly to Lucian's liking.

Suddenly a strange shudder rippled through the ship, and all four men jumped to their feet to find out what had happened. They quickly learned that an iceberg had scraped against the starboard side of the ship, and they discovered hundreds of ice pieces scattered across the deck, clear evidence of the encounter. A brief discussion and orders for the passengers to return to their cabins to retrieve their life jackets sent all four of the men below. While there seemed to be no immediate danger, it was clearly in their best interest to follow the order.

The three Frenchmen were each traveling alone and returned quickly, meeting up with one another on the starboard side of the ship. When the order of "women and children first" rang out, First Officer William Murdoch struggled to find even a few individuals willing to climb into lifeboats. He encouraged a small number of unaccompanied women to board and had even admitted some married couples. Because so much room remained after he loaded the women and children who were willing to get in, Murdoch opened up the additional space in boat 7 to any men waiting nearby who were interested in doing so. The three French card players seized the opportunity.

For Lucian, the story was quite different, for he needed to alert his wife first. Eloise had awakened twice by that time, first when the collision occurred and, after falling back asleep, when the engines stopped. When Lucian opened the cabin door and turned on the lights, Eloise quickly awoke and shielded her eyes from the glare. "What's going on, Lucian?" she mumbled, half asleep but nevertheless awake enough to know that it was not his custom to disturb her this way when he returned to the cabin after she was already sleeping.

"We are in the north and have struck an iceberg," he informed her. "It does not amount to anything, but will probably delay us a day getting into New York. However, as a matter of form, the Captain has ordered all ladies on deck." The news was unexpected, of course, but Eloise was not about to argue. She got out of bed and got dressed while Lucian casually munched on an apple. *At least he looks calm,* she thought, *so there must not be anything to worry about*. The only things she took from their cabin beyond what she was wearing were two rings. including the diamond one Lucian bought for her in Amsterdam. Otherwise, Lucian felt rounding up any more of the jewelry would be a foolish delay, and he told her, "Don't worry about such trifles."

For some reason after they left their starboard-side cabin, the Smiths crossed over to the port side as they headed up to the Boat Deck. Calm prevailed here like what the Frenchmen had found on the opposite side, but the order of "women and children first" took on an entirely different interpretation. Second Officer Charles Lightoller was in charge on this side of the ship, and to him the Captain's order meant that he was not to admit any men (other than some necessary crewmen to row) until every woman and child had been vacated from the entire ship. Upon learning this, Eloise's eyes welled with tears, and with great determination she let Lucian know she was not about to leave without him. When she spotted Captain Smith, she asked him directly if Lucian could join her in the lifeboat. However, the Captain continued shouting "women and children first" through his megaphone without acknowledging her or giving her a reply.

Lucian spoke up, saying "Never mind, Captain, about that; I will see that she gets in the boat." Whether the Captain heard Lucian's words was unclear, but Lucian knew he needed to fully focus on his wife, who was still uncertain about climbing into lifeboat 6. He looked into her eyes and tenderly told her, "I never expected to ask you to obey, but this is one time you must; it is only a matter of form to have the women and children first. The boat is thoroughly equipped, and everybody on her will be saved."

"Are you being absolutely honest with me?" Eloise asked, and Lucian assured her that he was. She felt better upon hearing his response, being absolutely confident in his words. Despite her attempt to smile bravely, tears welled up once again as the crew started to lower lifeboat 6. "How is this possible?" she wondered. "He just kissed me goodbye and warned me to keep my hands in my pockets to keep them warm, and now I'm so alone." Those promises to "love, honor, and obey" from their wedding vows just nine weeks earlier suddenly seemed so wrong, despite his assurance that all would work out. Her teary view of her husband, calmly waving goodbye, was seared into her brain.

For the next hour Eloise sat shivering in the lifeboat, but she kept her eyes riveted on the *Titanic*. Boat after boat were released, the ship visibly dipped deeper into the ocean, and faint sounds of yelling and even an occasional gunshot could be heard. All the while she prayed for Lucian's survival, whispering to herself, "Let him be safe." Occasionally her thoughts turned to her unborn baby, with the fervent hope that her anxiety and the intense cold would do the child no harm. To avoid being overwhelmed by the situation, she did everything she could to keep her worried thoughts in check.

Unfortunately, Eloise's wholehearted feelings could not offset the annoyance that welled up from deep within as she observed Quartermaster Robert Hichens, who had been put in charge of the lifeboat. She would later state, "Our seaman was Hichens, who refused to row, but sat in the end of the boat wrapped in a blanket that one of the women had given him. I am not of the opinion that he was intoxicated, but a lazy uncouth man, who had no respect for the ladies, and who was a thorough coward." Eventually she would refute this earlier claim.

When the *Titanic* finally sank, Eloise was startled to hear cries and shouts and wails as victims were tossed haphazardly into the icy ocean. Lucian's reassuring words that everybody would be saved were refuted by this new reality. The hours dragged on until the *Carpathia* arrived, and once Eloise was taken aboard she saw that, unlike her own lifeboat, many of the other boats had rescued male passengers. Encouraged but nervous, she searched for her husband until it became clear that Lucian was not among them, and hope turned into devastation. Her only consolation was that another survivor, Robert Daniel, had sensed her overwhelming grief and looked after her as the rescue ship headed to New York. Daniel also physically supported the weakened young woman as she went down the gangway of the *Carpathia* when it reached New York, turning her over to her parents and her uncle, Z. Taylor Vinson, who were there to meet her. At that point, Eloise struggled to control her near-hysteria.

Although she was spent both emotionally and physically, Eloise remained intent on learning as much as she could about the disaster while she was still aboard the *Carpathia.* Information and clear-headed thinking are crucial, she told herself, these being lessons she had learned from her Congressman father. Of course, questionable rumors were wide-spread among the survivors who shared their stories with one another, but one thing was unarguably true. White Star Chairman J. Bruce Ismay had survived. The stories she heard convinced her that he was a major factor behind the accident. The claim was circulating that he had ordered the ship to sail at top speed despite the ice warnings. And then after the collision occurred, he simply took the coward's way out and sneaked in to one of the earliest lifeboats to leave the doomed ship. How could he have escaped the horrors of the sinking, while her beloved husband bravely went to his death? And now he had hidden himself away on the *Carpathia*, sequestered behind locked doors, unwilling to see anybody. She had to make this travesty known.

Eloise submitted her affidavit for the United States Senate Hearings, a much calmer summary than what she had shared with the press earlier. "I know many women who slept on the floor in the smoking room while Mr. Ismay occupied the best room on the *Carpathia*, being in the center of the boat, with every attention, and a sign on the door [which said 'Please do not knock.']." But when she talked to the press, she made a point to include her angry charge that several seamen had actually escorted Ismay to one of the first lifeboats to be launched, while the women were left to their own devices to seek safety. Her allegations that Ismay remained hidden away on the *Carpathia* were certainly true, but the reality about his departure from the sinking ship was not. The White Star President was actually asked if he wished to climb into collapsible C, the last lifeboat to be properly launched on the starboard side. Reliable accounts suggest that he was offered the opportunity get in only after all the women and children waiting nearby had been seated. But none of this mattered to Eloise. She wanted to clearly state what she "knew" to be true.

The family returned to Huntington by train, and Eloise kept waiting and praying for Lucian's body to be recovered by the *Mackay-Bennett*. When this did not occur, Eloise wanted to find some meaningful closure regarding his death. Without any remains to be buried, there was no need to erect the large mausoleum she had been planning. Instead, she arranged for a memorial service to be held for him in the Central Huntington Church at 3:00 p.m. on Sunday, May 12. "How unfair it is," she thought, "that we have been forced into such a tragic remembrance here in the same church where we had our wedding just three months ago?" It was impossible for Eloise to ever forget her beloved Lucian, and tears ran down her cheeks during the service. But she also realized she had to get on with her life and prepare for the birth of her child. This would be his legacy.

The Hughes family took steps to make sure the finest healthcare was made available to Eloise while she awaited the day the baby would be born. Her friends and family supported her in every way they could, and even that nice man from the *Carpathia,* Robert Daniel, traveled from Philadelphia several times to visit her. Many pregnant women in the early decades of the twentieth century gave birth at home, but Eloise and her parents decided that she needed to be in a hospital when the time came. Knowing that larger cities boasted hospitals which were best prepared to high level medical care, Eloise entered a Cincinnati facility described as "the Jewish hospital in Avondale" by the press more than a week before her son was born on November 29, 1912.

Newspaper coverage ballyhooed the baby's arrival and even shared the fact that Madeleine Astor, whose own son was born three months earlier, had sent Eloise a congratulatory telegram. The press erred in reporting that the babies were the first and second born of mothers who had been on the *Titanic*, but such a mistake was trivial to Eloise. All she cared about at the point was that her son was alive and healthy.

*Eloise Smith with Lucian Philip Smith II (Source: Downtown Morgantown Walking Tours, The Clio)*

In later years, Z. Taylor Vinson, Eloise's uncle, enjoyed pointing out that "...Eloise was probably the only woman in the world who in just a year's time made her debut, got engaged, married, survived the *Titanic,* became a widow, and then a mother." But such a summary was of no importance when Eloise held her cherished son in her arms for the first time. She looked at him lovingly, and there was no doubt in her mind. "His name shall be Lucian Philip Smith II." Pride filled her soul as she continued to gaze at her baby son. Then she turned her eyes heavenward as she said, "Lucian, I miss you so much."

# Catherine McHugh Bourke

## Possibly Less Than Two Months Pregnant

*"Mother: The most beautiful word on the lips of mankind."*
*--Khalil Gibran*

Catherine McGowan was excited to be returning to her friends in Chicago and even looked forward to resuming the responsibilities at the boarding house she ran, but right now her main feeling was frustration. When she journeyed home to Ireland for a visit last year, she figured others would join her for the return trip to America – particularly her niece, Annie McGowan – but never did she imagine there would be a contingent of fourteen traveling together from Addergoole Parish. Of course, she was not actually responsible to watch over them, but with more than one hundred passengers milling about Queenstown's White Star Line building, waiting for the tender to carry them out to the *Titanic,* she at least wanted to keep them close together. This simply was not happening.

Catherine looked around for John Bourke. Perhaps his voice would carry better than her own, and he could call them together. But John and his wife, also named Catherine but better known as Kate, were some distance away, and it was not worth the effort to force her way through the crowd to reach him. Maybe it would be easier to pull everybody together once they boarded the tender.

John and Kate were waiting patiently with his sister, Mary. The Bourke siblings were 42 and 40 years old, respectively, but it was 32-year-old Kate who was far calmer at this moment. She had past experience crossing the Atlantic, and this transit was far more joyous for her than before. She found herself growing a bit nostalgic just thinking about all that had happened to her.

*A total of 123 passengers waited at the White Star Office in Queenstown before being transported to the* Titanic *by tender (Source: Visitcobh.com)*

In January of 1886, three months after Kate turned six years old, her mother died. Kate was really too young at the time to fully understand why her mother had become so debilitated, and then she was forced to face her father's death from cancer just eight months later. The loss of both parents in such a short period of time and the hardscrabble existence endured by her family, like so many others in Ireland, had taken its toll. Somehow her 16-year-old sister, Mary McHugh, assumed the initial responsibility for Kate and the other five children who were still at home.

As the McHugh children grew up and married they gradually moved away, and the younger children often found themselves relocating. Earning a livelihood was extremely challenging and included such grueling trades for women like working in the cotton mills. At the age of 16 Kate moved to Chicago, hoping the alternatives would be far brighter. However, she quickly learned that the fabled "streets of gold" in America were an exaggeration, and hard work was required if one wanted to survive. At least she could depend on the support of family members who were also living there in the Windy City.

In 1910 and still single, Kate headed back to Ireland. While her main intention was to visit relatives and friends from nearly half a lifetime ago, she certainly found an added bonus when she encountered John Bourke. He was an acquaintance she only vaguely recalled from her past, not surprising since he was ten years older than she, but they quickly became attracted to one another. "St. Patrick be praised," she thought to herself over and over as their love for one another continued to blossom, and on January 17, 1911, they married. The newlyweds lived together along with John's sister, Mary, and Kate learned a great deal about farming that year. But when Catherine McGowan returned from Chicago, the three Bourkes started seriously talking about moving to America together. This would not be an easy decision, despite the fact that Kate had already lived there.

Because John and Mary were used to their lives on the farm, they knew all too well how uncertain harvest yield and income could be, but they really had no other experience to draw from. A move to America was a bit frightening. For Kate, however, the thought of heading back to Chicago and once again being near her own sister, Ellen, was a major draw. Meanwhile, when they learned that Catherine McGowan continued to find an increasing number of Addergoole residents to head to America together, John and Kate's discussion grew more spirited.

One obvious issue was that a move to Chicago meant that John would not be engaged in farming at all. Kate was realistic and carefully explained the challenges that such a move would entail. "I know you're used to hard work as a farmer, John, but in Chicago you'll probably be working for someone else. If they don't like the way you are working, you'll find yourself out of a job, so we need to think about this carefully. Money flows quickly in America."

John figured that he would be well-suited for a position shoeing horses, still very much needed in the city. While he had never worked as a farrier, he certainly had enough experience trimming hooves and shoeing his own animals, so this would be a reasonable path to pursue. Or perhaps he could purchase some horses and set up his own teaming business. John and Kate's discussion continued almost relentlessly, and the thought of moving to America was gradually becoming more attractive. Even Mary was warming to the idea. How quickly everything seemed to progress after they finally made their decision. The Bourkes needed to sell their property, equipment, and whatever belongings that they were not taking with them to Queenstown when they prepared to board the ship.

And now here they were, holding hands as the appropriately named tender, *America,* made its way through the harbor to the *Titanic.* Kate realized from John's sweaty palms how nervous he was, and smiled a bit when he whispered, "Katie, it's so large," as they drew closer to the ship. Even though Kate had crossed the Atlantic twice before, she also found herself overwhelmed by the size of the ship. They both had learned that this was the largest ship in the world, but Kate was startled at how much larger it was than those she had sailed on previously. The closer the *America* got to the *Titanic,* the bigger it seemed to be. To Kate it seemed that the giant smokestacks reached the sky!

Catherine McGowen's earlier concern about trying to keep the 14 passengers from Addergoole together had become a lost cause even on the tender, but as it turned out they would often meet together during their voyage. With so many from Lahardane alone and with almost everybody in their group able to call someone else a relative, it was only natural that they would join one another on the outer deck area or in the third class general room. However, their cabins were scattered throughout the length of the ship, as the White Star Line had arranged the quarters so that single men were housed in the bow and the women in the stern.

Third class passengers were only permitted to enter certain restricted sections of the ship, but there was still plenty to explore. Kate and John headed out before dinner to do some investigating and to look at the wide-open ocean. The view almost rendered John speechless at first. For a farmer whose entire life had been tied to the land, the wide expanse of open ocean seemed nearly impossible to grasp. The enormity of their decision had finally become fully apparent, and he truly realized that they might never see their homeland again. But it was time to look forward to a new life with his wife.

Of course, Kate was fully prepared for the view of the sea, but a much simpler discovery took her by surprise. When they first entered the third class dining saloon, Kate grabbed John's arm and exclaimed, "They have chairs!" Her outburst puzzled John, but then Kate explained that steerage passengers were usually seated on benches that were fastened to the floor when they dined. By comparison, this was surprisingly inviting and fully indicative of how well White Star was treating the passengers of their class.

The dinner was quite good, exceeding what the Bourkes had expected, and they were especially delighted to learn that a generous supply of fresh fruit and warm bread would be available at every meal. The next morning at breakfast they found the oatmeal porridge to be quite filling and comforting, although Kate had to admit that slathering butter and orange marmalade on a thick slice of just-baked brown bread was a wonderful bonus.

Kate, John, and Mary enjoyed their time on the outer deck and chatting with their friends from back home, but they also found pleasure whenever they went to the general room. This was especially true when other Irish travelers commandeered the piano (which was most of the time, given the number of them aboard!). While Kate would have liked to join in dancing, John and Mary held back. After all, they were twice the age of most of those young people who seemingly never stopped their lively steps, and it was just easier for the older folks to sit along the outer edge of the room.

The familiar Irish tunes were wonderful. Kate often found her feet moving in time with the rhythm, and she had to smile whenever she noticed John's right hand keeping time as well. Even Mary, the most reserved of the three of them, would let a smile flicker across her lips when a particularly meaningful song was being sung, especially "The Rose of Tralee." Kate leaned over to be heard above the music and said to John, "Do you think they are having this much fun in first class?" John shook his head no and continued tapping his fingers to the rhythm.

The three Bourkes spent part of the evening of April 14th in the general room, but soon realized how tired they were. Because they had been on the outside deck when the colder weather moved in earlier that afternoon, the net effect had apparently been a bit wearing. Fighting the urge to fall asleep, they headed back to their quarters earlier than usual, and the sounds of the rich Irish ballads gradually faded away as they left the piano far behind. It did not take long before they settled down for the night and fell asleep.

The sudden pounding at the door and the abrupt shouts of the room steward were startling. This should not be happening in the middle of the night. They were quickly informed that the *Titanic* had struck an iceberg, and that all passengers were to put on their life vests and head up to the Boat Deck. The Bourses quickly complied, although the sight of a priest leading the penitent surrounding him in earnest prayer stopped them briefly. However, John did not let the women linger for long.

With the assistance of Pat Canavan, John led some of the Addergoole passengers through the mysterious maze of corridors, stairways, ladders, and upper class promenades. Finally, they reached a confusing scene of frightened passengers, hard-at-work crew members, and the final few lifeboats still waiting to be filled.

Not all of the Addergoole passengers were on hand, and it was impossible to know if some had already left the ship or if others were still trying to navigate their way through the lower decks. Annie McGowan climbed into a lifeboat along with Annie Kelly, but her aunt, Catherine McGowan, was missing, as they had gotten separated in the confusion. Delia McDermott joined them in the lifeboat by facing the frightening ordeal of dropping 15 feet downward from a rope ladder.

However, the Bourkes found that any possibility of leaving the ship was thwarted by the announcement that only women and children were being permitted into the boats. Kate's decision was instantaneous. Her eyes flashed as she looked at John and declared, "I'll not leave my husband." Mary was just as adamant as she announced, "I'll not leave my brother." Their decisions were final, and they awaited their fate as rockets from the *Titanic's* deck shot upward, bursting into sparkling stars and illuminating the night sky above them.

---

Addergoole was rocked by the news that the *Titanic* had sunk. Hardly a person existed in the countryside who did not know at least one of the victims; most knew several. Only three of the fourteen survived, and the other eleven needed to be properly mourned. Irish wakes continued for days, a curious blend of sorrow and grief, eating and drinking, remembrances and gentle laughter. Of course, there were no bodies to be buried and therefore the normal sense of closure was impacted, but cherished photographs were prominently displayed. What should have been a heartfelt, glorious sending off that was typical for such wakes became far more somber than usual. Pure white quilts covered what had been the victims' beds, and shadows from the burning candles cast gloomy shadows along the walls. It was so difficult to believe that just weeks ago they were in Castlebar, enjoying a fond farewell party for these very same individuals before they left Addergoole. Dancing and singing and the fond farewells had now been replaced by tragic good-byes and tears.

*Kate and John Bourke (Source: Encyclopedia Titanica)*

Stories about the *Titanic* victims went on for weeks as the County Mayo residents seemed unable to find anything else to talk about. A small group of older women lingered after mass several Sundays later, and the Bourkes' names cropped up.

"I heard that John and his sister had been having trouble maintaining the farm for the past three years. Besides, is it true that his step-mother really owned the land?" asked one the women. One of the others immediately spoke up.

"Oh, I don't know about the step-mother, but I really don't believe the farm was in trouble. John just purchased a new spade earlier this spring. 'Tis a major expense to invest in one if the farm was really doing poorly. I guess they had not yet made up their mind about traveling to America and this was an expense that seemed to be a wise one."

The women grew silent for a few moments, until a somewhat distant relative of the Bourkes quietly entered the discussion. "The family believes that Kate was with child." Again, silence took over, and two of the women raised their eyes heavenward as they made the sign of the cross. In that moment it appeared that Addergoole had lost one more.

# Argene Genovesi del Carlo

## Two Months Pregnant

*Every child born into the world is a new thought of God, an ever fresh and radiant possibility.*

*--Kate Douglas Wiggin*

Frank Aks was enjoying the attentive audience before him. Most of the attendees at the *Titanic* International convention already knew his story, of course, but he was well aware of the fact that hearing it from an actual *Titanic* survivor made it all the more special for them. In fairness, he had no actual memory of his own story as he was only ten months old when it happened. But his mother, Leah, had repeated it to him so many times that it almost seemed like he was delivering it from direct recall.

Frank's parents were originally from Poland, although they moved to England the year before he was born. Then in January of 1912, Sam Aks immigrated to Virginia and quickly earned enough money as a tailor for his wife and son to join him. Frank paused briefly before restarting his delivery. "Of course, my mother and I stayed in third class, and even that was a stretch on our finances, but my father wanted us to be reunited as quickly as possible."

The crux of Frank's story really began, unsurprisingly, when his mother carried him to the lifeboats after the *Titanic* hit the iceberg. Somehow little Filly, as she called him, was taken from her arms and put into lifeboat 11, and she was left behind. Frantically, Leah made her way to lifeboat 13. The night was a long one, and she was inconsolable, uncertain whether anybody was actually watching over Filly or if he would be able to survive the frigid conditions. Seated next to her was Ruth Becker, a 12-year-old missionary's daughter, who was on her way to Michigan along with her two siblings and her mother. Coincidentally, Ruth had been separated from the rest of her own family who were also in the same lifeboat as Filly.

Ruth did the best she could to comfort the "German woman," as she later referred to Leah, and promised to help her find baby Filly when they reached safety. Of course, once they boarded the *Carpathia,* Ruth located her own family first, but then she remained true to her promise by rejoining Leah. By that time, another woman had come to Leah's aid, namely Selena Cook, an English woman on her way to New York to visit her mother and who would later return to America and settle in northeastern Pennsylvania. The frantic search was on.

Once again Frank stopped talking briefly, and an impish grin crossed his face. "As it turned out, I found my mother before she spotted me. I cried out and reached my arms toward her. After all, I knew where my next meal was coming from." The audience laughed appreciatively, and Frank went on to describe the final part of the tale. The Italian woman holding him insisted that the infant was her own child (as did Leah, of course), and the crew member trying to sort out the messy situation finally called upon Captain Rostron to resolve the matter. Leah told the captain that her son had a red birthmark on his chest, and the issue was resolved at last. Mother and son were reunited. With that, the other woman faded back into the rest of the crowd nearby.

Frank made no attempt to identify the other woman during his presentation, but many believe she was probably Argene del Carlo. She was also believed to have been rescued in lifeboat 11, while her husband Sebastiano was left behind. Argene was two months pregnant at the time, and apparently her fragile mental stability was put to the test. By the time she reached the *Carpathia* she had no idea where her husband was, and the thoughts of her yet-to-be-born child weighed heavily in her mind. It is feasible that she managed to contort the presence of Filly in her arms as being her own child.

-----------------------------------

While Argene and Sebastiano were waiting for the arrival of the *Titanic* back in Cherbourg, she became somewhat unnerved. The ship was late arriving and that gave her enough time to again review the enormity of all that had been going on in her life over the past twelve weeks. Before that, the couple had known each other by sight, but they never formally met until January 20, 1912, during the celebration of the Feast of St. Sebastian. They fell in love almost instantaneously and the following month they got married. In the fast-paced days that followed, Argene found herself adjusting to married life, packing to go to America, saying goodbye to her friends, and coming to terms with the fact that she might never see her own parents ever again.

*Wedding picture, Argene and Sebastiano del Carlo (Source: titanic.pagesperson-orange.fr)*

Sebastiano told Argene that they would head to Chicago first, where he had lived for the past nine years, working most recently as a mechanic. He had been so successful that he was able to afford five trips back home to Italy to visit. Argene was convinced that their financial well-being was assured, but she had to admit she was nervous about his descriptions of the horrendously cold and snowy winters there. She hoped that they would quickly follow through with their eventual move to California. Her husband assured her that the conditions along the Pacific were similar to the pleasant Mediterranean climate of Montecarlo, their Italian home town. As an added bonus, Argene had two sisters living in Fresno, and it would be wonderful to be reunited with them.

Argene was suddenly aware that she was nervously clenching her hands again. She quickly released them and glanced up at Sebastiano, but he seemed unaware of how tense she had become. The crowd around them started to stir, and Argene peered out to the ocean. Something appeared to be moving toward them, although it was still far out on the horizon. "Sebastiano. È la nostra nave?" she asked. Her husband did not reply as he was busy listening to what the others around them were saying. She repeated, "Is that our ship?"

Sebastiano turned towards his wife and noticed the deep creases of worry lines playing across her forehead. "Si, mio caro," he replied. *Yes, my darling*. At last Argene began to relax, and the anxiety of the unknown began to be replaced by the anticipation of the future.

Much to her delight, Argene quickly fell into the rhythm of life at sea. Their second class cabin was quite nice, and it was incredibly relaxing just to rest on the outer decks and enjoy the lovely sea breezes. As to the meals, she was pleasantly surprised. The galley was located between the first and second class dining saloons, which meant that many of the finest of dining options were available for both. She had no idea that first class had a larger menu and more courses, but that really would not have mattered to her.

Some of the foods were unfamiliar to Argene, of course. *Probably English or American*, she decided. But they were quite delicious and made for an interesting change from the Italian cuisine she had grown up with. On the other hand, she was less enthralled with the music played by the small orchestra that periodically performed in the second class public areas.

The classical pieces were familiar enough, but many of the so-called popular tunes were not at all soothing. The lively music was a fine excuse for dancing, but Argene resisted joining in because of her pregnancy. "How nice it would be to hear some tunes from back home," she commented to Sebastiano.

How abruptly things changed on Sunday night. The ship shuddered when the *Titanic* hit the iceberg, room stewards informed the passengers that they were to put on their life vests and head up to the lifeboats, and the corridors filled with noisy, confused individuals. Argene had great trouble comprehending exactly what was going on, despite the fact that Sebastiano kept updating her about what he had learned. He was only sharing bits and pieces of the English chatter he was listening to, which she could not understand.

The one thing that soon became painfully obvious was that men were not being permitted into the lifeboats. As Sebastiano moved Argene closer to boat 11, she resisted the actions of the nearby sailors. "Il nostro bambino," Argene exclaimed. "Our baby. My husband must come too!" but the crew members had no idea what her Italian meant, nor would they have allowed him to get in anyway. Sebastiano gave his wife a parting kiss and gently told her, "Do not be afraid, Argenia, I shall come later."

Suddenly the pace intensified. Argene was convinced that she was practically thrown into the boat while her husband was shoved away, and all she could do was look back in stunned confusion. Woman after woman after woman were placed into the boat, and even a baby was handed down, seemingly coming out of nowhere. Suddenly the lifeboat lurched, and the long process began to lower it to the ocean far below. Argene searched for Sebastiano's face in the crowd, but she was unable to locate him. Hours of discomfort and confusion followed, made all the more frightening when the *Titanic* sank.

When she was finally hauled up to the *Carpathia* on a bosun's chair, Argene felt entirely isolated. The language barrier was a major problem and she had no idea where Sebastiano was. Should she walk around and look for him? Should she stay in one place until he found her? Neither alternative seemed ideal, and her worry continued to grow with each passing hour. She spent four long days on the rescue ship, alone, confused, and emotionally drained.

When she went ashore in New York, a kind person who was able to translate for her made sure that Argene was taken to one of the local hospitals so her condition could be assessed. Only then did she learn that Sebastiano had died when the *Titanic* went down, and her uncertain confusion finally turned into grief. Tears flowed and her body was wracked by her sobs.

Argene later was told that a ship from Canada, the *Mackay-Bennett*, was exploring the site of the wreck for bodies, and she would have to wait to learn if Sebastiano would be found. The sailors of the *Mackay-Bennett* spent seven gruesome days on their mission, ultimately recovering 306 bodies. Number 295 was Sebastiano del Carlo, and his was one of the 190 still on board when the recovery ship returned to Halifax, the rest being buried at sea.

Arrangements for Sebastiano's body were made on Argene's behalf, and she was already aboard the train when his remains were shipped to Boston. She walked slowly back to the baggage car, accompanied by Rev. G. Moretto of the St. Raphael Society for Italian Immigrants. Three black coffins were unloaded, and Argene walked beside Sebastiano's as it was moved by truck to the baggage room. Her deep sorrow was apparent to all who were gathered there, and the image of the former newlywed, now a 24-year-old widow, was sobering.

"My husband was a prosperous mechanic in Chicago and loved America. We were just married and he said 'Our wedding trip will be to the great United States.'" Argene paused for a moment as tears welled in her eyes. "Little did I expect to come into one of your great railway stations with my husband a victim of the cruelest disaster that the sea has exacted. I'd like to show you two watches which he carried at the time the great ship was on her way to America."

The watches, one silver and one gold and both stopped at 4:15, did not seem overly important to some, but they were among the very few tangible items that remained for Argene to treasure. Also found on Sebastiano's body were a pair of earrings, a pocket knife, a pin, and a few other minor items, but the watches were the items that truly captured his very essence in Argene's mind.

*Argene del Carlo with one of the nuns from the Saint Raphael Society for the Protection of Italian Immigrants in New York City. (Source: The Center for Migration Studies Archives)*

Only seven dollars and 37 French francs had been found stuffed away in Sebastiano's pockets. The $2500 they were bringing with them to America was now at the bottom of the Atlantic. Destitute and alone, Argene decided she had no interest in continuing on to Chicago, as she had no personal connections there. Heading to her sisters in California was a possibility, but she also realized that this would be too difficult a journey, especially in light of continuing communication problems and the fact that by then she was three months pregnant. "No," she decided, "I really only have one option. I need to return to my parents in Italy." On May 18, she started the journey home aboard the *Cretic* along with Sebastiano's remains.

Sebastiano was buried in Cimitero Comunale Altopascio, in Toscana, more than 70 kilometers from Montecarlo. Argene decided that it was probably for the best that he was so far away. That way she could turn her attention to the impending birth of her child, rather than repeatedly grieving at his gravesite. She discovered a newfound resilience as her pregnancy progressed, gaining confidence that she would be able to well-provide for the baby, thanks to her parents' help. While she had lost her husband, it was so wonderful having this life growing inside her: a life that was part her and part Sebastiano.

On November 14, 1912, Argene's daughter was born. Having long ago decided that if it were a girl she would name the baby Maria after the Blessed Virgin, Argene made a particularly decisive choice about her full name. The birth certificate would forever show her precious little girl's identity as Maria Salvata del Carlo, the middle name meaning "saved."

# Second Trimester

During the span from the 13th to the 27th weeks of pregnancy, the fetus increases in length from slightly over three inches to nine inches from crown to rump. Bones harden, the hair pattern on the scalp forms, rudimentary fingerprints begin to appear, the digestive system starts working, and both the lungs and the nervous system are clearly developing. The unborn child begins to respond to sound, and his or her eyes show rapid eye movement during the sleep cycle. Many mothers find this to be the easiest trimester, primarily because the initial tendency toward nausea, exhaustion, and anxiety generally dissipate. The baby starts to move and stretch within the amniotic sac, which eventually can also be felt by the expectant mother, a clear indicator of the precious life within.

# Mary Graham Carmichael Farquharson Marvin

## Three Months Pregnant

*A baby is born with the need to be loved – and never outgrows it.*
*--Frank A. Clark*

Mary Marvin's unbridled laughter filled the air, and a well-heeled, matronly woman standing nearby instantly stared in her direction. "There they are again," she sniffed. "She and her husband and that contraption of his seem to be everywhere." Fortunately, many of the other first class passengers found Mary and Daniel's youthful exuberance refreshing as they headed from one place to the next, filming for posterity their passage home from their honeymoon. By then it was Thursday, April 12, 1912, their second full day aboard the *Titanic,* and the Marvins were still managing to find new locations to shoot. Today they planned to go to the Boat Deck where they could focus on the lifeboats, the funnels, and all kinds of metal casings and vents that they knew they would not be able to identify on their own.

Although it was only mid-afternoon, Mary was already wearing her dinner gown. It was clearly too early to be so dressed up, but Daniel wanted to make sure he had adequate light to capture her image on film as she posed for him and waved to the camera. Mary was more than happy to do so, especially since she still felt sleek and beautiful. Now that she was more than three months pregnant, it would not be long before her figure would visibly start to thicken as their baby grew.

Mary recalled with a bit of amusement how stiff she was in front of the camera exactly one month ago when they restaged their wedding at her parent's home. Of course, Mary and Daniel would forever celebrate their anniversary date as January 8, when they secretly got married at a civil ceremony. They were still a few weeks away from their eighteenth birthdays, and it was so difficult for them to tell their parents about their marriage. In fact, after the original ceremony the two of them each returned to their own parents' homes. In the coming days they had to inform their families about what they had done, and what a difficult task it was. Mary felt overjoyed at the time, yet she could not stop her hands from trembling when she and Daniel delivered the news.

Everything considered, the Farquharsons and the Marvins took the announcement rather well, and in the days that followed, Daniel's father, Henry "Harry" Marvin, came up with a suggestion, or perhaps an order, depending on whose perspective one used. "Let's restage your wedding," he offered. "We could hold the ceremony at your parents' home, Mary, complete with a wedding gown for you, formal wear for Daniel, floral arrangements…." Harry continued talking. The Farquharsons chimed in, suggesting that Rev. Dr. John Caughey of the Harlem Presbyterian Church could officiate, and added that Mary's mother, Jessie, an accomplished dressmaker and shop-owner, would be able to design a special gown. Mary's head began to spin. Then came the clincher, once again from Harry. As an American Mutograph and Biograph Company executive, Harry's connections in the film industry ran deep. "We could film the ceremony, and yours would be the first wedding ever to be cinematographed. Daniel's Uncle Arthur could be the photographer."

Knowing that their much-needed finances for a real honeymoon would come primarily from the senior Marvins and that Daniel would soon be joining the business with the hopes of becoming a successful filmmaker, what choice did the newlyweds have? Harry was used to getting his way, and in fairness, the idea of a filmed wedding was intriguing, albeit a bit frightening. With some reluctance, the younger Marvins agreed, and in the end the ceremony was quite lovely. However, by then Mary suspected that she was in a family way. For the time being the best course of action seemed to be one of remaining quiet about this, as such news would complicate the wedding celebration itself. At least her pregnancy was not yet apparent, which would have been an embarrassing and unwanted addition to the wedding film being produced. Ultimately, on April 5, an article appeared in the newspaper under the headline of "Young Couple Wed Twice," explaining that Mary and Daniel had two weddings, claiming that this was surprising news even to their closest friends.

*Two frames from the cinematograph of Mary and Daniel Marvin's March 12, 1912, restaged wedding (Source: Encyclopedia Titanica, originally published in the Daily Mirror, May 15, 1912)*

The multiple-wedding announcement appeared in the press several weeks after the Marvins had left for their honeymoon. Theirs was not one of the multiple-month excursions that the wealthiest couples could afford, but Mary really did not mind. The ceremony was behind them, and two ocean crossings along with several weeks in Europe would be grand. But there was also a bit of an interloper, which at times seemed like a third party to their trip. Harry gave the honeymooners a motion picture camera as a wedding gift, and he insisted that they take lots of footage of the ships and their travel abroad.

Daniel was excited about the prospect. He received some quick lessons on filmmaking from Uncle Arthur, and then eagerly set up shots of their departure from their New York City home, their arrival at the pier, and their first views of the *Mauretania.* Mary would not have minded so much if Daniel had not insisted that she appear in so many of the moving pictures. The same stiff poses and awkward feelings she experienced during the wedding were still evident in this new round of photography. Then Daniel started to worry aloud that the rolling motion of the ship might compromise the clarity of his results. "Will any of this work out?" she wondered.

Fortunately, Mary finally began to relax in front of the camera, and by the end of their time aboard the *Mauretania* she actually felt that she appeared reasonably natural. Once they reached England, Daniel was quite interested in photographing the well-known sites they visited, but Mary had other ideas as well. She began to fully realize the memories these cinematographs would capture, and she suggested that he should also photograph some of the ordinary street scenes, including houses, vendors selling their wares, horse-drawn carriages, automobiles, and even well-manicured shrubbery.

At first Daniel was confused by her request, but Mary quickly provided the answer. She was only six when she and her parents moved from Edinburgh, Scotland, to the United States. These pictures would one day be a wonderful honeymoon keepsake for them to look at fondly in the years to come, and she was convinced they could also bring back some special memories for her mother and father. Her own recollections of life in the United Kingdom were limited, of course, but her parents had been born and raised there. Why not include some common sights along with the more famous locations, both to remind themselves of places they had seen as well as potential opportunities for her parents to reminisce over? And naturally, they would also enjoy the films of some of their Farquharson relatives who still lived in Britain.

When the honeymooners boarded the *Titanic* in Southampton for their trip home, the Marvins' baggage was delivered to their cabin, number D30, but Daniel made sure their precious camera was not packed away. He started filming in earnest almost immediately upon boarding, and by then Mary did not mind at all posing for him. She was just as eager as Daniel to choose locations for picture-taking, and the ship provided incredible opportunities. The *Titanic* was brand new. Like every other ship it could only have one maiden voyage, so the opportunity to film such an event was truly special. Mary headed from one spot to the next, with Daniel trailing behind, lugging the heavy, wooden Pathé camera which by then had become a curious combination of being both a blessing and a curse. Oh, yes, the pictures would be great, but the hefty load he was carrying and the relentless turning of the hand crank could get a bit tiresome at times.

"Over here, darling," Mary called out as she secured an open spot by the railing. She knew Daniel wanted to get some unhindered shots of their departure from Southampton. He definitely intended to include pictures of the sailors as the lines were cast off, engines were started, and tugboats guided the *Titanic* through the channel. Suddenly, Mary gasped, "Daniel! Look!" and she pointed at a fairly good-sized ship that seemed to be heading toward them. They did not realize at the time that the SS *New York* had broken loose from its moorings due to the strong undercurrent created by the *Titanic*, but Daniel instantly sensed that he had to take pictures of this. He repositioned the camera as quickly as he could and strained to keep the encroaching ship in his field of vision. "Surely father will be pleased with these shots," he called out to his wife. Fortunately, one of the tugboats managed to prevent the *New York* from colliding with the *Titanic*.

The subsequent delay before the ship could start moving again provided the Marvins with plenty of time for more picture-taking. During this long wait as the ship remained perfectly still in the harbor, the crowd on deck began to thin out as the passengers headed below to unpack. This provided lots of open space and unhindered opportunities for Daniel. The few who still lingered nearby could hardly avoid noticing the activities of the newlyweds, who seemed so very young, so clearly in love, and so excited by their cinematographic mission.

In actuality, the newlyweds only spent a small part of their time aboard the *Titanic* making films. The *Titanic* was so much more luxurious than the *Mauretania*, and they did not want to squander the opportunity of what the White Star liner had to offer. They enjoyed playing shuffleboard, sought out the ship's orchestra, and joined other young people in the Café Parisien for lively conversation. Sometimes they would just look out at the sea, embrace lovingly, engage in simple conversations, and ponder the far more important topic of the birth of their child. This would not occur for another six months, but there was so much to consider, especially since they really had not yet made a home for themselves. There was no question, however, that Mary was quite excited about their wedded future, and she was surprised at the maternal instincts that already seemed to be welling up from within.

*Mary and Daniel Marvin (Source: Rmstitanichotel.co.uk)*

When Sunday rolled around, Daniel decided to forego any late afternoon photography. Although the ocean was smooth as glass which would work to his advantage in terms of the ship's stability for picture clarity, the temperature had started to drop noticeably. He was uncertain whether the cold air would have a detrimental effect on the celluloid film, making it too brittle to safely use. Certainly, he did not want to add this risk to the other issue that continued to perturb him. Daniel had no idea how successful he had been with his entire photographic endeavor, because the film would not be developed until they reached New York. The great unknown of the quality of his efforts was simply hidden away in the metal canisters stored in their cabin.

An odd noise occurred that night shortly before midnight, although Mary and Daniel did not give it much thought at first. Forty-five minutes later, their room steward came pounding on their door, alerting them to put on their life vests and report to the Boat Deck. The news was startling, and as they got dressed their conversation disclosed their confusion and nervousness. They carried very few items from the cabin, but Daniel made the last-minute decision to take the film that was still in the camera and place it in a canister, which he then tucked under his arm.

Once the Marvins reached the lifeboats, they discovered a most unnerving scene. People seemed to be milling everywhere, crew members were intensely uncovering the boats and filling them with passengers, and emotions ran the gamut from stoic calm to frantic cries. Mary could hardly believe that Daniel expected her to actually get into lifeboat 10 without him, but somehow that is where she ended up. He called out, clearly and lovingly, "It's alright, little girl. You go. I will stay." Much to her surprise, she suddenly realized he had transferred the film canister to her when she got in the boat, a reality that mystified her. She looked up once again, and there stood Daniel, all alone, blowing her a kiss as a parting gesture. "Why don't they let him get in with me?" she wondered, looking about the boat that could have held a few more passengers. He had even indicated that he could help row, but his offer was ignored.

The rest of the night became a blur. For the next four days Mary sat aboard the rescue ship *Carpathia,* uncertain about what had happened to Daniel. He was nowhere to be found, and she could only cling to the idea that he had been rescued by some other ship. How quickly she had been transformed from a light-hearted, eighteen-year-old newlywed into a confused, lonely young girl. Her thoughts, silent prayers, and fervent hopes were focused completely on Daniel, with the baby inside relegated into the background of her considerations.

When the *Carpathia* reached New York, both the Farquharsons and the Marvins were waiting on the pier. The information that had been wired by telegraph and the confusing newspaper listings that followed made it clear that one of their children had survived, but they were uncertain as to which one. When Mary made her way down the gangway, both sets of parents had their answer, with relief and sorrow flooding over them accordingly. But at this point, Mary still believed that Daniel had somehow survived. When her parents broke the horrible news to her, Mary collapsed to the ground in a faint; her worst fears had become true.

In the weeks that followed, Mary moved back into her parents' home, awaiting the birth of her child. At some point Mary suddenly thought of the bulky film canister which Daniel had tossed to her once she was in the lifeboat. The night of the collision had been so confusing and the days that followed so empty, that she was unsure what happened to it. Could she have left it in the lifeboat? Did it fall by the wayside on the *Carpathia*? Had she actually managed to carry it off the rescue ship and pass it on to Daniel's father who then stored it away? Frankly, it no longer mattered to her, as there was no way to replace Daniel and the film seemed unimportant. To see those happy images of their honeymoon or to look at their earlier wedding motion pictures would have been too difficult to bear.

Mary finally realized that their baby would be Daniel's final gift to her. The next six months slowly went by, a troubling period that filled her with both mourning and anticipation. As her delivery date drew near, she made a firm decision as to what to name the child. Daniel was the obvious choice if she had a son, but on October 21 Mary gave birth to a baby girl. She named her Mary Margaret Elizabeth Marvin, and the family soon settled on "Peggy." Sadly, eighteen-year-old Daniel never lived to see his daughter, but his very essence lived on, a reality which finally brought a sense of comfort to Mary.

# Ada Mary Worth West

## Four Months Pregnant

*A baby is an inestimable blessing.*

*--Mark Twain*

"Mama! Look at me! Mama! Mama!" Ada West glanced up just in time to see her four-year-old toss a rope quoit into the air. It wobbled and fell to the deck quickly, but that did not matter to Constance. She clapped her hands together in pure delight, gave two excited hops, and bent down to pick up the next quoit. Edwy stood behind her, smiling broadly, and Ada gave her husband a quick wink. After feeling guilty about the way some of the *Titanic* passengers were forced to take a slight detour around Constance during playtime on the second class promenade deck yesterday, the Wests knew that they needed to locate a more out-of-the-way spot. Edwy's discovery of the game area for deck quoits was ideal.

Ada turned her attention back to Barbara, only to discover that the ten-month-old had something clenched into her hand and was raising it to her mouth. "Why is it that babies at this age want to try to eat everything they touch," Ada said to Edwy as she removed the foreign object from the tiny fist, "and why am I staring at it to figure out what it is? I'm certainly not going to give it back to her if it turns out to be edible!"

Ada gave a contented sigh. She and Edwy were so much in love. Today, April 12, was their six-and-a-half-year anniversary, not that this necessarily warranted a special celebration. Their marriage had been everything they hoped it would be, and they felt so blessed by their two daughters and the baby on its way. She gently dropped her hand to her stomach, as if to feel the baby within, although being only four months pregnant made it borderline that she would feel her child's subtle flutters. Realizing that Edwy was watching her every move, Ada smiled at him. "A boy would be wonderful, but so would another girl. Just so long as the baby is healthy."

The Wests' decision to emigrate from England and travel to America had not be made rashly. Life in Bournemouth had been good to them, but they were concerned that Edwy's job as a store floor walker in J. J. Allen's house furnishings department would not continue to support them, especially with a new addition on the way. They knew it would be a simple thirty-mile trip to board a ship in Southampton bound for the United States, but how would they support themselves once they got there? Rumors and promises of financial success on the other side of the Atlantic made the thought attractive, but obviously, it made no sense to do so if he simply would end up in another store as a floor walker.

Somehow, Edwy latched on to the idea of beginning his own fruit culture business in Gainesville, Florida. Such a thought startled Ada at first. After all, what did he know about citrus crops? But as their discussions continued, the idea began to sound quite feasible. As an added plus, the notion of raising their two (soon to be three) children in the warm and sunny climate of Florida was quite exciting. It would be beneficial for Edwy as well, given his ongoing respiratory problems. Eventually their decision seemed like the obvious thing to do, and the Wests began the challenging task of ending their lives in Bournemouth and preparing for their journey.

So far, the Wests' voyage on the *Titanic* exceeded their expectations. They knew from word-of-mouth, White Star Line advertising, and newspaper coverage how grand the ship was supposed to be, but those comments usually focused on the first class experience. Because they were housed in second class, they had been curious to see what the ship would have to offer. What a pleasant surprise this turned out to be. Here they were, more than two days into their voyage from England with another five to go, and they were still making new discoveries, like that day's deck quoits area. Ada particularly wanted to see what the library was like, hoping that perhaps some children's books might be in the collection which would provide yet another way to entertain Constance. Maybe they would head there tomorrow.

Space in the Wests' cabin was limited, but that was to be expected of most passenger ship staterooms. Nevertheless, when they learned from their room steward that some of the second class E-deck cabins could also be assigned to first class passengers if the demand warranted, they truly understood how special their experience on the *Titanic* actually was. With the four of them in the cabin together, the wardrobe and dressing table had already proven invaluable. Of course, they had to share bathroom facilities with other passengers who had rooms along the corridor, but the presence of the retractable washbasin in their own room was something Ada deeply appreciated, especially with Barbara still wearing nappies. And thank goodness for the linoleum floors. Ada was not expecting any problematic spills or messes, but these floors would be so much easier to clean than would carpeting, which she had naively anticipated.

*Period depiction of a second class stateroom on the* Titanic *(Source: Wikipedia)*

The next two days went smoothly for the family, although Ada was still a bit concerned that their daily routine might become a bit stale for Constance. At least the baby was much easier to entertain. But any concern about routine came to an abrupt end shortly before midnight on the 14th when Ada felt a slight jostling of the ship. Neither Edwy nor the girls were awakened. Ada lay there quietly, pondering what that could have been but not overly concerned. However, that soon changed, and afterwards she would remember that "it was only the hurrying of passengers outside the cabin that caused alarm. The steward bade us to all get up and dress thoroughly with plenty of warm things."

It took time for Ada to get both girls dressed appropriately. Actually, baby Barbara was the simple one to bundle up. Poor Constance, more asleep than awake, was in no condition to be cooperative as Ada struggled to get her fully dressed. Then there was her unborn child to think about. Ada decided to wear an extra layer of clothing for herself as added protection. The weather had grown quite chilly by nightfall, and certainly the outer deck would be even more frigid by now. She finished dressing herself while Edwy put lifebelts on the children, and then they all left the stateroom together.

Edwy managed to carry both children as they made their way up the stairwell, driven by uncertainty, and Ada trailed two steps behind, clutching her handbag. The second class lifeboats were located towards the stern, and she and the girls were soon directed to lifeboat 10, where they were awkwardly lifted aboard. Once they were safely seated, Edwy shouted above the ongoing noise that he was heading back to their room to fetch a thermos of hot milk.

Ada positioned herself and the girls as comfortably as possible. The only option was to cradle baby Barbara in one arm, and to carefully drape her other arm as reassuringly as possible around Constance's shoulder. Still waiting for Edwy to return, she looked at the other passengers seated about her. A few other mothers and their children were also present, which she found strangely comforting. But what was taking Edwy so long to return?

Suddenly, the lifeboat gave a slight pitch, and the crew members started to lower it. Only then did Edwy reappear, vacuum flask in hand. Of course, there was no way for him to climb aboard now that the boat was descending, although the earlier cries of "women and children first" would probably have thwarted his entry anyway. At least he was quick-witted enough to find a rope that he tied around the thermos so he could lower it to Ada. Although she would have been much happier to have her husband sitting with them, she was not overly concerned. He would simply be able to get into one of the other lifeboats once the men were allowed to do so.

Shortly afterwards, and to the dismay of the women seated in the lifeboat, two men were discovered, secluded away in the bottom. Ada was shocked. They "had concealed themselves under the ladies' skirts and had to be asked to stop lighting cigarettes as there was a danger of the dresses becoming ignited." A stray flame or bit of ash might be enough to set their clothing afire, and Ada was as adamant as the other women who were insisting that they be stopped. She needed to keep her daughters and herself safe at all costs. Ada once again wished Edwy was with her, somewhat resentful that these two foreigners, later identified as Masabumi Hosono from Japan and Neshan Krekorian from Turkey, had managed to get in.

Ada intently watched the *Titanic* and finally became convinced that the ship was actually settling lower in the water at a somewhat alarming rate. She was absolutely certain that the rows of lights on the ship were steadily becoming ever more submerged. Her confidence that Edwy would be all right started to weaken, and her resolve all but vanished when the ship upended itself and broke in half, with each portion disappearing into the sea. The terrible groans and cries that immediately followed finally made Ada realize that her husband's survival was in real danger. She gasped, held each of her daughters more tightly for a few minutes, and then released her arm briefly from Constance's shoulder. As if to comfort her unborn child, Ada moved her hand to her stomach, let it rest there for a few minutes, and then wrapped her arm about Constance once again.

By the time the Cunard liner *Carpathia* arrived, Ada's fear for her husband had reached a terrible threshold. "What if Edwy is not in one of the other lifeboats?" she asked herself, with no real answer to the question. As it turned out, her worst fears were affirmed as she searched the decks of the *Carpathia* only to learn that he was nowhere to be found.

The journey to New York seemed endless. Ada fought back her tears as much as she could while she tended the children, although she lost the battle each time Constance asked about Daddy. There simply was no good way to explain death to a four-year-old. Each time her daughter seemed to understand that Daddy was in heaven now, it was only a matter of time before the question "Will we see Daddy soon?" would resurface.

Even before the *Carpathia* reached New York City, Ada knew that she and the girls needed to return to England. Continuing on to Florida was simply not feasible. Being pregnant and having two other daughters under the age of five did not leave Ada in a position to head there, moving to a location where she knew nobody and facing a business venture about which she knew nothing. Thank goodness for the Red Cross and the many volunteers who were helping the *Titanic* survivors deal with their new realities. Ada was so grateful for their aid in lining up passage back to England aboard another White Star liner, the *Celtic.*

Titanic *passengers aboard the* Carpathia *(Source: Wikimedia Commons)*

Of course, the Wests could not return to their old home in Bournemouth. They made their way to Truro, the small Land's End city where both Ada and Edwy had been raised. Her father had passed away eight years ago, but her mother still lived there, as did Edwy's parents. Ada knew that with their assistance and the support of other family members and friends, she and her children would be able to make a new home for themselves.

On September 14, 1912, Ada's third daughter was born, and with no delay she named her Edwyna Joan West, a fitting tribute to the husband lost at sea. In the coming days, Ada thought long and hard about the *Titanic* tragedy and her own family's loss. As she gazed upon her delicate little girl, she realized that Edwyna was also a survivor in her own right, even though she was born five months to the day after the ship hit the iceberg. Edwyna's tiny hand suddenly curled around her mother's finger, and Ada smiled at the little blessing before her.

Her newborn would never know her father, but it was equally impossible for Barbara to have any memory of him either, given her age at the time of the sinking. Even Constance would be hard-pressed to preserve any memory of her beloved Daddy, and Ada could already sense that the little girl's recollections were fading with each passing day. Ada vowed that she would not let his memory die, and she would make sure that each of the girls would learn about him as they got older. He needed to be more than just "some man" associated with the vacuum flask that returned to England with them.

Ada soon discovered that she could not fulfill this promise to herself as completely as she wished. The memory of his loss and that horrible night at sea were too difficult for her to deal with, and only rarely could she bring herself to share even the smallest thoughts of their father and their mutually-shared *Titanic* ordeal.

# Hannah Godfrey O'Brien

## Four-and-a-Half Months Pregnant

*Honey is sweet. A little baby is even sweeter.*
*--Asian Proverb*

Hannah stormed out of the third class dining saloon, leaving Thomas behind, a shocked look on his face. "I'm gobsmacked," he muttered to himself. "What just happened?" He replayed the conversation through his mind. It had started so happily, with his wife describing how active the baby was that morning. Hannah was four-and-a-half months pregnant, and the baby's movements were starting to become quite evident.

"That's when I made my mistake," Thomas decided. In what should have been a thoroughly delightful conversation, he foolishly referred to their departure from Ireland as an "elopement" and added that his four sisters in Chicago did not know he was bringing his new wife with him, let alone that she was pregnant. Had he only known ahead of time how sharply Hannah would react to that news. At least he knew he had to keep his mouth shut in the future.

The O'Briens recognized that having their first child when Hannah was 27 and Thomas was 26 made them older than the typical first-time parents in Ireland, and her pregnancy should have been exciting news. Unfortunately, the fact that Thomas's relatives did not even know about her, nor that she was in a family way, seemed unbelievable to Hannah. This startling reality had been enough to set her off, making her totally confused as to why he had not even mentioned her to them.

At least Thomas knew that his wife's normally good-natured personality meant she would get over it quickly, so there was no point running after her. Instead, he turned back to his lunch. Today's roast beef was a special treat, as it was not something he would typically ever have back home. What seemed even more amazing was that the string beans tasted as fresh as if they had just been picked from a garden, even though they had been at sea for two days since they boarded in Queenstown on the 11th.

Stabbing his fork into a potato, Thomas glanced up in time to see Hannah walking back toward him, a somewhat embarrassed half-smile on her face. "I'm sorry, mo ghrá. I feel so foolish."

"Thank goodness," Thomas thought to himself. "Just hearing her using a bit of Irish to call me 'my love' means this argument is over." Thomas assured her not to worry about it, and motioned for her to sit down to finish her lunch. The two ate silently at first, searching for a new topic to talk about. Because they had been together non-stop since leaving Ireland – in their cabin, during meals, singing and dancing in the lounge, roaming outside on the deck – it seemed that there was little which remained undiscussed. "Should I talk about my old job at the creamery?" Thomas wondered to himself. "Maybe I could mention once again how lucky we were to get passage on the *Titanic,* after our voyage on the *Cymric* was canceled due to the coal strike." All he knew for sure was that he wanted any topic he broached to be a safe one. Finally, Hannah spoke up.

*Thomas and Hannah O'Brien (Source: Geni.com)*

"I wonder if we will be having mass tomorrow," she asked. Because the *Titanic* was a British ship, it was clear that some sort of Church of England service would be held, but what would be available for the Catholics? The O'Briens had heard that there were several priests in second class, so perhaps one of them would come down to steerage and conduct mass. Most of the Roman Catholics on board were Irish, but they also noticed a couple of Italians and maybe there were others whose nationalities they had not been able to determine.

As it turned out, Father Thomas Byles conducted mass on Sunday morning, and Hannah felt comforted by the familiar Latin liturgy. But how startling the next encounter with the priest turned out to be. It was the middle of the night, and Father Byles, along with another priest the O'Briens did not recognize, were leading the frightened Catholics in the Our Father and other prayers, speaking loudly enough so that those in the back of the crowd might hear them. By then, word had reached third class that the *Titanic* had hit an iceberg, a reality known all too well by those who had already run from the rising water in the bow of the ship. Hannah wanted to join the prayers, but her husband pulled her away.

"Hannah! We need to get to the lifeboats. We have to save ourselves and the baby." This simple reference to their unborn child was all she needed to hear, and the two of them continued their journey to the upper decks. As third class passengers they had not been anywhere remotely close to the lifeboats, and they faced a confusing path to get there. Their route was complicated by closed gates, dead-end corridors, and even a metal ladder along one outer wall that they had to climb in order to gain access to the next deck up.

What Hannah and Thomas never anticipated, however, was that only women and children were being allowed into the lifeboats, and most of the boats had already left the ship. Fortunately, they found a spot for Hannah which she slipped into just before the crew started lowering the boat to the Atlantic. When she vanished from his line of sight, Thomas stepped back and found his mind overwhelmed by that timeworn phrase, "the luck of the Irish." Hannah and the baby would be safe, but he fully recognized his own doom. Hearing Father Byles's voice in the distance, Thomas decided that it was time to head back for his own absolution.

Hannah and her unborn baby were rescued, but how ugly life had suddenly become. To lose her beloved Thomas was a cruel turn of fate, and the challenge of raising her yet-to-be-born baby would be daunting. Returning to Ireland and her own aged mother did not seem to be an option at this point especially because of limited finances, so she would need to figure out what choices might be available to her in America. With Thomas gone, she scuttled their original plan of continuing on to Chicago to live with Thomas's sister, Mary Hunt. This seemed a thoroughly impractical alternative, given the fact that her very existence was still unknown to them. Besides, Hannah was also concerned that being around those sisters-in-law would be too difficult a reminder of her dead husband.

Once the *Carpathia* reached New York, Hannah was relieved to learn that a number of organizations, both volunteer and professional, had joined forces to provide assistance to those survivors who needed such support. Hannah certainly was a case in point, and they aided her by arranging short-term housing at the Foundling Asylum. Normally the facility cared for infants who had been abandoned on the streets of New York, but Hannah's dilemma certainly dovetailed with their mission, at least for the early assistance she needed.

One horrible reality was yet to be revealed to Hannah. Various relief efforts provided funds for the families of *Titanic* survivors as well as for those who had lived through the crisis. Unfortunately, Thomas's extended family had also put in a claim for what they assumed would be their share, not knowing about Hannah's existence, her status as Thomas's widow, and the upcoming birth of their child. A long-distance tug-of-war ensued, with accusations raging between Hannah in New York, Thomas's sisters in Chicago, and his mother in Ireland.

The discord continued while Hannah just wanted to turn all of her attention to the upcoming birth of her baby. On September 3, 1912, Marion Columba O'Brien was born, a healthy, lovely, Irish lass. The two of them resided in Brooklyn, and Hannah finally experienced the proverbial ray of sunshine in a life that had become so heavily clouded. How could she feel otherwise, with such a beautiful daughter as the legacy Hannah shared with her beloved Thomas?

*Hannah O'Brien and her daughter, Marion (Source: Timesunion.com)*

Yet Hannah's argument with the O'Brien clan continued for another six months, although the sisters-in-law in Chicago eventually reached out to Hannah, inviting her and Marion to travel west and live with them. Finally, the disagreement drew to a close when Hannah wrote an abruptly short letter to her sister-in-law in Chicago on March 20, 1913, informing her that the issue was now settled.

"My dear Mrs. Hunt,

"I have just received your letter this morning, you need not bother yourself about that lawsuit. I have all that filed long ago. I settled with them, you needn't worry about me. My baby & myself will be alright. I knew ye were all trying to get some money. I produced my marriage certificate, & I had the nearest claim, so you nor the lawyer needn't bother…

"With love from baby & myself your fond Sister

"Hannah O'Brien"

The settlement did not make Hannah a wealthy woman, but the income was enough to ease some immediate financial pressures. At last the future seemed a bit brighter for herself and baby Marion.

# Madeleine Talmage Force Astor

## Five Months Pregnant

*Every baby born into the world is a finer one than the last.*
--*Charles Dickens*

"It always makes me nervous when she stands there, watching my every move," Rosalie Bidois thought to herself. Under normal circumstances, she got along well with Caroline Endres, and she truly appreciated Carrie's role as Mrs. Astor's nurse. But the maid simply found her presence to be a bit disconcerting at times like this. Rosalie was always careful when tightening the pregnancy corset, so as to meet Mrs. Astor's needs while not causing any potential harm to the baby. And she realized that nobody was better suited to monitor this than Carrie. At least when Rosalie finished fastening the corset about Mrs. Astor, Carrie excused herself as she headed out of the suite and crossed the corridor to her own quarters.

Rosalie relaxed a bit, pleased that her adjustments to the corset met Carrie's tacit approval. She had succeeded, as always, in fastening the girdle to the appropriate level of tightness, especially now that Mrs. Astor was five months pregnant. "Carrie should realize that I know what I'm doing, but at least she leaves us alone once we move on to the gown," she thought to herself. "Everything considered, Carrie and I usually function very well together. Maybe it's just because I'm not used to working so closely together with her in the limited space of this stateroom. It's considerably easier when we're in a spacious hotel suite or back home at the mansion. Travel just adds an extra level of stress."

Madeleine Astor chose a lovely, neutral-colored evening dress for Saturday night's dinner. Its loose folds would help mask her thickening waist. She was not at all embarrassed to be seen in a family way, but she still wanted her appearance to disclose the pretty young 18-year-old woman that she was. That said, she was actually thrilled to be having this baby and had not been overly annoyed when gossip began to circulate about her pregnancy.

Rosalie finished fastening the back of the gown, and Madeleine debated which of several necklaces she might wear this evening. The glass bead-work of the gown would reflect brilliantly in the light, so she wanted to select an appropriate necklace that would add a touch of color without creating a conflicting level of sparkle. She finally chose one of the darker pieces and had Rosalie fasten the clasp behind her neck. Satisfied by the effect, Madeleine dismissed the maid and attended to a few stray strands of hair while looking over her image in the mirror. "Imagine! You are going to be a mother in four months," she voiced to her reflection.

Suddenly the door to suite C17 swung open, and in walked Colonel Astor. "Darling, you look gorgeous!" he exclaimed, meaning every word of it. Madeleine performed a quick twirl, flashed a broad smile, and replied happily, "Thank you, John." They left their suite and headed arm-in-arm along the corridor, proceeding to the luxurious a la carte restaurant one deck above.

The Astors appreciated the extra bit of privacy that the restaurant afforded in contrast to the regular first class dining saloon. When they entered the room they detected the delicate aroma of the white roses, which dominated the arrangements on the center of each table. The French walnut paneling added a welcome degree of elegance to the room, further enhanced by gilt trim and exquisite carvings. Madeleine, always fashion conscious, looked about at the bright reflections from the necklaces and the beadwork on the other ladies' evening gowns, which added a wonderful sense of life and vibrancy to all those gathered here.

Their dining steward immediately greeted the Astors, carefully holding their chairs in place and then arranging the linen napkins across their laps. As expected, the dinner choices were marvelous, and the Astors took their time in making their selections for the evening. They anticipated that tomorrow's options would be even more incredible. Such was the case when they had traveled aboard the *Olympic* on their way to Europe several months ago, and White Star was known for extraordinary Sunday dinners, both in the regular dining saloon as well as in the a la carte restaurant. Unfortunately, the steward had no definite information as to what the next night's meal might include.

With their dinner ordered, Colonel Astor started talking about his visit with Captain Smith earlier in the day. John had known Captain Smith for many years, and Madeleine enjoyed meeting him during their earlier voyage on the *Olympic*. As John continued his discussion, he brought up many details which he was clearly fascinated with but which Madeleine did not particularly care about. He had learned that the ship had traveled 519 nautical miles by noon that day, and he started speculating about what the mileage would be by noon on Sunday. The Captain had made it clear that he would order the ship to sail at a higher speed, given how pleased he was with the *Titanic*'s performance so far. He then added that he naturally would not subject it to the highest speed the ship was capable of. Such an act would be foolhardy on a maiden voyage.

John was having a great time talking about all of this, but because Madeleine was not particularly interested, she allowed herself to slowly gaze about the room. Several of the women seated nearby pleasantly nodded in her direction, and she responded accordingly. Madeleine was encouraged by the fact that she was no longer feeling as snubbed as she had been at the start of her marriage to John. Most of the couples who knew the Colonel and his first wife, Ava, had reached the point of at least being cordial in their presence, but Madeleine still remained cautious. Some of the women who hailed from the highest levels of society still would not accept John and Ava's 1909 divorce.

When the Colonel wedded Madeline in November 1911, far too many were scandalized by the disparity in their ages. Haughty society matrons clucked to one another, "Imagine a 47-year-old divorced man marrying an 18-year-old woman. She's even younger than his son, Vincent!" For this reason, Madeleine was glad to have met some other first class passengers on the voyage who had not known John from his "earlier life," and she especially enjoyed many of the discussions she had with Helen Bishop from Michigan and others who were not part of the New York City social scene.

Madeleine continued looking about when she suddenly noticed a woman staring at her and then averting her eyes, her actions betraying her feelings about the Astors' marriage. "John!" Madeleine exclaimed quietly. "It's happening again. That woman is glaring at us." John did not even bother to turn his head.

*John and Madeleine Astor (Source: Wikimedia Commons)*

"Madeleine, don't worry about it. You know how much better things have become," he replied, and she realized he was quite correct about that. She thought back to their very beginning together, when the two of them met in Bar Harbor, Maine, in the summer of 1910. How surprising their mutual attraction had been. Madeleine was only 17 at the time and would not even be introduced to society until later that year. Never did she imagine that she would fall in love with a man more than twice her age, who had a son one year older than she. At first many of the onlookers did not fully grasp that the two of them were really becoming quite serious about each other, given that John had a bit of a reputation as a playboy. All the while the society page editors seized the opportunity to casually weave details into their columns about them, alluding to the difference in their ages and reminding readers about John's first marriage and divorce. This just stirred the pot, and others in their social circle responded accordingly.

Some of the doyennes of high society simply snubbed the couple. Others were cordial, but initially there existed a definite stiffness to their interactions. Many were convinced that Madeleine was feigning love for the Colonel solely on account of his wealth and that she really just came from rather common stock in their eyes. Actually, Madeleine's parents, William and Katherine Force, had often appeared in the Brooklyn society pages, but their status in Manhattan did not warrant the kind of coverage that John Jacob Astor IV attracted. John despised such attention, but as head of the Astor family it was inevitable and the press was relentless. Madeleine soon discovered that simple things like the outfit she wore when she and John attended Newport tennis matches had suddenly become newsworthy. Articles appeared describing casual get-togethers between the entire Force family and John when vacationing in Maine or upstate New York, and even dining at a simple social event became sufficiently important to keep them under the microscope of the press.

Worst of all was the month before their wedding. Unsavory gossip about the couple finally led William Force to contact John in August 1911, asking his permission to formally announce his daughter's engagement to the Colonel. Afterwards, the press managed to became even more relentless. All John had to do was move his yacht, *Noma,* between Newport, Rhode Island, and New York City and speculation would begin anew that the wedding was imminent. The reporters figured that the date would be during the fall with the assumption that the ceremony would be a quiet one, not that the Colonel would confirm such thoughts when they questioned him. One of the conditions of his divorce from Ava required that he could not remarry in New York, so the Astor Newport cottage, Beechwood, seemed like a strong possibility as a wedding venue.

"Do you agree, Madeleine?" She suddenly snapped back from her wandering thoughts about the past. John was talking to her directly, and she needed to respond, although she had no idea what he had been saying. The safest thing to do was to indicate that she agreed and then reach for one of the dinner rolls that the a la carte restaurant had provided. Slowly she began to butter the roll, and her thoughts once again drifted back to the days leading up to their wedding.

So much needed to be accomplished, and Madeleine was mortified to learn that their prenuptial financial arrangements even made the newspapers. This was standard for all Astor marriages, and in her mind this should not have warranted any press coverage. Then there was the issue of finding a minister to marry them. The Forces insisted on a religious service, adamant that a civil ceremony would not do. They wanted their younger daughter's wedding handled by a man of the cloth, but John's divorced status was a major roadblock. Even though he was offering a princely sum of $1000 to the man who would officiate at their wedding, a series of individuals kept turning him down on moral grounds. And, yes, the newspapers carried that information as well, much to Madeleine and John's chagrin. September 1, September 2, September 3, ..., day after day their impending marriage made the news.

Finally, on the morning of September 8 the *New York Times* reported that Rev. Percy Stickney Grant was in Newport and was expected to perform the ceremony, although he had not yet been contacted to do so. Another article told about the congratulations Rev. Edward A. Johnson was receiving because he had turned down the opportunity. The next day, attention in the papers had shifted to Rev. Edwin Straight, but as readers sipped their morning coffee while reading this news, the wedding was taking place with Rev. Joseph Lambert of Providence officiating. The upper crust was treated to this unexpected twist of information when the Sunday newspaper became available. The report indicated that the Astor-Force wedding took place at Beechwood and was conducted by a Congregationalist minister, far less appropriate in society's collective eyes than an Episcopalian priest would have been.

At least the speculation was over, Madeleine and John had married, and she finally felt a bit of relief. The newspapers did a nice job talking about her black Empire gown and its crêpe de chine fabric, the pearls she wore around her neck, and the American Beauty rose she added as a corsage after taking it from their breakfast table afterwards. "At last," she figured, "the press coverage has started to change and will wind down in just a few days."

Madeleine was wrong. Other ministers criticized Rev. Lambert for performing the wedding service and even included attacks in their sermons. Rev. Straight's name appeared in articles describing how humiliated he felt after he had agreed to officiate only to be snubbed at the last minute, and then Rev. Lambert's name reappeared when the press carried the story of his resignation from the pulpit of his church due to the controversy. Madeleine began to believe that these attacks would never go away.

The next two months continued to create a strain on Madeleine, but at long last they boarded the *Olympic* on January 24, 1912. Just getting away from the fishbowl pressures of New York society and having an extended stay in Egypt, far from this turmoil, was such a welcome change. How wonderful their time in Alexandria was, and the warm climate proved to be beneficial for her health. What a surprise it was when John let her know that they would be spending time sailing on a dahabeah, and the leisurely days traveling on the Nile were unbelievably restorative. Better still, Madeleine's pregnancy was proceeding nicely, and she fell into a wonderfully relaxed, uncomplicated existence. Life was good.

Madeleine's attention suddenly refocused on her husband when their meals arrived. John had continued carrying on the one-sided conversation while she had let her mind stray, but now with the fabulous dinner before them, she once again entered the discussion. How glad she was by their decision to dine in the more exclusive a la carte restaurant and to keep to themselves as much as possible on the voyage.

Yet thirty hours later, the Astors found themselves in the middle of a growing group of many of the most prestigious passengers on the *Titanic*. Even such noteworthy individuals as George and Eleanor Widener of Elkins Park and John and Marian Thayer of Haverford, Pennsylvania, gravitated toward them, and it was clear that they expected the Colonel to approach Captain Smith to find out what the status of the ship was. By then, they all understood that the *Titanic* had struck an iceberg, but other than some stray shards of ice scattered on the deck and a barely noticeable list to starboard, there seemed to be no major problem. Indeed, even the crew seemed calm as they informed the passengers that nothing was seriously amiss.

John left the group to speak to the Captain and soon returned with the news that they were all to head to their cabins, don their life jackets and make their way back to the Boat Deck. What he did not tell them was how serious things actually were; the Captain made it clear that the ship was in a delicate situation from which they would not recover. On their way to their C-deck suite, John assured Madeleine that all of this was just precautionary, and this seemed very believable at first. Only when the crew started uncovering the lifeboats and preparing them for passengers to board did Madeleine become concerned. However, she was not about to leave the solid safety of the *Titanic* and board one of those flimsy, wooden boats. John once again stated that all was well, but there was something about his facial expression that caused her to wonder. Had he disclosed everything that Captain Smith had told him?

Time passed and the angle of the ship became more disturbing. The group of extremely wealthy first-class passengers began to seriously discuss the prospect of actually getting into the lifeboats, and Madeleine looked up at John, her eyes widening with confusion. The ongoing cries of "women and children first" continued to raise their concerns. At one point their group even followed one of the sailors down to A-deck where they were to actually get into lifeboat 4, only to discover that the promenade windows blocked their access. They were led away once again, with Marian Thayer speaking up, "Tell us where to go, and we will follow."

Madeleine still maintained that it would be foolish to get into the lifeboat when it was finally readied, but she had to admit she was beginning to lose her resolve. The passage of time and the growing sense of danger combined to raise clear doubts. Amazingly, the ongoing discussions rambled onward, avoiding the reality of what was at hand.

At one point, she and the Colonel retreated to the gymnasium for a bit of warmth. They seated themselves on the mechanical horses, an action that was a bit awkward for Madeleine given the fact that she was five months pregnant, but this really was intended to serve as nothing more than a temporary seat and not as a means of exercise. When John spotted an extra life vest, he retrieved it and brought it closer to Madeleine. He figured he could use it to help pass some time. The Colonel pulled a pen knife out of his pocket and cut into the vest, exposing its cork interior and explaining how this was sufficient to keep a person afloat.

At long last boat 4 was readied, and the trek to A-deck began once again. By this time Madeleine was really minding the cold night air. She had no regrets over the fact that she had given her scarf to a stranger so that she might bundle her baby boy with it in order for him to stay warm, but she had to admit that the chill was now becoming bothersome. She shivered a bit, unsure whether it was because of the cold or because she was about to get into the lifeboat.

Access into the boat was ridiculously cumbersome. Because the listing of the ship had become so pronounced, the women and children had to crawl over a makeshift bridge of deck chairs to get from the deck into the boat. Once again Madeleine became hesitant at the thought of leaving the *Titanic*. John gently placed his hands on her shoulders, gazed into her eyes, and gently said, "Get into the lifeboat to please me." With that, Madeleine agreed to do so and managed to crawl across the awkward bridge fairly gracefully, everything considered, but her nurse watched on in dismay. Carrie Endres had no idea how long that the three of them, Mrs. Astor and the maid and herself, would be in this little boat, nor was she certain how she would be able to effectively watch over Mrs. Astor and the baby.

Colonel Astor had been a paragon of bravery all night, but he still thought it would be wise to turn to Second Officer Charles Lightoller and make a request. He asked if he might get in the lifeboat with his wife, pointing out that she was in a delicate condition and would need his attention. Lightoller was not swayed and would not allow it. Astor put up no fuss and backed away, much to Madeleine's shock. "Oh, John!" she mouthed softly to herself, and as the boat was lowered, she had her final glimpse of her husband.

Madeleine remained bravely stoic as the disaster continued to play out. Suddenly an explosion burst forth when the icy sea water swirled around the heated furnaces. A sharp sound escaped from her lips – not quite a sob nor a distinct cry, but clearly an acknowledgment of what had just occurred. As the *Titanic* lifted up, broke in half, and sank into the sea, Madeleine buried her face in her hands. It was undeniable that joy had left her life.

Hours passed as the lifeboat bobbed about on the ocean, the freezing cold water beneath them seeming to turn their feet to ice. Rosalie and Carrie did what they could to keep Mrs. Astor comfortable, but their options were limited. When they were lifted by the bosun's chair to the *Carpathia* their relief was palpable, and the crew of the rescue ship quickly learned what an important person Mrs. Astor was. She was moved to a vacant cabin, one of the finer ones the *Carpathia* had to offer, although it was not remotely similar to even the most ordinary of first class rooms on the *Titanic*. However, at least the nurse and maid could once again attend to Mrs. Astor in the manner that her position called for.

Madeleine decided to stay sequestered for most of the trip to New York. Several times she would quietly assure Rosalie and Carrie, "I'm okay. I'm okay," although there was no sense of conviction to back up her words. She was trying to come to terms with the fact that she had lost John, and that emptiness seemed insurmountable. Added to this was the reality of the baby which she was carrying. Of course, there would be no financial problems to face, but the thought of raising a child without a father was concerning. Yet she was still sensitive of others. In the midst of dealing with her personal grief, she asked Rosalie, "Have you heard anything of Victor?" The women informed her that Victor Robins, Mr. Astor's valet, was not aboard the *Carpathia*, adding another layer to the grievous loss.

Because Madeleine remained hidden away in her cabin most of the time, this opened up idle speculation and rumors about her well-being. Conflicting messages were telegraphed to New York, reporters tried to cobble together stories about the survivors, and misguided intentions played havoc with the articles carried by the newspapers. Mrs. Astor's condition was reported over the full range from seriously ill to healthy but grieving. One paper went so far as printing the claim that she died just as the *Carpathia* pulled into New York harbor.

The family members awaiting the arrival of the *Carpathia* at the Cunard pier in New York were uncertain what condition Madeleine would be in. It was with great relief that they saw her stride confidently toward them, virtually unaided, her white sweater and stylish white turban easily visible in the distance.

"Oh, Katherine!" Madeleine exclaimed, throwing her arms around her sister, tightly hugging her long enough to recover from the tears she was shedding. "Thank you for being here, Vincent. I'm so sorry," she said to

John's son. The awkwardness of their ages was swept away in the moment, and they clasped hands, sharing a deep understanding of their mutual loss. Watching the scene unfold were two other men, Raoul Kimbell, the family doctor, and Nicholas Biddle, a doctor in his own right but also a trustee of the estate and John's private secretary.

The *Washington Herald* reported that Madeleine was near collapse and hysterical as she called out "Have you heard from anyone?" For her to ask such a question was perfectly reasonable, but once again the description of her condition was clearly an exaggeration, probably designed to sell papers. Because there were no immediate medical needs on Madeleine's part, the entire entourage, including Rosalie Bidois and Carrie Endres, climbed into the three Astor vehicles waiting nearby.

Before proceeding to the Astor mansion at Fifth Avenue and Sixty-fifth Street, they made one other stop. Madeleine was escorted into the home of her parents, where she greeted them and reassured them that she was feeling fine, despite her ordeal. Because William Force had not been well for the past few months, the intense uncertainty surrounding her well-being had been especially difficult for him. Just seeing his daughter for those brief minutes was all that he and his wife needed.

On they continued to the Astor mansion, where Nicholas Biddle issued a statement that Mrs. Astor was in excellent health and that she just needed some time to rest and deal with her grief. Katherine spent the night with her sister. Poor Vincent, overwrought and still harboring a hope that somehow his father might have survived and was rescued by some other ship, finally began to accept that such would not be the case. There were already many reports that the Colonel had last been seen on deck with his valet and Kitty, the family wired-hair Airedale, and had not managed to climb into a lifeboat.

Unfortunately, William Dobbyn, one of the Colonel's secretaries, released a statement after Madeleine arrived home, claiming that "Mrs. Astor is very ill and under the care of a physician. It will be impossible for her to be interviewed or to give out any statement." Once again, an incorrect and extreme position had to be counterbalanced, and the next day the newspaper pulled back this initial statement with Dr. Kimball's assessment that "Mrs. Astor is perfectly well, and suffering only from grief. She arrived in as good health as any one could be who had undergone such strain. The reports that she has been seriously ill at any time during the last few days are incorrect." The only consistent stories were those involving Colonel Astor, praising him for his gallant bravery as the doomed ship foundered.

*Madeleine and John Jacob Astor IV with Kitty (Source: Wikimedia Commons)*

Madeleine decided she needed to observe deep mourning in her attire and keep social contacts to a minimum, a practice highly appropriate for high society widows. Upon the recovery of John's body by the *Mackay-Bennett,* his remains were delivered to New York and Madeleine made a rare appearance at his funeral service, held on May 4 at the Astor family plot at Manhattan's Trinity Church Cemetery.

Madeleine wanted to find a way to personally thank Captain Arthur Rostron and Dr. Frank McGee of the *Carpathia* for the successful rescue of the *Titanic* survivors and the care extended to them during their journey to New York. Although she was still wearing deep mourning, she decided to invite the men to a dinner party at her home. She also wanted to include three other *Titanic* widows, namely Florence Cumings of Boston; Marian Thayer of Haverford, Pennsylvania; and Eleanor Widener of Elkins Park, Pennsylvania; all of whom had been rescued in the same lifeboat as Madeleine. Unfortunately, Mrs. Widener needed to decline due to illness.

The Astor mansion was a beehive of activity for days before the May 31 dinner. Madeleine designed a simple menu for the kitchen staff to prepare, and she made sure that the house staff selected appropriate china, flowers, and other decorations to help her maintain that delicate balance between being in mourning and being a gracious hostess. Madeleine made it clear to the staff that arrangements of pink roses and wild flowers would provide the casually formal appearance that she wanted to achieve.

Newspaper photographers had to remain outside the home, of course, but they had plenty of opportunity to take photographs and moving pictures of the women, dressed in black, as well as the two guests of honor as they arrived at the house. Madeleine presented the men with small tokens of appreciation, indicating that they were being given on behalf of the women and children who had been rescued by the *Carpathia* and its crew. In order to appease the press and take the pressure off of his hostess, Captain Rostron made some remarks, expressing his delight with being Mrs. Astor's guest and seeing the other two women. He also confessed to feeling slightly embarrassed by all the attention resulting from what had been just a fortuitous proximity of his ship at the time of the *Titanic* tragedy.

Afterwards, Madeleine would have then preferred to simply prepare for the birth of her child over the coming months, but nothing would be that easy. Ava, the Colonel's first wife, had been heard from. She had settled in England with daughter Alice after the divorce, but his death had changed everything. Because her son, Vincent, had been thrust into the position of the head of the Astor family with his father's demise, this meant he would be put firmly into the middle of the New York social scene. Vincent disdained such attention, and the further fact that he was not yet married meant that there would be a void in terms of who would take the female lead over many of the social events of the city.

Ava was not about to let this opportunity pass. She moved back to New York with ten-year-old Alice. Quite legitimately, part of this return was intended as support for her son. But Ava also made it immediately obvious that, as the true Mrs. Astor, she was also prepared to assume the social mantle that this would entail. Upon learning of this news, Madeleine sighed deeply. She wanted no part of such a struggle, which was made all the more exasperating with both Mrs. Astors still formally being in mourning. Madeleine had no firm notion on what the best alternative would be at this point.

The contentious situation simmered all summer long. Their social counterparts avoided making any public statements about the situation, in deference to mourning the Colonel's death that they were also compelled to observe. As for Vincent, still twenty years old, he tried to distance himself from the controversy as much as possible. As an obvious first step he moved out of the Fifth Avenue mansion to avoid the awkwardness of remaining in the same domicile as Madeleine, and this naturally meant he ended up spending considerably more time with his mother.

In order to maintain privacy and to observe an appropriate period of mourning, Madeleine was determined to try to ignore whatever stories the press might carry about herself or John, and indeed there were plenty of them for many weeks. Some of the most bizarre ones involved third class passengers. Normally such individuals would have no interaction with those from first class, but the *Titanic* disaster brought together individuals from truly disparate paths of life.

When Adele Nasser wrote a letter to Madeleine, the press found the story of this missive from "Mrs. Nasrallah" to be newsworthy. Adele explained that she was also pregnant and had also lost her husband when the *Titanic* went down. She then added that she had no money and no means of supporting herself, although she stopped short of explicitly asking for funds.

Harry Miller claimed that he jumped from the *Titanic* and onto an ice floe while holding his baby sister, with his story appearing in a July 29, *New York Sun* article. It explained that Harry then slipped off the ice and lost his grasp of his sister. Resorting to his very limited ability to swim and having the good fortune of reaching a nearby lifeboat combined to save his own life, and it was supposedly Madeleine Astor who pulled him aboard. A social worker advised him to approach Mrs. Astor for some aid in pursuing his suit against the White Star Line. Interestingly, Harry's name did not even appear on the list of *Titanic* passengers.

The *New York Tribune* carried a story in August about Hadne Mamee, a Syrian who traveled third class on the *Titanic* and who had filed a $25,000 claim against the White Star Line for the loss of precious jewels. He claimed that he had pushed his way into Mrs. Astor's lifeboat immediately after she was seated. Crew members tried to force him to leave the boat, but he insisted that he was saved by Mrs. Astor when she hid him beneath her wraps.

Madeleine simply did not respond to or acknowledge any of these stories. Thank goodness that amidst this turmoil, Madeleine had the birth of her child to look forward to, a much more joyous aspect of life and a clear fulfillment of her destiny with John Jacob Astor IV. As the date grew closer, Madeleine needed the full support of her family, so her mother moved in and remained there continuously during the week before the child was born. Her sister Katherine was generally on hand as well. They remained in the Astor mansion under the encouragement of her step-son, Vincent, who pointed out how appropriate it always had been for Astor heirs to be born in the Astor mansion.

On August 14, 1912, Madeleine gave birth to a son, and naturally she wanted to name him after his father. Because John Jacob Astor V, the first Baron of Astor of Hever was alive and well and living in England, there was only one obvious option remaining. Madeleine's beautiful baby boy would become John Jacob Astor VI, but she would call him Jakey. Congratulatory notes and telegrams poured in, including one from Vincent, who also sent a huge bouquet of American Beauty roses. He did so while on a European tour with his mother. Madeleine found Vincent's gesture to be quite touching.

*Madeleine Astor and John Jacob "Jakey" Astor VI (Source: Encyclopedia Titanica)*

Of course, Jakey lived in great luxury, as had the last several generations of Astors, and Madeleine was so grateful to have her nurse and maid to help care for him from the very beginning. Soon she would need to obtain a governess for her son, but that could wait a bit. Life had turned around with his birth, and the world seemed brighter and more hopeful.

The settlement of the Colonel's estate several weeks before Jakey was born provided financial bequests for all three of his children as well as his widow. Ironically, in the eyes of the law, all four of them were considered infants, as none had yet reached the age of twenty-one. John had finalized his will on September 18, 1911, shortly after he and Madeleine married, and he anticipated the possibility of yet-to-be-born children of their marriage. Madeleine's share was a generous $5,000,000 trust account as tied to their prenuptial agreement, although a provision required that the remainder of the fund would revert to Vincent should she remarry after the Colonel's death.

Because Jakey was born several months after his father's will had been admitted to probate, a special guardian was named on August 31, 1912, to protect the baby's interests. Egerton L. Winthrop Jr. was appointed to this position. Interestingly, Winthrop himself had been scheduled to board the *Titanic* for its first return trip from New York. When the will was admitted to probate once again that December, Winthrop reported that Jakey's rights had been properly attended to. As a result, tiny Jakey, the son John Jacob Astor IV would never meet, had a $3,000,000 trust fund established with a clearly stipulated amount that could be drawn off of the account each year. Jakey would also inherit a large portion of real estate, probably worth more than $10,000,000, when he would turn 21.

"Yes, indeed," Madeleine thought to herself as she gazed down at her son, "You will never have any worries in this life as long as I can help it." That thought quickly dissolved into pure love as Jakey's eyes locked on hers and as his tiny hand curled around her index finger. Surely no baby had ever been as wonderful as he.

# Third Trimester

Between the 28th and the 40th week of pregnancy, the baby grows from 2½ pounds to its full delivery weight around 6 to 9 pounds and increases in length from 9 inches to roughly 19 to 22 inches. Cartilage transforms into bone, translucent skin becomes opaque, and the five senses truly begin to send messages to the rapidly developing brain. Even dreams occur. Heroic medical efforts are needed for an early-delivered fetus to survive at the start of this trimester, while each additional week of continued pregnancy contributes to the viability of the child at the time of birth.

# Marion Estelle Stauffer Kenyon

## No More Than Six Months Pregnant

*I carried you every second of your life, and I will love you every second of mine.*

*--Unknown*

Marion Kenyon burst out laughing, delighted by her husband's story. Frederick never told her this tale of his youth before, and the surprising ending was truly funny. Their tablemates and friends, Dr. Alice Leader and Margaret Smith, chortled just as heartily. Alice even needed to wipe tears from her eyes, and when she finally gained enough control she cheerfully exclaimed, "Fred, you are so charming! You were so lucky to marry this one, Marion."

Marion readily agreed, fully cognizant of the innocence of Alice's remark. The good doctor did not know that Marion had been married twice previously, each one fairly quickly followed by divorce, before she and Frederick wed in 1904. At no point did she feel any reason to divulge this information to the other women, especially considering the social implications this might impart.

Their laughter finally subsided, and they continued telling other stories while enjoying their Sunday evening meal. Service was phenomenal. Oysters, salmon, lamb, roast duckling, sirloin of beef, roast squab, filet mignons lili topped with seared pate de foie gras and sliced truffles. So many choices and so little room. And those vanilla and chocolate eclairs for dessert were especially tempting, with a choux dough that somehow managed to be delicate and airy. How was that possible?

They lingered over coffee and tea afterwards, and the conversation turned to fond recollections of their holiday trips which were rapidly drawing to a close. The excursion to Panama was eye-opening, especially with the opportunity to see the work being done on the Canal. The first ships would not be passing through for another two years, but already the Kenyons were talking about returning there. "But will it be safe for the baby?" Marion asked, realizing that the tropical climate and threats of insect-borne disease could truly be dangerous. Frederick assured her that they would look into that concern long before scheduling such an excursion. Clearly the baby's safety would far outweigh a Panama Canal transit.

The foursome then started reminiscing about their time spent in Paris, and all of them chimed in about the Louvre, the Eiffel Tower, and many of the quaint boulangeries they had discovered. Finally, after a bit of silence, they decided that they had dawdled long enough in the dining saloon and prepared to head back to their cabins.

When she stood up, Marion felt slightly awkward, and a twinge of discomfort rippled across her back. She still had several months to go before the baby would be born, and she found true joy in these minor annoyances. After all, she and Frederick had just celebrated their eighth anniversary three days earlier, and their long wait for the arrival of a child had become such a blessing. To be in a family way at the age of 40 after all that time was a delightful surprise and an unbelievable gift. Frederick noticed Marion's slight grimace as she arose. "Are you okay, dear?" Frederick asked.

"Yes, I believe so. All that rich food for dinner has apparently made the baby a little more active than usual!" she replied with a smile.

It was a short walk from the dining saloon to their rooms which were situated directly opposite from each other, with Alice and Margaret in cabin D17, and Marion and Frederick in D21. However, none of them were ready to turn in for the night, and they decided to meet shortly afterwards in the first class lounge. As the Kenyons entered their room, Marion was suddenly struck by an unexpected urge.

"Frederick. Do you think we could go up to the A-deck promenade and look at the stars?" He was a bit surprised at her request but was also open to the possibility.

"Be sure to put on a coat, darling. It's cold out there tonight, and I want you and the baby to stay warm." She smiled at her husband as he helped her put it on, making sure that she was bundled up against the nighttime chill.

The view from the promenade was breathtaking. The stars glimmered brightly, seemingly in numbers that far exceeded any night sky they had witnessed in the past. Marion shifted her eyes to look straight ahead and was almost startled at how intensely black the open ocean looked. Yet it was not foreboding. The dark expanse simply spread out, reaching its indistinct edge along the horizon where it met the sky. Only by looking straight down from the railing could she make out the water itself. Light from the portholes reflected off the wake of the *Titanic* as the ship sped ahead. Despite the chill, it all seemed so peaceful.

Marion's thoughts turned to the baby who had stopped actively stirring, and she quietly began to hum a lullaby as she stared into the vast darkness of the night. She shivered slightly, suddenly bothered by the near-freezing temperature, and she suggested to Frederick that it was time to head to their friends in the lounge. Once again, their conversation with Alice and Margaret was a lively one, as expected. Between Alice's experiences as a doctor, Margaret's law background, Frederick's career in the iron trade, and Marion's general zest for life, their exchange was a wide-ranging one.

Once more they started thinking seriously about how quickly the journey was drawing to a close. Today was the 14th and they would be docking in New York City on Wednesday morning, so there were only two more full days in between. Of course, Frederick needed to get back to his job as vice president of Leechburg Steel, in Pittsburgh. However, when the ship docked it would be an easy side trip to Noank, Connecticut. It would be pleasant to extend their trip for just a few more days so they could visit his mother and their vacation home.

They chatted a bit longer until Marion decided she was ready to turn in. Excusing herself, she encouraged Frederick to stay a while longer and keep Alice and Margaret company, but shortly before 11:30 they also decided to call it a night. It had been a wonderful day at sea.

When Frederick returned to the cabin, he was surprised to see that Marion was still not ready for bed, but it was late and clearly it made sense to start changing into their bedclothes. Then came the collision between the *Titanic* and the iceberg. The Kenyons sensed an impact that was very loud and heavy. Across the hall, Margaret Swift noticed "an indescribable wrenching followed by a fearful recoil." Together they went out into the main corridor, hoping to find out what had just occurred. To their shock, several men appeared with handfuls of ice from a starboard side porthole. Yet an overall sense of calm prevailed. The early word coming back for those who ventured out for more details suggested that everything was fine, and they returned to their rooms, convinced that they were safe.

About twenty minutes later the room steward came along, banging on the stateroom doors and spreading the word that the Captain had ordered all passengers to head to the upper deck with their life vests. The Kenyons and their friends checked on one another and prepared accordingly. None of them had yet fully changed for the night, so they were able to get completely dressed in short order. They knew that coats would be needed, and then faced the awful challenge of figuring out how to don the life vests. The tangle of cloth-covered cork, dangling straps, and unfamiliar fasteners did not seem well-suited to put on while still in the close quarters of their rooms or the hallways. Perhaps it would be better to carry them along and figure out how to wear them once they had more space available to work with.

The scene on the port side of the outer deck was remarkably calm, and Second Officer Charles Lightoller patiently directed his crew to get lifeboat 8 ready for launching under Captain Smith's watchful eye. This boat was the first to be readied on that side of the ship, and for Alice and Margaret it was an easy decision to climb in. However, as Marion stepped forward, she immediately realized that Frederick was holding back. She turned to him inquisitively. Frederick, who had already taken the initiative to talk to the Captain about the evacuation, explained that he would need to stay aboard until all the women and children were taken care of first. He pointed out that there were very few people standing nearby, lots of lifeboats were still to be launched, and clearly this unexpected middle-of-the-night procedure was simply precautionary. Marion glanced down the deck in both directions to see the full complement of lifeboats on the port side waiting to be loaded, and that reassured her.

"The Captain has ordered that he wants to make sure that all the women take to the lifeboats and wait for a little while." Frederick then kissed Marion, and she climbed into the lifeboat with her friends. "I will take another lifeboat and meet you in the morning," he called out to her.

The three women talked with one another over the next eighty minutes, nervously watching how steadily the *Titanic* was sinking into the water. The rows of lights made this reality abundantly obvious. Marion's worry level rose accordingly. She had no way of telling whether her husband was safely in one of the other boats. Suddenly the ship started to rise vertically in the water. It tore in half, explosions sounded, and each portion sank separately. Human cries filled the air, and any sense of calm which Marion had clung to earlier was now gone. "What about Frederick?" she asked in pure fright, and her friends had no ready answer. The three women sat in silence, listening to the distant cries for help. All Marion could do at that point was to focus her thoughts on her husband's safety.

*Marion Kenyon (Source: picswe.com)*

The hours passed slowly, and Marion joined the effort in helping to row the lifeboat, despite the fact that she was in a delicate condition. The crew members assigned to the lifeboat were simply not up to the task, and only when the Countess of Rothes assumed control of the rowing detail was any real progress made.

All were so relieved to spot the rescue ship when it first appeared on the horizon. Of course, they had to wait their turn until, finally, their lifeboat was alongside the *Carpathia*. The women were taken up one at a time, hauled up on a bosun's chair or with ropes tied about their waists. Marion's concerns immediately turned to her baby, fearful that harm could occur as she was hoisted upward. More than once she crashed into the side of the ship, and she did everything she could to keep her unborn child away from the solid metal wall. Bruises to her arms, legs, sides, or back were far preferable to endangering her child.

Once aboard the rescue ship, the three women searched unsuccessfully for Frederick. Marion remained surprisingly strong throughout the ordeal while they continued to look for him, but once it became clear that he was not aboard, she was devastated. She grieved the death of her husband, and she had to come to terms that the baby, their first-born, would be his legacy. The days at sea that followed were excruciatingly lonely.

On Thursday evening, George Baldwin, who was married to Marion's sister, glumly waited on pier 54. He and his friend had taken a taxi ride from their hotel in the drenching rain, reaching the dock shortly after 8:30 p.m. and nervously anticipating the arrival of the *Carpathia* and its contingent of *Titanic* survivors. He had obtained passes in advance, knowing they were being issued to prevent the crowd of curious onlookers from getting too close, and the scene around him was sobering. "It was a positive leveling of wealth, a sight never to be forgotten, and agony was expressed in almost every face." Rich and poor, famous and obscure, all were awaiting their first reassuring glimpses of their loved ones, and all were reduced to the same level of anxiety.

"A short time afterwards the United States senate committee sent on from Washington elbowed its way thru the gates to be ready to go aboard immediately on the arrival of the steamer, and to interview Mr. Ismay."

While he found their behavior to be a bit boorish, George's main concern was that of locating Marion as soon as possible.

"The survivors came out in single file; there were first two men and then a woman with a hood; I saw her face, it was Mrs. Kenyon, but I did not know her.... All faces seemed the same, devoid of understanding, a pathetic laxity of thought after their terrible experiences. Had a composite picture been made of all these people, it would have given a perfect expression of two things, horror and agony.

"Fearing that I might not be near enough I went around to meet the first of them again as they were coming thru the lines and again looked into the face of Mrs. Kenyon, but did not recognize her, so swollen were her features from weeping; but I recognized the four-leaf clover on her hood and called her by name and I caught her as she staggered out of the line.

"I asked her if she came alone and she could only bow assent; and I knew she was a widow."

In the days that followed, Marion's story gradually unfolded. While she was still on the *Carpathia,* Marion found she was unable to write about what had occurred to her, so she dictated a letter to one of her friends. Marion's sister, who was at her home in Oak Park, Illinois, soon found herself reading those heart-wrenching words explaining that Frederick had died in the disaster. Of course, this fact was all too well known by then, but just seeing those words intensified her sorrow.

Marion had little interest in returning directly to her home in Pittsburgh, where she would be very much alone. However, instead of going to her sister in Illinois right away, she first traveled to Connecticut to be with Fred's mother, Emma. They fell into one another's arms, sobbing and grieving and talking and sobbing once again. Only the thoughts of the baby seemed to provide any sense of calm and restoration to a world that had suddenly become so unfair. As mother- and daughter-in-law finally adjusted to their shared sense of loss, Marion invited Emma to come live with her.

But fate was not finished with Marion Kenyon. In the days that followed, Marion refocused her attention away from grieving for her lost husband and towards the preparations that needed to be addressed for the arrival of her child. One day, shortly after she sat down in a favorite chair, she quietly began humming the same lullaby that she had hummed on the deck of the *Titanic,* this time with a tear in her eye. Suddenly, she felt something was wrong. Shortly afterwards, while just beyond her sixth month of pregnancy, Marion suffered a miscarriage. The hope for a child and the promise of Frederick's legacy had been dashed.

# Mary Emma Miller Corey and Claire Bennett Karnes

## Seven Months Pregnant and Less Than Three Months Pregnant

*It is important that children, even when babes, should never be spectators of anger, or any real passion. They come to us from heaven, with their little souls full of innocence and peace; and as far as possible, a mother's influence should not interfere with the influence of angels.*

*--Lydia Child*

"We really need to get moving, Mayme!" Claire Karnes was startled by the intensity of her own voice, but she was getting nervous. Yet Mary Corey barely responded. She remained seated on the bed, and merely looked up. A few seconds passed and finally she replied, "Not yet. Let the crowd die down a little." Defeated, at least for the time being, Claire sat down next to her friend. It was clear from the noise level that there were far fewer people in the corridors than before, but she also understood Mayme's hesitance. Because she was nearly eight months pregnant, Mayme was simply not moving as easily as before. Besides that, she wanted to protect her unborn child at all costs from being jostled by any out-of-control passerby who might push through. Claire was in a delicate condition as well, but she was only several months along.

Claire was willing to wait with her friend a bit longer and searched for something to talk about. "I wonder what our husbands are doing right now," she pondered, raising a topic that was sure to generate some discussion. Mayme's husband, Percy, was a superintendent for the British Indio-Burma Petroleum Company near Youngala, Burma, and she had traveled to India last August after marrying him in Ontario, Canada. The trek to that faraway outpost was far more grueling that she expected, but love was a powerful motivator. She had even given up her teaching job near Pittsburgh to be with him.

Claire's story was similarly dramatic. She met her future husband aboard a ship when both were sailing home from Liverpool. Within just a few months they married, and the two of them traveled to Burma together, where he returned to his job as a driller. Jacob never anticipated that his taking leave of absence would lead him to a wife, and Claire found herself moving half way around the word. Love was grand!

Considering the rough-and-tumble conditions surrounding the petroleum fields, the Coreys' and the Karneses' living conditions were far better than the women had anticipated. Unfortunately, Mayme had been terribly homesick and thoroughly bored for almost the entire time she was in Burma. What a change this was from her teaching days, when she was constantly preparing lessons for her students and enjoying a vibrant life in a major city. She wrote home that she did not have "anything much to do, having five servants, a cook, a boy to clean the house, a boy to wait on the table, and a woman to wait on me." The one gloriously bright spot was how soon she had learned that she was in a family way. She and Percy celebrated their anticipation of this tiny blessing, but it also got them thinking about whether it would be wise for her to remain in the tropical Burmese climate until the baby was born.

As Claire continued to listen to her friend's story, Mayme reminded her about the letter she wrote home to her parents in October. "I shared the exciting news of their future grandchild, you know, and I asked them whether I should return to Pittsburgh. I couldn't believe it when my mother wrote back, recommending that I remain in Burma and have our baby there." Of course, Claire had heard this story before, but Mayme pressed on anyway, explaining how her desire to have the baby born in America continued to grow. "I was so conflicted over my parents' advice. Thank goodness when I found out that you were in a delicate condition too, Claire."

Because Claire had recently endured a serious fever, the Karneses figured it would be far safer for her and their unborn baby to return to Pittsburgh. Using the excuse that it would be unwise for a pregnant woman to travel all that distance alone, the Coreys decided that Mayme should join her friend for the long journey back to America. They could travel together all the way to Pennsylvania and their respective parents' homes. Mayme would be back in time for her baby's birth, and Claire would have the added joy of seeing her parents' faces when she surprised them with the news that she was in a family way. They would provide one another with company and mutual support as needed throughout the long journey, but never did they envision the challenge they now faced on the *Titanic*.

*Mary Emma "Mayme" Corey (Source: Encyclopedia Titanica)*

Their discussion stalled for a moment as Mayme reached up to her face, adjusting her pince-nez glasses across the bridge of her nose. This brought a smile to Claire's face, as it reminded her of Mayme's former status for twelve years as a fifth-grade teacher. "Are you ready to leave?" Claire asked, but Mayme simply responded, "Not yet." This certainly did not make Claire happy as the slope of the floor beneath them had become distinctly more pronounced. "Doesn't she realize that we need to get moving?" she wondered, but she was not about to argue. Even though the two women had grown to be friends, Claire could not ignore the fact that 32-year-old Mayme was ten years older than she was, and besides that, she was also the wife of a far more important employee of the oil company. Status has it privilege, even in this circumstance, so Claire remained in place.

Once again, Claire searched for a subject for the two of them to chat about, but Mayme beat her to the punch. "Didn't we have the grandest time once we reached Europe?" she asked. "And isn't the *Titanic* so much more gorgeous than that ship we took from India? I certainly hope that whatever repairs are needed do not spoil its appearance." Claire immediately agreed, and this lead-in was enough to launch them into a discussion about the gleaming coats of paint, the crisp linens in the second class dining saloon, and the beautifully polished brass accessories throughout the ship. They had even joked throughout the voyage that this ship was White Star's new baby, but it could not begin to hold a candle to the beautiful new babies that they would soon be having.

The only thing negative in Clair's mind prior to the collision was a peculiar uneasiness she started to experience soon after they were at sea. Somehow, she felt alone and empty, which was ridiculous, given the presence of her friend and with the reality of a baby on the way. Most of the time that feeling went away quickly, only to return hours later. Unable to explain the strange impression, she never mentioned it to Mayme. "Oh, if only Jacob were with me," she thought to herself several times. "I would certainly have told him about it."

Their conversation continued, and they agreed that their time on the *Titanic* had been splendid, until now. Their cabin was quite nice, the food excellent, and the occasional music provided by the ship's orchestra was a welcome change, especially in comparison to the exotic tunes they never got used to in Burma. They also agreed it was wonderful to stand on the promenade deck and stare out at the ocean, but it was the library that they both fell in love with.

The library was conveniently located fairly far aft on C-deck along the promenade and near the second class entrance. It was amazing what a broad spectrum of activities the room could provide. The women read books, enjoyed afternoon tea, wrote cards, and simply relaxed. But most of the time they simply chatted with each other about Burma or Pittsburgh or their babies or their trip home or whatever else might come to mind.

*The Library on the Olympic, very similar to that of the Titanic (Source: SSmaritime.com)*

Mayme and Claire were regulars in the library, and other passengers even began to take notice of them. A British science teacher, Lawrence Beesley, never introduced himself to the women – in his mind such action would have been far too forward – but the ladies made a distinct impression on him, sufficiently strong enough to write about them.

"Close beside me—so near I cannot avoid hearing scraps of their conversations—are two American ladies, both dressed in white, young, probably friends only," Beesley penned. "One has been in India and is returning by way of England, the other is a schoolteacher in America, a graceful girl with a distinguished air heightened by a pair of pince-nez." He was a bit off in some of his details, but it was clear that the women were memorable.

How much more relaxed their discussions were in the library compared to their current one, seated beside one another on the bed in their cabin. Claire suddenly felt that strange, empty impression she had been having on and off for several days, and it snapped her back to their present situation. "Mayme, I think we really need to get going. It is very quiet out in the corridor now, so it should be safe for the two of us and our babies to head out." At long last, Mayme agreed.

------------------------------------

Hundreds of families mourned the loss of their loved ones because of the *Titanic* disaster, but two families in Pittsburgh could not imagine anybody feeling a level of grief greater than their own. The Millers had been awaiting the return of Mayme and the joy of a new grandchild who would soon be born there, but now their wonderful anticipation had been destroyed. For personal reasons, they decided to avoid mentioning anything about Mayme's pregnancy to the press; their pain did not need to be intensified by sensationalistic news coverage.

The Bennetts had not yet learned that Claire was with child – this fact would come out later – but their grief had also been doubled. Not only was their daughter lost to the ages, but they also learned that her husband, Jacob, had died from smallpox around the same time that Claire boarded the *Titanic*. There was only slight comfort in knowing that she had not learned of this. The news had not reached her while she was aboard the ship.

The mystery for both families centered on why their daughters never made it to the safety of a lifeboat. Why in the world were their daughters among the twelve second class women who were not saved? Had all the boats left the ship before they arrived at the Boat Deck? Did they lose their way in the confusion? Had they never even left their room? The questions remained unanswered, and the loss of their two wonderful young daughters and their unborn children was tragic beyond belief.

# Maria Mathilda Gustafsson Backström

## Seven Months Pregnant

*A baby fills a place in your heart that you never knew was empty.*

*--Unknown*

"Mama! Tell me the story!" Alfhild's eyes twinkled as she looked up at her mother. Mathilda Backström knew she would end up giving in to her daughter, even though she was really much too busy to do so. And, even worse, Mathilda knew that her little girl would not settle for just any tale. The way she worded her request made it clear that she wanted "the" story.

Mathilda placed the bread dough on the floured bread-board, and started the tale, hoping that a greatly abbreviated version would suffice. "Well, Alfhild, it was such a cold, cold night when I was standing by the lifeboat, and I was wearing only my nightgown and life belt...."

"No, Mama!" I want to hear the whole story!" interrupted Alfhild, her mouth drawn into a tiny pout.

"So much for trying to shorten things," thought Mathilda, "and I know she's going to want all the hand motions." She smiled broadly at her daughter and started once again, "Okay, darling. Well, do you remember that I used to work as a maid in America, but that I had just come back to Finland and I had to cross the entire ocean?" As she spoke that final phrase, Mathilda swept her arms in a wide semi-circle, and Alfhild mimicked the gesture, symbolizing that long voyage home from America. Mathilda continued the story, including details about how nice it was to be back home with her mother once again, and she included a few scattered descriptions of the town that her daughter would recognize.

Mathilda started kneading the dough as she continued, finally reaching the part that introduced Alfred into the story. "Now remember, I was only in the United States for a few years, but your father had been there for many years, even living all the way across the country in San Francisco at one time. And when he came back to Finland to see his mother in 1911, he also had to cross the entire ocean." Once again Alfhild's arms swept out the wide semi-circle that represented the Atlantic voyage, and so did Mathilda. Unfortunately, a remnant of bread dough flew off her fingers and landed somewhere on the other side of the room. Mathilda figured she could just look for it later and continued the story.

"Do you remember your father's name, Alfhild?"

"Yes! He was Alfred, and my uncles were Birger and Vilhelm," came the instantaneous reply.

Of course, Alfhild never knew any of them as she was not born until after the *Titanic* disaster, but Mathilda found comfort in the fact that they seemed very alive and very real in her daughter's mind. In fact, this was one of the main reasons she started telling the little girl the story in the first place. Alfhild was growing up without a father, but it was important to make sure that he was still part of her life.

Mathilda punched down the dough, and a white cloud of flour filled the air. She continued the story, supplying details about leaving Kejtala along with Alfhild's father and two uncles. Mathilda's brother Viktor drove them in his horse carriage for the first ten kilometers to Loviisa. Then they took a train to Lahti, where they spent the night, before continuing on to Hangö. Mother and daughter made the clip-clop sounds of the horses' hooves and the chugga-chugga noise of the train, as the story progressed.

Mathilda continued on, talking about boarding the *Polaris,* which transported them through the Baltic and North Seas to Hull. As always, she asked her daughter for the name of the Finnish steamship, mostly because of the cute way Alfhild sounded out the "r." She also introduced a new name and talked just a bit about Erna Andersson. There were still parts of the *Titanic* story that Alfhild was probably too young to hear about, but Mathilda decided to bring up Erna's name for the first time. She added that many of the Finns aboard the *Polaris* only spoke Finnish, so it was nice to let Erna join their group of Swedish-speaking passengers.

The reason they were heading to New York where Alfred had lived and worked in the past was because he had been offered a position as a foreman on a construction project there. Knowing that he would have a free hand in hiring many of the laborers that were needed, he suggested that

Mathilda's brothers, Birger and Vilhelm Gustafsson, should travel with them to America so they could join his work-crew. These were details Mathilda thought she might add to the story next time.

*Karl Alfred Backström, the father Alfhild never met (Source: Annaevaa.wordpress.com)*

"How long did we stay in Hull?"

"A week" came her daughter's reply, "and you wrote home to your Mama to tell her that everything was fine!"

"And where did we go next?"

Alfhild looked puzzled. She recalled that her mother had to take another train ride to get there, but she simply could not remember the name of Southampton. But really, that did not matter to Alfhild. The really fun part was coming up. Knowing what was about to happen next, Mathilda quickly reached for a cloth to wipe off her hands. She did not need to hurl more loose dough through the air.

*The* Titanic *at Southampton (Source: Wikimedia Commons)*

"And what did I say when I saw the *Titanic* for the first time?"

In unison, mother and daughter rose on their tip-toes, raised their hands above their heads, and sang out, "It's so big!" Alfhild burst out in a giggle and her little feet stepped up and down. Meanwhile, Mathilda scooped up the dough, dropped it into the bowl, and covered it with a clean cloth to let it rise a second time.

The story continued, the particulars a bit more random than before. For whatever reason, Mathilda's details about being at sea seemed to shift each time she told the tale. Scattered memories about hearing the band play when they boarded the ship, viewing the ocean, conversing with their fellow travelers, singing and dancing in the public rooms, enjoying huge quantities of food at the vast tables in the dining saloon, and describing the long corridors and their small but very clean quarters were always topics worth including. Not surprisingly, given today's activity in the kitchen, she decided to talk at length about the wide varieties of fresh-baked bread that were served at every meal.

Finally, it was time to talk about crisis, including how the *Titanic* hit the iceberg. Mathilda did not want to make these details too gruesome, mostly for the sake of her daughter but also because after all these years they were still difficult memories. At least she no longer teared up every time she told about the disaster.

"There was such a big bang," Mathilda continued, "but your father didn't even hear it. I had to wake him up and send him out to learn what was going on." How frightening it was when he returned to tell her that the ship had hit an iceberg. He insisted that there was no time to dress properly, and they left their room immediately. Why it never occurred to her to at least grab her coat still remained a mystery in her own mind. Apparently, her fear and the urgency of the situation completely overwhelmed the obvious.

It was all so confusing. They quickly discovered that only women and children were being allowed into the lifeboats, and many of those near the Backströms hesitated to climb in. Wives would simply not leave their husbands, and sisters would not leave their brothers. With each passing minute the crowd grew more restless. "One could hear panic-stricken yells and there was jostling and pushing," was the way she shared her memories about this moment. However, Mathilda felt such detail was still much too graphic for Alfhild. But, as always, she included the part about the signal rockets being launched into the air, and the two of them arced their arms accordingly to mimic the paths they made.

Finally, Mathilda steered her story back to the way she had started it earlier. "It was such a cold, cold night when I was standing by the lifeboat, and I was wearing only my nightgown and life belt. I really did not want to leave your father and get into the boat, but he said to me...."

Alfhild immediately interrupted with the words which she had heard so many times. "'I promise you that I will get into the next boat.' And then you kissed him, right Mama?" She nodded her head up and down so rapidly that her curls bounced about accordingly.

"That's right," Mathilda replied, and she hesitated for a few moments, silently contemplating the bittersweet nature of the memory. While there was more she would add to the story in the future, it was time to end it now, at a point that was so familiar to the two of them.

"Do you remember being there, Alfhild?" The girl shook her head no, maintaining the earnest look she always showed at this stage. "Were you there, Alfhild?" came the next question.

Her daughter smiled broadly, pointed her finger at her mother, and replied, "Yes, I was. I was in your belly!" Then, anticipating the next question, she added, "And I was born on June 29th."

Mathilda reached out both hands and cupped her daughter's face, continuing their loving tradition. "Yes, you were, darling, and that's why you are so special to me. You are a survivor."

Alfhild clapped her hands and turned away, running and skipping off, shouting behind her, "Thank you, Mama. I love that story."

Mathilda searched the room for the glob of dough that she had accidentally dropped a few minutes earlier. Then she sat down briefly, thinking about the rest of the story which she would eventually share with her daughter. Getting into that lifeboat, collapsible D, was the most difficult thing she ever did in her life. At least Erna Andersson was there with her, and they clenched each other's hand watching the rest of the scene play out.

*Maria Mathilda Bergström (Source: Annaevaa.wordpress.com)*

It was obvious to Mathilda when she climbed into the boat that it was unlikely that Alfred would be able to get into another lifeboat and leave the ship, despite his promise. The only other one in sight was a similar collapsible which the crew was struggling to get off the roof over the officers' quarters. She would forever be angry about the fact that her husband was denied a place in the boat, yet several other men had managed to get in. One of them even hurled himself aboard at the last minute, too late for the sailors to pull him out. She remembered that he remained in the bottom, however, and she was convinced that he died during the night, probably from his injuries.

How peculiar it was to watch the rows of bright lights on the *Titanic* right until the very end, slanting so heavily downward and then suddenly disappearing. The ship was lost. Cries rang out, heart-breaking sounds that conflicted with the visually peaceful scene. The sea was so calm and the many stars shone incredibly brightly. She sat there for hours, shivering, crying, mourning the loss of her husband and brothers. How grateful she was for Erna's support, in the lifeboat, on the *Carpathia*, and later when they were housed together at the Union League Home once they reached New York. What unusual strength Erna had shown as a 16-year-old girl.

Mathilda knew her only choice was to return to Finland. She was without her family, in a strange country, pregnant, and expecting to deliver in June. She reached home in Kejtala on May 9. The journey to return to her mother was sorrowful and a bit frightening, both in terms of being alone and crossing those same waters which had previously proven to be so dangerous, but it was the wisest thing to do. Having reached the age of 33 before getting married to her childhood friend, Mathilda felt life had played a cruel trick on her, making her a widow just a year later. And how sad it was the first time she got together with Birger's widow and three children. She sighed briefly at the memory, and tears welled in her eyes. How would she ever be able to share the most horrific parts of the story with her daughter?

Suddenly, Alfhild appeared in the doorway. She called out, "I love you, Mama," and immediately ran off once again.

Mathilda smiled sadly, and replied in a hushed tone, too quiet for her daughter to hear, "I love you too, baby."

# Birth

The mother's body undergoes a number of changes just prior to the time of birth. The cervix become softer and thinner as it dilates, the baby shifts position toward the pelvis in preparation for being born, the sac of amniotic fluid breaks as contractions begin, and the uterus presses on the baby, directing the child down the birth canal.

# The *Titanic*'s Youngest Survivors

*I love these little people, and it is not a slight thing when they, who are so fresh from God, love us.*

*--Charles Dickens*

Ernest Brown managed to stifle a yawn. He had been sleeping soundly when the message reached the *Carpathia* that the *Titanic* was in serious trouble, and as Purser he had to immediately spring into action. With the aid of Assistant Purser Percy Barnett and Chief Steward Evan Hughes, he interacted with the arriving passengers from the *Titanic* lifeboats, recording their names and directing them to hot beverages and soup that the victualling department had prepared.

Brown looked over at the woman who was now being helped onto the deck of the *Carpathia* and noticed immediately that she was very much in a family way. He could see how exhausted she was, and a stunned look of confusion was clearly etched on her face, reflecting her uncertainty about the fate of her husband. With a blend of efficiency and compassion, he asked for her name. Quietly, the woman looked up and replied in a faint whisper, "Maria Mathilda Backström." Brown recorded her name, figuring he was close to the correct spelling, and then turned her over to another crew member who led her to the coffee and soup.

Ernest watched Mathilda as she walked away, wondering how soon her baby would be born. "Perhaps in a month or two," he thought to himself, and he hoped that the ordeal of this horrible night would not have a negative effect on the child's well-being. But he could not speculate on this any further, partly because he really had no medical expertise, and more importantly because another woman had just been taken aboard the *Carpathia* and he needed to return to the job at hand.

Maria Backström was fortunate, and on June 29, 1912, her daughter Alfhild was born in Finland. In the very truest sense of the word, Alfhild was a *Titanic* survivor, but her name would never be included in the listing of persons who were saved on April 15, 1912. When Ernest Brown and Percy Barnett cobbled together the survivor manifest to be presented to New York

City immigration officials, there was no need or consideration to include those not yet born. In particular, Maria's immigration entry simply listed her as a 33-year-old Finnish domestic with her closest relative living back in Finland, but there was no mention of her very obvious pregnancy.

Carpathia, *the rescue ship for the* Titanic *survivors (Source: Titanicfacts.net)*

Alfhild Backström was the first child born to a *Titanic* survivor, but her birth was not heralded by the world press at the time. Her delivery in a small Finnish town, far away from the major news agencies of England or the United States, preserved her anonymity, and such would be true of most of the children whose mothers were pregnant aboard the *Titanic*. Moreover, these children had very different experiences growing up in terms of what kind of link they felt to the *Titanic*. Some had mothers who provided them with many details about the ship (although not necessarily to the degree of the fictionalized account regarding Alfhild and the story-telling in the last chapter), while others grew up in households where the sinking was barely ever discussed.

In contrast to Alfhild's unnoticed birth, the next to be born attracted extreme media attention. John Jacob Astor VI, better known as Jakey to his family, was born on August 14, 1912, and was generally, but incorrectly, identified at the first-born of the *Titanic* babies. Of course, just being a member of the socially prominent Astor family would have attracted attention anywat, and his relationship to the *Titanic* made his arrival all the more enticing. The press seemed to take great pleasure in referring to him as "The Titanic Baby."

News reporters waited outside of the Astor mansion as details about the blessed event unfolded, and they gleefully reported such details as the baby's weight at seven and three-quarters pounds, the news bulletins from attending physician Dr. Edwin Craigin, the fact that roses were sent to Madeleine from her stepson Vincent, and even minor facts like the broad smiles on the faces of the servants.

"Both Mother and Baby Said to Be Very Well: The Child Strong and Well Formed" proclaimed the sub-headline regarding Jakey's birth in the *New York Times* on August 15. The opening sentence referenced the *Titanic,* followed in quick succession by the mention of the $3,000,000 trust account for the baby set up by his father's estate. The remainder of the article chronicled aspects of the Astor family history, recent legal proceedings regarding the settlement of Colonel Astor's estate as a result of his death on the *Titanic,* the need for a future financial guardian to protect the interests of Jakey's trust account, and text from one of the clauses of his father's will.

Jakey had two older step-siblings born during his father's first marriage, namely Vincent (who was slightly younger than Jakey's mother), and Alice. Madeleine and Jakey took up residence at Beechwood, the Astor cottage in Newport, Rhode Island, because of the family dynamic in New York City, especially with the return of Ava Astor, the Colonel's first wife,

After Jakey's mother married William Dick in 1916, the couple had two sons, William and John, providing Jakey with two more half-siblings. As a result of this marriage the remainder of Madeleine's inheritance was turned back to the Astor family, in line with a clear-cut clause in the Colonel's will. While this provision was well-known by Madeleine and even though William Dick was a wealthy man, one can still imagine that Jakey grew up hearing occasional, disgruntled comments about this "loss."

At least Jakey was fond of his step-father. But the Dick marriage ended in divorce, and when Madeleine married Enzo Fiermonte in 1933, Jakey was not at all pleased. In fact, when he was interviewed by the press as to rumors that his mother and Fiermonte were actually to be wed, his response was a sullen "Unfortunately, it's true." This third marriage ended by divorce in 1938, and Madeleine passed away in 1940 at the age of 46.

*Madeleine Astor Dick and John Jacob Astor VI in 1926 (Source: Encyclopedia Titanica)*

Jakey's own love life was also a rocky one. He was engaged to Eileen Gillespie, but she changed her mind and cancelled their wedding on January 22, 1934, just 15 days before their scheduled marriage. This prompted myriad journalistic jabs, including an article entitled "The Rich Boy Nobody Wants." Yet on June 30, 1934, he married Ellen "Tucky" French, a close friend of Eileen, in a truly beautiful ceremony.

During the course of Jakey and Tucky's marriage, he worked for the International Mercantile Marine, accepting a position arranged for him by his half-brother Vincent. This was the very company that owned the White Star Line and the *Titanic,* and he earned $25 per week. Vincent's intent was aimed at helping his step-brother become a responsible, dependable member of the Astor family, but the intended effect did not materialize. The step-brothers gradually grew further apart, with the final straw coming during World War II. Vincent was active with the Navy as he had also been during the Great War, and he was ever mindful that his father was known as the Colonel. At some point, a news reporter asked Vincent about the story that Jakey avoided military duty during World War II by claiming mental illness. Vincent was mortified by the allegation, and he subsequently cut his brother off, apparently not investigating the veracity of the claim.

As the war continued, Jakey's personal life also became a battleground. He and Tucky divorced in 1943, shortly before their only child, William Astor III, turned eight years old. Their separation was made all the more awkward by the fact that Ellen's sister, Virginia, married Jakey's half-brother William Dick in 1941, yet another marriage that was not destined to last.

A string of marriages and divorces followed for Jakey, and it seemed nothing would go smoothly for him. He married Gertrude Gretsch on September 18, 1944, but they separated in 1950, a year after the birth of their daughter, Mary. Jakey obtained a Mexican divorce from Gertie in 1954, but in the end the legality of that split was questioned because he alone filed the paperwork. As a result, they were formally divorced under American legislation in 1956. In the meantime, Jakey had married Dolores "Dolly" Fullman in 1954, but this ended quickly in divorce within a matter of weeks. With two overlapping marriages, it was little wonder that the world referred to him as a playboy and a bigamist. Fortunately, his fourth marriage, this time to Sue Sandford in 1956, was more successful, and they remained married until she passed away in 1985.

Not surprisingly, Jakey was comfortable financially, thanks to the bequest from his father, Colonel Astor. The original $3 million trust had grown to about $5 million when it was turned over to him at the age of 21. Even though he was not as wealthy as other members of the Astor family, this was still an enormous sum during the Depression, and he immediately pampered himself by purchasing ten automobiles in very quick succession.

But other issues swirled around Jakey when it came to the family fortune. His mother decided to leave money only to her two children born of her marriage to William Dick, figuring that Jakey already had inherited sufficient wealth from his father. Not surprisingly, Jakey felt hurt by her decision, and ultimately he received only a few pieces of his mother's jewelry when she passed away.

The second blow came in 1959 when Jakey's half-brother, Vincent, died childless in 1959. There was no love lost between the two of them, and by then Vincent had even suggested that Colonel Astor never actually fathered Jakey. Vincent completely omitted his younger half-brother from his final will, which was written in 1958. Jakey contested the instrument, claiming that Vincent's third wife, Brooke, had continuously plied her alcoholic husband with liquor which clouded his mind when he prepared his will. During the pre-trial hearing, Vincent's widow went so far as to say that Vincent "thought he [Jakey] was the most useless, worthless member of society and he despised him because he was a slacker and a draft evader." In the end, Jakey was awarded with $250,000, a truly small amount in comparison to the full estate.

Jakey's roller-coaster of a life came to an end on June 26, 1992, when he died at 79, and "The Titanic Baby" was buried in Manhattan's Trinity Church Cemetery, where both of his parents had also been laid to rest. As Derek Wilson pointed out in his biography of the Astor family, "Thus, ironically, it is only through the disowned, disinherited, posthumous son of Colonel Jack that the Astor line has been maintained in the USA."

When Marion Columba O'Brien was born on September 3, 1912, she was in a similar position to Jakey's, given that her father had also perished when the *Titanic* went down. However, her parents, Hannah and Thomas O'Brien, were third class passengers aboard the fated ship, which makes it immediately obvious that the lives of Marion and Jakey shared virtually no other similarities.

The O'Briens originally planned to settle in Chicago, but with Thomas's death in the disaster, Hannah decided to remain in Brooklyn. When Hannah married James Quinn, a fireman and future dockworker, he became the only father Marion would ever know. A son, also named James, was born in 1918, and it seemed that the family was complete and happy. But disaster would strike again, this time in the form of the Spanish influenza, and the worldwide epidemic claimed Marion's mother as another victim.

*Marion O'Brien (Source: Timesunion.com)*

James moved himself and the children into the home of his sister, Mary, and with her assistance he was able to continue raising them. He decided to burn all of Hannah's papers, effectively erasing any trace of Marion's extended family back in Ireland. It is impossible to conclude exactly what motivated James to do this, but he clearly did not want to open up any contact between Marion and her Irish relatives.

James married another woman from Ireland, Catherine by name, and the two of them had a daughter, Mae, who was added to the family in 1921. Of course, they felt blessed by her birth, but the sad reality was that the Quinns were not well off financially. Marion was forced to leave school and started working in 1926 at the age of 14. She became a telephone operator while still in her teens.

Fortunately, Marion was not doomed to a life of poverty. She met William Hanlon, yet another Irish immigrant, whose studies had led him to a career as a civil engineer. Marion and Willie fell in love, married, and raised a family of three children, a boy and two girls. The Hanlons lived in Albany, New York, and this was where Marion and Willie remained after their son, William Jr., died during the Vietnam War and their daughters grew up and left home.

Marion obviously could not have had any personal recollections about the *Titanic*, nor had she been raised with ongoing tales of the disaster, given her own mother's death at such an early age. She knew about the ship, of course, but it certainly was not subject to much discussion as she was growing up. But late in the 1950s, after movies and books began to spread the incredible story of the ill-fated ship, Marion finally told her own children about her personal connection to the ship. Over the years that followed, Marion's children and grandchildren would ask for details which she would answer the best she could. However, Marion forever avoided joining any of the *Titanic* historical societies, and she had no interest in traveling aboard any boats or ships. In fact, she even kept her distance from the ocean, the very thought of which made her nervous.

Despite the records destroyed by her step-father many years before, Marion eventually managed to gather details about her mother's family. At long last the opportunity presented itself to visit Ireland, and she met with members of the Godfrey family, finally creating some direct ties with her maternal relatives. However, she never visited any of the O'Briens, perhaps assuming that they did not want to meet her, perhaps feeling that his death before her birth created a permanent barrier, or perhaps discovering that a lack of details made it seem impossible to track them down.

After Willie Hanlon died in 1975, Marion moved to Manchester, Tennessee, to live with her daughter, Catherine Fisher. The pace in this small Southern town was far more subdued than her former life back in New York, and it suited her quite well. After Marion passed away at the age of 81 on July 4, 1994, the family made sure that she was buried with her husband and son at St. Agnes' Cemetery, Menards, New York, just a few miles north of Albany.

During the two months following Marion's birth, three more girls were born to women who were with child when they traveled aboard the *Titanic*. All of these babies had also lost their fathers when the ship went down.

Ada West's child, Edwyna Joan West, was born on September 14, 1912 and was named in memory of her father, Edwy. The Wests' plan to settle in Florida was dashed when Edwy perished, and so Ada returned to Cornwall, England. She remained there with her first two daughters, awaiting the arrival of the baby, and she was confident that her deceased husband's parents who lived nearby would provide her with much needed support.

Sadly, Edwyna and her older sisters, Constance and Barbara, were destined to lose all three of their living grandparents in 1915, including Ada's mother Ruth Worth, and both of Edwy's parents, Edwy Sr. and Elizabeth. At least one bright spot shone forth thanks to the Worshipful Company of Drapers, which covered the educational costs for the three girls until they reached the age of 12.

Growing up was undoubtedly a challenge for Edwyna, but when she married Clarence Patrick Erskine-Lindop in 1941 things certainly moved in a positive direction. He eventually became Permanent Secretary for the Ministry of Agriculture, Fisheries, and Local Government in the Bahamas, and in 1977 he was awarded the status of an Officer of the Order of the British Empire (OBE). Edwyna passed away in 1969, at which time she was living in Plymouth, England.

Relatively little is known about Mary Margaret "Peggy" Marvin and Maria Salvata del Carlo, the next two *Titanic* babies. Peggy was born on October 21, 1912, the baby daughter of Mary and *Titanic* victim Daniel Marvin. After the disaster, Mary returned to her parents' home in Manhattan, once again a case of a *Titanic* survivor finding comfort and support from her own family. However, unlike Edwyna West, Peggy grew up in a household with a father when Mary married Horace DeKamp in 1913. The DeKamps had a daughter, Julie, in 1915, and the following year Horace formally adopted Peggy. When Frank was born in 1920, the family was complete. Peggy lived until October 7, 1993, when she passed away in Massachusetts.

Maria del Carlo was born on November 14, 1912, in Montecarlo, Italy, a small town in the Lucca province. In a situation reminiscent of what Ada

West faced, Argene del Carlo knew it made no sense to continue on to Chicago where she and Sebastiano were planning on settling. With the death of her husband on the *Titanic,* Argene returned to her own father's home in Montecarlo, Italy, to await the birth of her Maria. As a matter of record, Argene made sure that her daughter was properly documented at the Office of the Civil State. Argene did not remarry until after Maria was fully grown, so father-like influences for the little girl had to come from her maternal grandfather and other male relatives or friends who lived nearby in Tuscany. In the 1930s, Maria married Guido Triboli and went on to have two children. Sebastiano was born in 1936 and was given the name of his grandfather who died on the *Titanic;* and Sabatino was born in 1940.

By the end of November, 1912, six babies had been born whose mothers had been pregnant while aboard the *Titanic.* Nevertheless, the November 30 edition of the *Washington Herald* published an upbeat article under the numerically incorrect headline "Third Widow, Due to Titanic Wreck, Becomes a Mother." The previous day Eloise Smith gave birth to Lucian Philip Smith II, named for his father who had died in the disaster. Not only had the reporter been unaware about most of the other births, he also included Mrs. George T. Widener as one of the survivors to have given birth under these circumstances. However, it is completely unclear who this was referring to. The similarly-named Mrs. George D. Widener was a *Titanic* survivor, but Eleanor's last child was born in 1891.

The next day, the *Chicago Examiner* ran a similar article entitled "Second Titanic Baby Born," still showing the lack of awareness of the other *Titanic* babies, but at least the reference to Mrs. George T. Widener was not included. This article added the news that Eloise had received a congratulatory telegram from Madeleine Astor the previous day, linking the two as the *Titanic* mothers being referenced in the headline. The newspaper errors reflected the fact that those *Titanic* children born overseas remained unheralded (at least by the American press), and the stateside births of Peggy Marvin (whose mother was an American citizen) and Marion O'Brien (whose mother was an Irish immigrant living in New York) did not gather any major media attention either. Social connections mattered, and both Madeleine Astor and Eloise Smith had them.

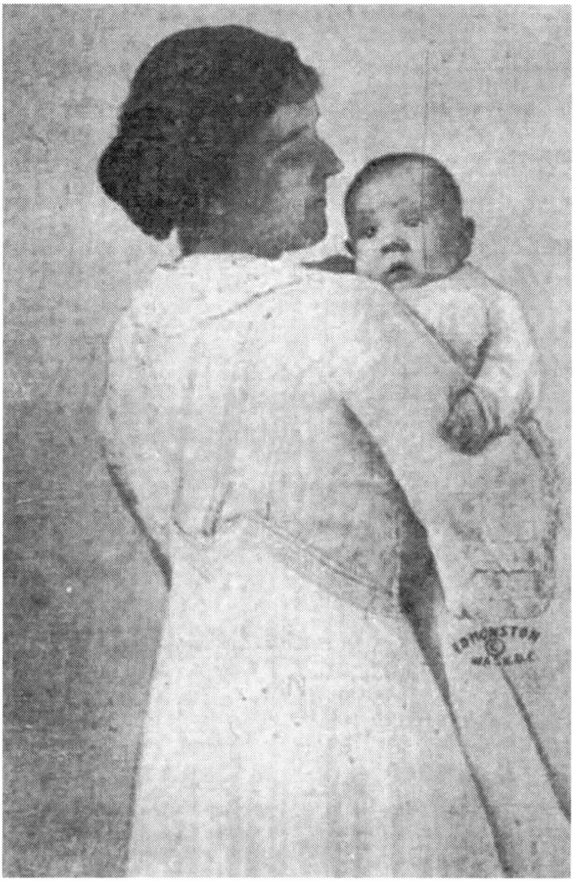

*Lucian Smith II, held by his mother Eloise.* (Source: Encyclopedia Titanica)

While Lucian Smith II was born in the Jewish Hospital at Avondale, near Cincinnati, he and his mother soon headed to the Hughes family home in Huntington, West Virginia, where Eloise's parents lived. Of course, over the years that followed there were also trips to Washington, D.C., where his grandfather, James Hughes, was a Congressman.

One particularly contentious issue during Lucian's childhood was something he was probably unaware of at the time. When his paternal grandmother, Anna Smith, passed away, it was disputed whether Lucian, by then seven years old, should inherit any part of the estate. Legal language stemming back to Lucian's great-grandfather James Cochran's will complicated the matter. Anna's father had left a sizable amount of money when he passed away, and one of the provisions stated that upon her death equal shares of the remaining amount should eventually be turned over to his surviving grandchildren. Lucian's uncle, James Smith and his aunt, Mrs. Paul McKeel, (that is, the brother and sister of Lucian Smith Sr.) maintained that young Lucian should not receive any of the inheritance on the grounds that Lucian Smith Sr. had not survived the sinking of the *Titanic*. Congressman Hughes obtained the best legal counsel he could find to argue the case on behalf of his grandson, and in the end the boy was granted an equal share of the estate, valued at $165,083.

By the time Lucian was seventeen, he had had three different step-fathers. The first one, Robert Daniel, was arguably the most noteworthy in that he was also a *Titanic* survivor. Eloise's marriage to Daniel ended in divorce, as did her final marriage. Lucian's second step-father passed away in 1929 on his 36th birthday. While these fatherly changes and losses undoubtedly uprooted Lucian's life, there was a comforting aspect when Eloise decided to revert her surname to Smith after the final divorce. This rather touching gesture returned her surname to that of the true love of her life, and once again her identity and the last name of young Lucian were the same.

Since Lucian was 17 by then, he soon would be making his own way in the world, which would find him in Huntington, West Virginia; Uniontown, Pennsylvania; Dallas, Texas; and Venice, Florida, over the course of his lifetime. When his mother died in 1940, her funeral service had to be delayed slightly due to difficulties locating Lucian. He had piloted his plane from Lynchburg, Virginia, to Miami, Florida, in the days just before his mother's death, and the family was unable to locate him at first. Thanks to the concerted efforts of the family lawyer he was finally contacted, and Lucian returned to Huntington for the service.

During the 1940s Lucian married Catherine Scates, and the couple went on to have two daughters, Cathy and Betsy. While it is a shame that Eloise did not live long enough to know them, there is still a wonderful reality that the family touched by the *Titanic* tragedy had continued on to a new generation. Fate has an odd way of twisting itself about in unexpected ways, and such was especially the case on April 8, 1966, when Lucian and family was aboard the Norwegian ship MS *Viking Princess* when it caught on fire. Not surprisingly, Lucian and the other male passengers had no problem boarding lifeboats for the evacuation and all were safe, thanks to policy changes that had taken place as a result of the *Titanic* disaster 54 year before. The number of lifeboat seats available were required to meet the needs of all passengers and crew members aboard.

Retirement from a 25-year real estate career in Uniontown, Pennsylvania, eventually found Lucian and Catherine settling down in Venice, Florida. Warm weather was a much-appreciated change from the northern winters, and he became active in the city's Elks Lodge as well as the local Veterans of Foreign Wars Post, an outgrowth of his service in World War II. He passed away on October 24, 1971, at the relatively young age of 58, and was buried nearby in Sarasota Memorial Park.

In many respects Lucian Smith II and the other *Titanic* babies born before him represent a celebration of life growing out of tragedy, but a terrible change was about to take place with the next two tiny *Titanic* survivors. Infant mortality in 1912 was a legitimate concern. As many as 10% of newborns never reached their first birthday, even in the most developed countries. Then there was the lingering question whether the harsh conditions and stress associated with the sinking of the *Titanic* might have led to a disproportionately large number of deaths among those unborn children whose mothers were in a delicate condition when they were aboard the ship.

Marion Kenyon's miscarriage in the weeks following the disaster was probably the result of issues not directly related to the *Titanic,* but one has to wonder about two of the other women who were only a month pregnant at the time the ship sailed. Helen Bishop's son, Randall Walton Bishop, was born on December 8, 1912, a *Titanic* survivor in his own right, but he died two days later. Adele Nasser gave birth to a boy on December 9, 1912, but he died within a few hours. Helen's husband, Dickinson, had managed to survive the sinking of the ship and was on hand to help comfort his wife at the time of their tragic loss, but Adele Nasser was alone in that regard, suffering her pain with the help of family members but without her husband. In fact, of all the pregnant women who were traveling with their husbands on the fated ship, the only ones whose spouses also survived were

Helen Bishop and Ethel Beane. In another cruel twist of irony, Ethel and Edward Beane's child was stillborn on January 13, 1913.

Yet in the midst of all of these tiny *Titanic* survivors whose lives were cut short following their births, there were still some happier outcomes. On December 17, 1912, Joseph LeMercier Laroche Jr. was born to Juliette Laroche, her third child and first son. There was little doubt that he would be named after his father who had lost his life when the *Titanic* foundered. Baby Joseph was born in France, to which Juliette and her daughters returned after the *Carpathia* reached New York. There was little point for the Laroches to continue on to Haiti as originally planned now that Juliette's husband had died, and at least back in France her father could help support the family directly. Ultimately, neither of Joseph's sisters married, but he and Claudine Laroche went on to have several children. Joseph passed away on January 17, 1987.

All three of the *Titanic* baby boys who survived into adulthood were named after their fathers as was Edwyna West, but Kate Phillips's daughter suffered a very different reality. Ellen Mary Phillips, also known as Betty, never even had her father's name included on her birth certificate. Despite a life-long quest to have him legally recognized as her biological father, this was never granted and it remained an emotional challenge for her to accept.

Ellen's childhood was very difficult. After her daughter's birth on January 11, 1913, Kate decided to move away from Worcester, leaving the girl under the care of her parents, Thomas and Mary Phillips. Society could treat a child born out of wedlock quite harshly during that era, so perhaps this decision made things slightly better for Ellen, given that her mother was out of the immediate picture and living in London.

However, until she was nearly ten years old, Ellen was confused by annual visits by a stranger, a woman from London whose identity the young girl was not privy to. This visitor smothered her with hugs and kisses and then would leave again, a puzzling reality. Ellen would much rather be out on the River Severn on the family punt, strapped carefully in place, with her grandfather promising her that she would not drown. His tone sometimes seemed quite serious, but that was okay to her. These excursions were truly fun.

*Ellen Phillips (Source:* The Sun*)*

The situation changed in 1922, four years after Kate married Frederick Watson. At long last Ellen's confusion about the mysterious visitor were made abundantly clear when she learned that this woman was her mother, and she was taking her away from her grandparents so they could live together in South Ealing, London. Unfortunately, this reunion of mother and daughter was far from a dream fulfilled. Almost immediately after reaching her new home, Ellen's fine outfits that her grandparents had provided for her were taken away. Even her footwear was replaced by black stockings and uncomfortable boots.

Ellen was forced to do so much housework that she felt more of a servant than a daughter, while her mother spent incredible amounts of time in bed, claiming to be ill. Of course, some might imagine Ellen was clinging to this memory as an exaggerated assessment of her duties, but what seemed to be forced servitude was only the tip of the iceberg. Breaking a cup meant she would be beaten. Corporal punishment continued for the slightest infraction even when her grandparents visited each August. Reprimands were not always physical, however, and it was not unusual for Ellen to be locked in her bedroom all day, with her mother delivering an occasional piece of dry bread as her only nourishment.

Fortunately for Ellen, others outside of the family eventually noticed something was amiss. A schoolmate, Elsie, saw some loose, fluffy material stuck in the cuts on the back of Ellen's legs and was curious what it was. After Ellen explained that it had come off of her fleece-lined knickers when her mother caned her legs, Elsie was alarmed. She told her own mother who in turn informed the authorities. A short time later, Ellen was called to the headmistress's office at school, a frightening prospect that made Ellen fear more abuse might be coming her way when her mother learned about this. To her surprise, Ellen received the headmistress's promises that her mother "will never touch you from this day." As it turned out, the beatings came to an immediate stop, and years later Ellen learned that her mother had been taken to court over these allegations.

Until Ellen was twelve, she had no idea who her actual father was. Kate Phillips never mentioned Henry Morely's name, nor had her grandparents. Then one of Ellen's aunts told her the story of how her mother and Henry had run off together aboard the *Titanic* and that she had been born almost exactly nine months after the ship had left Queenstown. Pieces of the story were added over the next few years, and by the time Ellen turned 15, her aunt came across a picture of Morely and passed it on to her. Shortly afterwards, the photograph disappeared. Ellen realized that she could not ask her mother about the picture, nor could she ask about further details regarding Henry Morely or the *Titanic.*

What a cruel twist of fate for Ellen. Henry Morely had been a wealthy man, and while it would be impossible to know how Kate's mental state would play out had he survived the sinking, it still seems reasonable to assume that Ellen's early life would have been far better. Ellen's one bright spot beyond her grandparents was that her step-father treated her well. However, he was an uneducated window-washer who could neither read nor write, and as such he was limited in what he could offer her.

Despite her efforts to get Morely's name added to her birth certificate, Ellen never tried to contact anybody in his family, not even her own half-sister Doris. The great unknown was whether the Morelys would welcome Ellen into their lives or reject her due to the embarrassing and insulting circumstances regarding her very existence. After all, Morely had run off with Kate while leaving his wife and young daughter behind in England.

As Ellen grew into adulthood, the distance between herself and her mother widened greatly, especially after Kate was institutionalized. Eventually, daughter and mother completely lost touch with one another. Ellen married a bus-driver named Lawrence Farmer in 1935, and she and her husband had a son, Robert. Sadly, widowhood soon followed. Ellen found love once again, and she married Frederick Walker in 1944. Over the years she also held a variety of jobs, including positions working for a florist, serving in the passport office, and taking on the physical challenge as a railroad porter during World War II.

Kate died in 1964, and it was months later until Ellen learned of her mother's death, a clear indication of how far the two of them had grown apart. Despite the wide gulf between them, Ellen still ended up with several *Titanic*-related objects she treasured throughout her life. These items included her mother's purse that she had used while on the ship, the cabin keys she had tucked away when she headed out to the lifeboats, and a sapphire necklace that Henry had given to Kate while they were at sea.

In 1989, 76-year-old Ellen moved back to Worcester, where she had spent her early days with her grandparents. Rekindled interest in the *Titanic* around that time led to occasional newspaper articles about the ship and its victims, and one of her acquaintances spotted a picture of Henry Morely in a human-interest story about local individuals who had been on the ship. The woman shared the article with Ellen. "I cried and cried and cried. It was the first clear picture I'd seen," Ellen stated. Then, with her *Titanic* background becoming more widely known, John Hodges approached her with the request that she write the foreword to his book *Titanic – The Story of a Maritime Tragedy.* She accepted the opportunity, providing a truly meaningful connection between herself and the ship.

Ellen understood that the Morely fortune was long gone and perhaps no other family members were still alive who might even remember him. Yet she remained saddened by the fact that she never managed to have him identified on her birth certificate, and even her son's efforts were to no avail. Her wish remained unfulfilled until the day she died in October 2005. Her long life made Ellen the final survivor among the yet-to-be-born *Titanic* passengers and the one individual who could best point to the possibility of having been conceived on the ship itself.

Many hundreds of individuals were born after the *Titanic* sailed, children and grandchildren and beyond, whose very existences hearken back to one or more ancestors who survived the disaster. This status particularly included David Baclini, who was born on January 26, 1913. His mother, Latifa Qurban Baclini, was reunited with her husband, Solomon, after she reached New York on the *Carpathia.* David is considered the first child conceived by a survivor after the *Titanic* went to its demise. But the final birth to a woman who might have been pregnant while aboard the ship involved Ida Doling, born on January 30, 1913.

Ida's status in this regard is open to question. She was the fifth child and only daughter of Ada and John Doling. John had remained in England with his four sons when Ada boarded the *Titanic* on April 10, 1912, for a visit with her own mother in New York. Because Ada did not return to England until May 11, this opens up interesting speculation as to whether she had been newly pregnant when she boarded the ship in Southampton. Ida was born 295 days later, about two weeks longer than the standard pregnancy, making her somewhat overdue. Of course, Ada could have become pregnant after her return, which would have meant that Ada was born about 264 days later, roughly two weeks shorter than expected. Suffice it to say that Ada welcomed baby Ida as a much beloved addition to her four sons in the household, a fitting ending to the story of the expectant women aboard the *Titanic.*

# Epilogue

# The Mothers' Lives after the *Titanic*

*The child supplies the power but the parents have to do the steering.*

*--Dr. Benjamin Spock*

Of the seventeen women known or believed to have been pregnant while aboard the *Titanic,* fourteen survived. The tragedy changed their lives dramatically, especially for the eleven whose partners were not saved that night. Some of these mothers-to-be, unexpectedly and horribly alone, returned to their parents for the help and support that they could provide. Others faced their futures in their former homes with the loving assistance of friends and families, and in some cases, their servants.

The women's lives eventually settled into the "new normal" that fate had handed them. Perhaps that meant living in relative obscurity. Maybe that meant remarrying and having additional children after their *Titanic* babies were born. Possibly it meant continuing in the public eye through the intrusive attention of the newspaper society pages. A few would face further tragedies with their own lives cut short, while others would enjoy far longer lives and the relative healing that the passage of time can offer.

What follows are brief summaries of the rest of the lives of these survivors:

**Madeleine Talmadge Force Astor** and her newborn son, Jakey, moved to Beechwood, the Astor family mansion in Newport, Rhode Island. This took her away from the ongoing forces at play in Manhattan where Ava Astor, Colonel John Astor's first wife, reclaimed her position at the head of the city's highest echelon of society. On June 22, 1916, Madeleine married William K. Dick at her estate in Bar Harbor, Maine. Dick was a childhood friend, worked successfully in finance, and served as a corporate official for a number of companies. He was also part of the social scene, although obviously not to the same level of the Astors. Madeleine and William added two sons to their family, William in 1917 and John in 1919. The Dicks divorced in Minden, Nevada, on July 21, 1933.

Rumors had been circulating that Madeleine was having an affair with boxer Enzo Fiermonte, whom the Dicks had hired to teach their younger boys basic fighting skills. She was wedded to Fiermonte on November 27, 1933. All three of her sons were present, with the ceremony held at New York's Doctors Hospital, where Madeleine was recovering from an injured shoulder. Social mavens viewed this marriage as a final blow to Madeleine's social standing, after which she faced further indignity when she finally realized that Enzo was really only after her money. A series of arguments and temporary separations plagued their marriage, and the fact that he was fifteen years her junior added to the discord. The Fiermontes divorced in 1938.

At this point in her life, Madeleine reassumed Dick as her last name. Heart disease ended her life in Palm Beach, Florida, on March 27, 1940, although there were rumors that an overdose of prescription drugs might also have been involved. She was buried at Trinity Church Cemetery and Mausoleum in Manhattan, not far from the final resting place of her first husband, Colonel John Jacob Astor.

**Maria Mathilda Gustafsson Backström's** return to Kejtala, Finland, to await the birth of her daughter, Alfhild, turned out to be permanent. Even though Mathilda was almost 34 by the time the baby was born, she much appreciated the caring help and support of her own mother. Mathilda never remarried, remaining in Kejtala until her death on June 30, 1947. She was buried next to her brother, Viktor, at the Abborfors burial grounds.

**Ethel Louise Clarke Beane** and her husband, Edward, had their world turned upside-down when their first child was still-born, a cruel blow to one of the relatively few couples to survive the sinking of the *Titanic.* Fortunately for them, their Rochester, New York, home was eventually filled with the sound of children's voices. Their son, Edward, was born in 1913, and three years later George was added to the family. The Beanes continued living at 44 Michigan Street in Rochester, never making a return to England, not even for a brief visit. On rare occasions they would grant an interview to a reporter about the *Titanic,* but otherwise this was a topic they generally avoided discussing.

Ethel was widowed in 1948 and remained in the family home until it became necessary for her to move into a nursing facility, where she resided until her death on September 17, 1983. She was the last of the expectant mothers on the *Titanic* to pass away. Always a bit vain about her age, those around her were convinced she was 90 years old at the time, and this was reflected in the newspaper accounts reporting her death, although in reality she was only two months away from her 94th birthday. Both Ethel and Edward were buried in White Haven Memorial Park in Pittsford, New York, about 14 miles from where they had lived.

**Helen Margaret Walton Bishop** and her husband, Dickinson, certainly were traumatized by the *Titanic* disaster and the loss of their son only two days after his birth. This created some marital pressure, but, in fairness, they continued trying to make their marriage work. However, surprising issues arose that dovetailed with the predictions made by the Egyptian fortune teller when they had been on their honeymoon. While on vacation in California in 1913 they experienced an earthquake, just as the seer said they would. Then on November 5, 1914, [some sources say 1913] the third prediction regarding her death in a car accident was almost fulfilled. The Bishops were returning to their home in Dowagiac, Michigan, from a country club dance in Kalamazoo. Dickinson lost control of their car and ran into a tree, causing extensive injuries to Helen's head. The doctors figured she would not recover, yet somehow she survived, and a metal plate was inserted into her skull. However, surviving was not the same as recovering, and Helen's condition deteriorated as she started experiencing episodes of Jacksonian epilepsy.

In the end, Helen and Dickinson got divorced in January of 1916, with Helen claiming cruelty and drunkenness on the part of her husband. Just two months later on March 15, Helen had a terrible fall while visiting friends in Danville, Michigan, causing her death at the age of 23. In an ironic twist, the front page of the *Dowagiac Daily News* that announced Helen's death also reported Dickinson's third marriage, this time to Sydney Boyce. Helen was buried next to her son at Oaklawn Cemetery in Sturgis, Michigan.

**Argene Genovesi del Carlo** gave some consideration to remaining in New York after losing her husband when the *Titanic* sank, but by July she returned to her parents' home in Montecarlo, Italy. It was here that her daughter Maria was born. It appears that Argene truly focused her attention on Maria and delayed remarrying until April 4, 1935, when she wed Antonio Casata. He was from Altopascio, another town in the Lucca Province, and this became Argene's new home until her death on October 8, 1970. She was buried nearby in Cimitero Comunale.

**Ada Julia Elizabeth Bone Doling** and her husband John felt truly blessed by the long-awaited addition of a daughter to the family. Fortunately, all five of their children reached adulthood before John passed away on April 1, 1938. Ada remained in Southampton for another 24 years until she died on April 11, 1962. Rather than having her buried, the family saw to it that she was cremated at the old Garden of Rest Crematorium, located in section 7 of South Stoneham Cemetery, in Southampton's Swaythling district.

**Marion Estelle Stauffer Kenyon** had to deal with the double blow of her husband's death on the *Titanic* and the loss of her child through a miscarriage. Correctly figuring that she could rely on the support of her sisters, Etta and Grace, she decided to leave the East Coast and moved to California where the two of them lived. On December 24, 1916, she married Owen Williams, her fourth husband, and the couple settled together in Santa Monica. Owen had been a friend of Marion's husband, Frederick, back in Noank, Connecticut, where the Kenyons had their summer home and where his mother still lived. Unfortunately, Marion and Owen were eventually divorced, and she decided to change her name back to Kenyon. In the years that followed, Marion lived with her sister, Dr. Grace Davis, along with their aged mother, Martha Stauffer. Upon Marion's death on October 3, 1958, her ashes were placed at Woodlawn Mausoleum in Santa Monica.

*Final resting place of Marion Kenyon's ashes at the Woodlawn Mausoleum, Santa Monica, California (Source: Photograph by the author)*

**Juliette Marie Louise Lafargue Laroche** remained at her father's home in Villejuif, France, after her son was born, both emotionally and financially destitute. Fortunately for the Laroches, her father was relentless in encouraging his daughter to pursue a settlement against the White Star Line on behalf of herself and his grandchildren, as his wine business was not sufficient to support all five of them. It took six long years for a settlement to finally be granted, with the family being awarded $22,000, which Juliette was able to use in starting up a small fabric-dying and craft business.

Financial realities were still challenging for the family, although inheriting her father's house when he passed away was obviously beneficial. Juliette was especially protective of her three children, the extra caution growing out of the loss of her husband and the ongoing health problems of her daughter Louise. Ironically, her sick little girl ended up living the longest of the three children. It is open to speculation what impact Juliette's overly protective nature may have had on her two daughters never marrying and the fact that she, herself, also remained single for the rest of her life. Juliette avoided discussing the *Titanic* as much as possible, haunted by the horrifying memories of that fated night. She passed away in Paris on January 10, 1980.

**Mary Graham Carmichael Farquharson Marvin** continued residing with her parents after her daughter was born. However, she soon fell in love and married Horace DeKamp on Christmas day 1913, and for much of their married lives they maintained two homes, one in Manhattan and the other upstate in Old Forge. Together they added two more children to the family, Julia in 1915 and Frank in 1920.

Not feeling restricted by the tragedy in her past, Mary frequently journeyed across the Atlantic with her family. However, she tended to be tight-lipped about the *Titanic* disaster itself, a subject she simply found too upsetting to discuss. Mary never remarried after Horace's death in 1954, and as she grew older, she settled permanently in Old Forge, appreciative of its small-town pace. She passed away on October 17, 1975, at the age of 81 and was buried beside her husband at the town's Riverview Cemetery.

**Adele Hakim Nasser** awaited the birth of her son in Cleveland, Ohio, where her sister Mahībā Anter lived. How fortunate Adele was that they were together for the extra support she needed when the baby died within a matter of hours after he was born. In 1914 Adele moved to Albuquerque, New Mexico, along with her brother Ilyās, and she soon fell in love with Albert Shamaley. He was a confectioner who was also from Lebanon and had lived in the United States since 1898. The Shamaleys moved to El Paso, Texas, at about the same time that Ilyās died. Looking for a way to increase the family income, Albert set up a successful company manufacturing office equipment.

Adele and Albert had five children together, Selma, Ayoub, Lee, Albert (who died a year after he was born), and Anne. Not only was Adele wonderfully surrounded by her husband and children, but more of her own siblings had also moved to America. Even her mother, Attur, came to the United States and lived with her for a while. Adele's husband was injured in an automobile accident and died 19 days later on August 18, 1969. Five months afterwards Adele passed away from a heart attack, dying on

January 20. Contributions in her memory were requested for two of her favorite causes, Jesuit High School and St. Joseph Borromeo Seminary, quite indicative of her solid ties to the Catholic church. The Shamaleys' crypts are next to one another in El Paso's Evergreen Mausoleum.

**Hannah Godfrey O'Brien** remained in Brooklyn after the birth of her daughter, enduring a battle with her deceased husband's relatives over the proceeds of the *Titanic* settlement. Fortunately, Hannah prevailed. She married James Quinn, a city fireman, and she became a mother again. The happy couple added a son, James Jr., to the family in 1918. Just months later Hannah fell victim to the worldwide influenza epidemic, and she died on October 17, 1918.

**Kate Florence Phillips** initially thought she would remain in the United States despite the death of Henry Morely on the *Titanic*, and family lore suggests that some Americans had agreed to take in the lovely young woman. However, that offer changed quickly when they learned Kate was pregnant, so she returned to her parents' home in Worcester, England. After her daughter was born, Kate left the girl in the care of her parents and moved to London, where she obtained a job selling shoes and hats.

In 1918 she married Frederick Watson who at the time was a café proprietor, and in 1922 Kate decided she and her husband would have Ellen move in with them in London. Unfortunately, Ellen was often physically abused, and such treatment would not end until Kate was hauled into court. Kate was an extreme hypochondriac and showed other signs of mental instability, eventually going to the extreme of swallowing corrosive acid. The authorities had her institutionalized, and she remained in an asylum for most of the rest of her life. Kate died in Herdon, Middlesex, on March 27, 1964, at a time when she was very much alone. By then her husband had left her, and mother and daughter were no longer keeping in touch with one another.

**Mary Eloise Hughes Smith's** marriage to Philadelphia banker Robert Daniel prompted a move for Eloise and her son from her parents' home in Huntington, West Virginia. Eloise met Robert on the *Carpathia* after both were rescued from the *Titanic* disaster, but apparently nothing would save their marriage. They separated in 1920, six years after they wed, and a divorce degree was issued in Charleston, West Virginia, on March 20, 1923. Accusations regarding "a blonde woman" were raised during the proceedings, and in the end provisions in the settlement forbid Eloise from marrying for at least six months and Robert for at least five years.

However, just weeks later the *New York Times* announced Eloise's marriage to Lewis Cort Jr., on April 7, and by year's end Daniel remarried as well. Lewis was head of the Cort Tire & Rubber Company, founded by his father, and the newlyweds made their home on the west side of Huntington, near Eloise's family. Unfortunately, Lewis died on his 36th birthday, November 24, 1929, making Eloise a widow for the second time. Twenty-six days later, she married Charles Wright in Washington D.C., but they divorced on April 19, 1930, just four months later. Back to Huntington she and her son went, this being her final major move, and she changed her last name back to Smith.

Eloise made many appearances in the years that followed, making speeches for the Republican Party and talking about her experiences on the *Titanic*. She also indicated that she was planning on writing a book about that fated night, although this never materialized. Shortly after taking a course in hotel management, Eloise was admitted to a Cincinnati hospital for a heart ailment, and she died unexpectedly of a heart attack May 3, 1940. She was buried at Springhill Cemetery in Huntington, laid to rest between her father's burial spot and the location where her mother would be interred ten years later.

**Ada Mary Worth West** and her two daughters returned to England after the *Titanic* disaster, awaiting the birth of her third girl. They resettled in their old hometown of Truro, where Ada's attention was focused on raising her family. She never remarried, and only under the rarest circumstances did she discuss the tragedy. One item she treasured all her life was the thermos flask which had been filled with hot milk when her husband lowered it by rope to her and the girls after the lifeboat they were in was already descending. This flask remained in her possession even when she moved into St. Vincent's Nursing Home in Plympton. She died on April 20, 1953.

*Gravesite of Eloise Hughes Smith at Springhill Cemetery, Huntington, West Virginia (Photograph by the author)*

# Widowed Mothers and Posthumous Fathers

*The most important thing a father can do for his children is to love their mother.*

*--Theodore Hesburgh*

As word spread among the passengers and crew members that the *Titanic* had collided with an iceberg, all struggled to understand what had occurred and how to respond. Thoughts turned to home and their loved ones, perhaps even before the intensity of the peril was fully understood. Women in the stern of third class struggled to unite with their adult sons and brothers who were located far away in the bow. Parents with young children woke up their offspring who were fast asleep, and struggled to get them dressed so they could head off to the Boat Deck. All the while they tried to balance a sense of urgency while soothing them the best they could. Even crew members who clearly did not have any children aboard found mental images of their sons and daughters filling their minds' eyes.

The extreme case might lie with James Witter, a second class smoke room steward, who rushed to his room where 32 men had already turned in for the night. He was driven to find out exactly what was going on down below, and once he understood the extent of the damage, he retrieved several things he felt he needed. As he would later indicate in a letter to Walter Lord, "...I opened my trunk and filled my pockets with cigarettes, and also taking the cowl of my first child, which I always carried with me." In the end, James was a fortunate father. He survived the sinking and returned to his eight-month-old son and the mother of his child back in England. Others were not so lucky.

In this moment of crisis, parental care and priorities rose to the foreground. There were so many loving mothers on board the *Titanic*. Some of these mothers had children back home and did all they could to be rescued in one of the lifeboats on the night of the disaster. The mothers who were traveling with their children on the doomed ship desperately did what they could to make sure their children would be saved. For some, especially in third class, there was little hope for survival, as circumstances made it nearly impossible to find their way to the Boat Deck.

The seventeen brave mothers-to-be who were in a delicate condition while aboard the *Titanic* ran the gamut from those who were expecting their first child to those who had already experienced the joys of motherhood as many as four times. A few would not learn that they were pregnant until later. Ten of them lost their husbands that night and one lost the man she had run off with, forcing them to face the rest of their pregnancies and the births of their children without their presence and loving support.

There were, however, many other women in a family way who were not even on the *Titanic* but who still had a direct connection to the ship. These expectant mothers remained at home when they lost their husbands who were aboard. Many of these men were young crew members, just starting to raise their families. Others were passengers, who lost their lives on April 15, 1912. They did not live to see the birth of the children they helped create.

Below is a listing of these women and men. This includes those who were fathers-to-be for the first time and those who were expecting an addition to their growing families. These fathers would never know their babies, and the babies would sadly never meet their dads. This listing also recognizes the mothers who brought their children into the world alone, suddenly forced into raising their sons or daughters under completely unexpected conditions, bravely facing what life had handed them.

The 46 women known to have been in a family way back home and their spouses or loved ones who were aboard the *Titanic* are as follows, grouped under the month in which their children were born:

## April

Esther Olsen gave birth to Charles Ernest shortly before or just after the *Titanic* foundered. Sadly, the baby died on May 16, 1912. The boy's father, Charles Olsen, was an engineer in the United States since 1894 and had briefly returned to Norway after his mother died. He was returning to America with his son, Artur, who had been living with his grandmother. Carl managed to see to it that nine-year-old Artur was rescued in lifeboat 13, and the boy was taken to his step-mother after reaching New York. Esther later remarried and added a daughter to the family.

Isabella Wyeth's daughter, Gladys, was born around the time of the *Titanic* disaster. Similar to the situation with Charles Olsen, the precise date for the birth of fireman James Wyeth's child is not readily known. Isabella never remarried and was left completely alone when Gladys passed away at the age of 11.

Edith May Hosgood gave birth to a son on April 18, 1912, and named him Richard William after his father. Richard Hosgood Sr. was a fireman aboard the *Titanic* and was one of six individuals hired at the last minute to replace crew members who arrived at the dock too late to board the ship. The couple also had a two-year-old daughter. In 1914 Edith once again married and gave birth to another son.

## May

Eliza Mayo was already the loving mother of a son, William, and was awaiting the birth of her second child when William Mayo Sr. headed for the *Titanic*. He signed on as a leading fireman on April 6. Sadly, their daughter, Evelyn, survived only for a day after her May 5, 1912, birth.

Catherine Jackopson well-understood the challenges inherent for the wives of sailors who often were away at sea for many weeks at a time. She already had three children and was awaiting the birth of her fourth when her husband, John Jackopson, left to assume his position as a fireman aboard the *Titanic*. When their son was born a few weeks after the ship sank, she named him after his father, but tragically the baby passed away a few months later. She remarried in 1913 and would go on to have two more children.

Mary Elizabeth Adams Rimmer, wife of Gilbert Rimmer, became the mother of Leslie Charles on May 29, 1912. Gilbert was a saloon steward aboard the *Titanic,* and the couple already had another son. Touchingly, she placed a memorial notice regarding Gilbert in the *Liverpool Echo,* ending with the words, "Deeply mourned by his loving wife and children."

## June

Ellen and Henry Charles Fairall had been married for twelve years when he departed for Belfast to participate in the delivery trip of the *Titanic* to Southampton and the maiden journey of the ill-fated ship. With three children aged eleven and younger, Ellen's responsibilities included caring for them and running the household, especially challenging with Henry at sea. The first class saloon steward lost his life when the ship went down on April 15, 1912, destined to never meet his firstborn son, Charles Anthony, who was born on June 12, 1912. Tragically, the boy died on November 7 of the same year, and both father and son are remembered on their shared tombstone. Ellen remained single for the rest of her life.

Florence Crisp married Albert Crisp late in 1911, and it was wonderful to be expecting a child with her new husband. She had been widowed in 1910 and was raising two daughters on her own until the Crisps married. Minnie Kathleen Joan was born on June 29, 1912, nearly eleven weeks after Albert lost his life on the *Titanic* as a saloon steward. Florence never remarried, raising all three girls on her own.

## July

Edith and Henry "Harry" Brewer were expecting their first child when he boarded the *Titanic* as a trimmer. Their son, Harry Marks, was born on

July 6, 1912. Edith remarried the next year and would have four more children while still living in Southampton, followed by an additional child after moving to Canada.

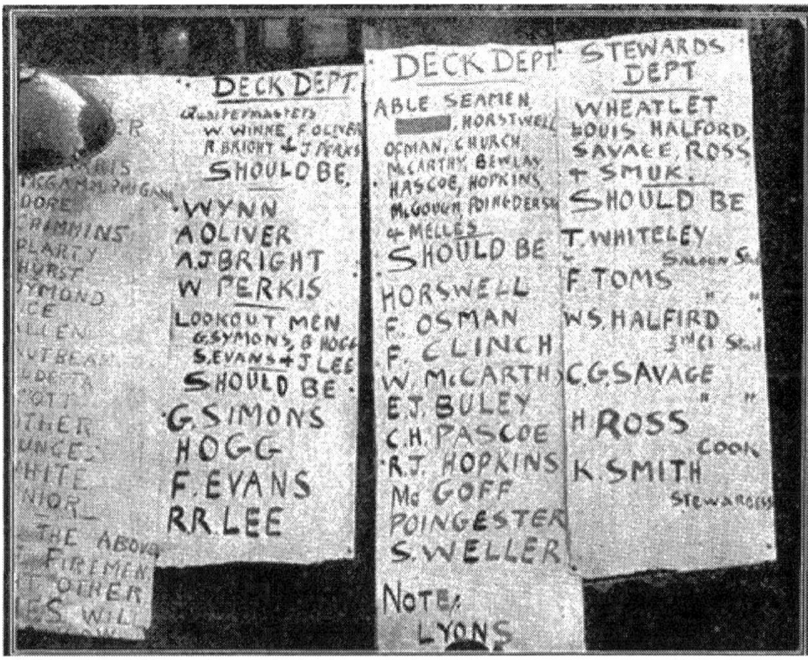


*Early lists posted in Southampton included names of crew members who were victims of the* Titanic *disaster. These often needed to be corrected due to transmission and spelling errors. Of the 908 total crew members, 724 had lived in Southampton. A total of 549 of these residents perished, including 26 whose widows would give birth in the coming months. (Source:* The Mirror)

Charlotte Willsher gave birth to a son on July 21, 1912, and named him William Herbert. She and the baby's father, William, a butcher aboard the *Titanic,* already had four other children by that time. Charlotte dedicated herself to raising the children on her own after losing her husband, and she did not remarry until 1928.

Lillie Williams was awaiting her second born, Harold Charles, when Leslie Williams left for the *Titanic*. He was one of two highly regarded Welsh boxers heading to Pennsylvania to engage in a series of exhibition bouts. Both men would lose their lives on the *Titanic*. Lillie and Harold's baby was born on July 25, 1912. Lillie remarried in 1915, and she is described as raising a large family with her second husband.

Mary and Richard Edward Burke had every right to feel a mix of joy and trepidation when they learned that she was in a family way. The couple dearly loved their daughter, but the memory of the painful August 1911 death of their four-month-old second child, also named Richard Edward, was still fresh in their minds. Richard Sr. was a first class lounge steward for the maiden voyage of the *Titanic* and had also been aboard for the delivery voyage of the ship when it traveled from Belfast to Southampton. When Richard Edmund was born on July 26, she named him after his deceased father and older brother. Fortunately, the baby lived a long and happy life. Mary would have another son in 1916 after remarrying that same year.

Alice and James Arthur Paintin were eagerly awaiting the birth of their first child. They had just been married on November 8, 1911, and with Alice being 30 years old, they were thrilled that a baby was already on the way. The father-to-be was highly regarded as a White Star Line steward, and on the upcoming voyage he was to serve as "Tiger," steward to Captain Edward Smith. Paintin lost his life when the ship went down, and when the baby was born on July 31, Alice named him Arthur James in his memory.

When Nella Mangiavacchi married her adventurous 39-year-old husband Emilio in 1903, he had returned to Italy from Chile after a career as a firefighter. She was fifteen years younger than he, and although he was ready to settle down, the couple and their firstborn son did so only after moving to the United States in 1904. Two more boys would be born in America in 1907 and 1910, and Emilio seemed content with working as a realtor at a New York bank. A troublesome illness led him to decide that he needed to return to Italy for an operation. Around the same time he was planning his trip, Nella became pregnant. Emilio traveled to Italy alone, the operation was successful, and he secured passage on the *Titanic* for a return that ended in tragedy. Their daughter, Maria Emilia, was born sometime later in 1912. Her birth was certainly before September as this was when Nella and all four children boarded a ship so they could resettle near Florence, Italy, where they lived near the home of Emilio's brother.

## September

Early in 1912 China Livshin, a young Russian woman, married David Livshin, who was a native of Latvia. The couple settled in Manchester, England, where David was a watchmaker, and they had plans to move to Montreal, Canada, where several of David's siblings already lived. For the time being, China would remain in England, awaiting the birth of their first child, while David would head to North America without her. For reasons that have never been fully resolved, David boarded the *Titanic* under the name of Abraham Harmer, perhaps using a ticket he had purchased from somebody else. Their baby was born on September 3, 1912, and China named her son David. In the end, mother and son moved back to Russia using the proceeds she received from the Liverpool relief fund.

Elizabeth and William Rogers were not married when their first son was born in 1901. The couple finally wed in the spring of 1911, only to have William abandon the family early in 1912. Shortly before he boarded the *Titanic,* a court order accusing him of desertion was issued. Clearly he was on the run, reflected in the fact that William's ultimate destination when he boarded the ship remains unknown to this day. Seemingly, the only certain aspect of his trans-Atlantic journey was that he was traveling with his nephew, Evan Davies, who was also a miner. By the time the ship departed Elizabeth was with child, and she gave birth to William Morgan on September 13.

Eva Ayling became the mother of a second daughter, Edna Rosina, on September 16, 1912. With the death of assistant vegetable cook Edwin

Ayling when the *Titanic* foundered, Eva was faced with raising the two girls on her own until she remarried in 1915, and she added two more sons to the family in the years that followed.

Julia and August Carlsson already had two sons when he left Sweden and headed to Tower, Minnesota, where his brother lived. Quite possibly August intended to continue laboring as a farmer in the new world. Julia gave birth to their third son, Karl August, on September 19, 1912, only days after the older of her two other sons passed away. The Mansion House Fund awarded an unusually large settlement to Julia, based on the fact that August had been the only source of income for his own family as well as for his parents. A rather quirky twist followed on September 11, 1919, when Julia gave birth to a daughter, and she had August was listed as the father. This action was tied to the fact that Swedish law did not declare him dead until 1920.

When Samuel Williams boarded the *Titanic* as a fireman, he left behind a young woman in England who was pregnant with his child, although her identity still remains uncertain. Their son was born about five months later, probably during the month of September, and he was named Samuel after this father. Despite the fact that the parents were unmarried, the woman (whose surname is thought to have been Gouge or Read) was still granted a settlement from the Mansion Fund after she initiated a court case. She produced signed affidavits from several of Sam's shipmates who swore that he had died when the *Titanic* went down.

## October

Daisy Coe was a loving mother of two boys under the age of four when she learned that she was once again in a family way. She and her husband, Harry, were quite happy about this future blessing, still nearly six months away at the time he boarded the *Titanic* as a trimmer. Their son, George Arthur, was born on October 5, 1912, giving Daisy three young sons to raise on her own. She would remarry in 1919 and add another son and two daughters to her family.

Florence Jones also gave birth to a baby boy on October 5 and named him Arthur Owen. Her husband, Harry Owen Jones, destined to die the night the *Titanic* sank, was a roast cook on the ship. The couple had just gotten married in early 1912, and with Harry already in his mid-thirties, the news that a baby was on the way was quite exciting. Florence never remarried.

*Fund raising groups like the Boy Scouts shown here helped collect funds to support the families of the* Titanic *victims (Source:* The Mirror)

Margaret and Hugh Fitzpatrick already had an 18-month-old son when Hugh left for his position as a junior boiler maker aboard the *Titanic*. Their daughter, Rose Ann Theresa, was born on October 10, 1912. Margaret would go on to marry another seaman in 1921 and became the dedicated mother to seven more children.

Large families were quite common in the early 1900s, and Rhoda Andrew would eventually give birth to nine children. However, when her husband, Frank Andrew, left Cornwall for America, the couple only had a three-year-old daughter. Frank was probably aware of the fact that another baby was on the way when he departed for the *Titanic,* intent on applying his tin-mining skills in the Upper Peninsula of Michigan near Houghton. Because he lost his life when the ship sank, he was robbed of the opportunity to see his second daughter, Clara, who was born on October 11. Rhoda married a stone-mason the following year.

Mary Costin had fallen deeply in love with John "Jock" Law Hume, a talented Scottish violinist. He had been booked through the Liverpool firm of C. W. and F. N. Black as one of eight musicians to perform during the maiden voyage of the *Titanic,* which spoke well of his abilities. The story of the orchestra members bravely and selflessly playing music during the sinking of the ship is well known, and all of them went to their deaths that night. Whether John was aware of the fact that Mary was with child remains uncertain, but it is known that their daughter was born on October 18, 1912. Mary named the girl Johnann Law Hume Costin in loving memory of the baby's father.

## November

Maria Sofia Rintamäki had faced the challenge of raising a large family for many years. She and Matti Rintamäki were married in the late 1890s, and by 1911 they had ten children, two of whom had died by the age of two. Matti was a farmer and general laborer at a time when obtaining any sort of steady income in Finland was incredibly challenging, and the family struggled to make ends meet on less than $300 per year. He boarded the *Titanic* with three acquaintances, on their way to Sudbury, Canada, with the goal of obtaining steadier and more lucrative income. All four of the Finnish friends perished when the *Titanic* went down. This tragedy left Maria alone to care for her nine surviving children plus a newborn son, Eino Aatos, who entered the world on November 12, 1912. Filing a suit against the White Star Line for manslaughter and grave neglect, she was awarded approximately $1400 early in 1913.

Cecelia Banfield was thrilled that she became pregnant when her husband, Frederick, returned to their home in Plymouth for a three-month holiday. He had been in America most of their married life, working as a mining engineer in Nevada, moving there less than one month after their September 22, 1907, wedding. Since the couple had already lost a child in infancy, their prayerful hope was that this next child would enjoy a full life. In April Fred headed off to the *Titanic* with two others from the area, intending to apply their mining skills near Houghton, Michigan, at the Isle Royale Copper Mine. All three of these second class passengers died when the *Titanic* sank, and Cecelia was left alone to raise her son Frederick James Jr., who was born on November 15, 1912. Fate smiled on this child, as he lived to the ripe old age of 89.

Winifred and Sidney Siebert married in 1907, and two years later suffered the tragic loss of their first daughter, who passed after only a few weeks. A second daughter, born in 1910, was far healthier, and the Sieberts were looking forward to increasing their family. It is not clear whether Sidney knew that another child was on the way when he departed for Belfast, where he was part of the crew of the *Titanic* during the transfer of the ship to Southampton. He continued on as a bedroom steward, serving along with his brother-in-law, Charles Savage. Charles survived the sinking, but the debilitating impact of the icy water was too much for Sidney. He was pulled from the Atlantic into lifeboat 4, but died during the night. Winifred gave birth to another daughter, Constance Winifred, on November 18 and raised both girls on her own, never remarrying.

When Margaret Dennison married William McQuillan on September 11, 1906, their first-born daughter was nearly 17 months old. Sadly, the girl passed away in July of 1910, suffering from complications related to convulsions that wracked her body. By then Margaret and William also had a one-year-old daughter, with another son added to the family a year later. The McQuillans lived in Belfast, where William boarded the ship as a fireman, initially as part of the delivery team involved in transferring the ship to Southampton. His widow Margaret gave birth to Gertrude Wilhelmina on November 20. Sadly, on April 3, 1919, 38-year-old Margaret encountered complications from another pregnancy, and she lost her life.

Ethel Saccaggi was English by birth but married Italian immigrant Giovanni Saccaggi in 1909. He boarded the *Titanic* as an assistant waiter, excited by the prospect of serving on the maiden voyage, but in the end he became a posthumous father to Beatrice Grace on November 29. Ethel raised her baby and a son who had been born three years earlier, never remarrying.

*Students leaving Southampton's Northern School after the day's lessons. One hundred pupils at that school lost one or more relatives when the* Titanic *foundered (Source:* The Independent *and* The Mirror)

Madge and Samuel "Sidney" Seduary married late in 1911, and when he left Southampton as the second third class steward aboard the *Titanic,* it is feasible that they did not yet know that Madge was with child. After his death when the ship sank, Madge received Sidney's personal items discovered on his body when it was recovered by the *Mackay-Bennett,* but these seemed trivial in comparison to the promise of his unborn child. Sidney Jr. was born sometime during November 1912, and Madge cared for him lovingly on her own until 1921. At that time she married her deceased husband's brother, Arthur, and they would go on to add another boy to the family five years later.

## December

Emily Ackerman was raising five children, with much of the responsibility falling on her own shoulders because her husband, Joseph, was away at sea for long stretches of time. A major tragedy during their 14 years of marriage was the loss of one other child when she was just an infant. Joseph left Southampton to board the *Titanic* as assistant pantryman steward, and it seemed like yet another routine departure. When the ship sank he lost his life as did his brother, Albert, a third class steward. Emily gave birth to a son on December 16, 1912, naming him Joseph Francis after his father.

Rose and George Evans got married early in 1912. When he left to join the *Titanic* crew for the delivery trip from Belfast and then as the first class saloon steward for the maiden voyage, the couple would not have known that Rose was in a delicate condition. Audrey Isobel was born on December 24, 1912. Rose would be widowed a second time when her second husband of seven years died in 1923.

Theodora Andersen already had two young sons living with her in Bergen, Norway, in 1912. Her husband, Albert, was often away from home for long stretches of time working on Norwegian ships as a trimmer, fireman, and donkeyman over the years. He eventually worked his way up to a more prestigious position by studying to become a ship's engineer, and he was on his way to New York to join the crew of the *Edda* as second engineer. He was lost at sea when the *Titanic* went down, making the situation particular difficult for the family as he was the sole source of income. The birth of Albertha Theodora the following December apparently brought her mother no comfort. Theodora's mental health was compromised, and she suffered a breakdown, lost her battle with alcohol, and neglected the care of her own children. She died in 1915, and the three children were then raised by Albert's family.

When Emma Maybery developed a serious eye condition in 1911 while she and her husband Frank were living in Moose Jaw, Saskatchewan, they decided the best course of action would be for her to return to England for the medical care she needed. The Mayberys settled in Weston-super-mare, Sussex, along with their two daughters, Joyce and Ruth. Early in 1912 Frank needed to return to Moose Jaw to temporarily help with the real estate business that he operated there, along with his brothers. Passage on the *Titanic* proved fatal to Frank when the ship went down, not knowing that Emma would give birth to the couple's third daughter, Nancy, the following December.

## Final Quarter of 1912

Mabel Abrams's married life was far from easy. Her husband, William Abrams, was a former seaman who had been in jail during 1911. In fact, Mabel's own father was imprisoned in a poorhouse at the same time, and she ended up listing her marital status as being single while working as a housemaid at Bournemouth's Grand Hotel. Upon his release, William decided to go back to sea and would eventually secure a position as a fireman on the *Titanic.* He was lost when the ship went down, and Mabel faced the prospect of her pregnancy alone. Her daughter, Nancy, was born late in 1912 but passed away before she reached the age of three. Mabel remarried in 1916, but was widowed three years later. She married for the third time later that same year and gave birth to another daughter.

Eleanor Early married Arthur Morgan late in 1908, and their son, who was born the next year, died in August 1911 at two years of age. Of course, they were grief-stricken. It is not certain whether Arthur knew that Eleanor was in a family way when he signed on as a trimmer for the *Titanic,* his first time serving on a ship, but how excited he would have been. Unfortunately, he died when the ship sank, and Eleanor was alone when daughter Mary was born in the final months of 1912. Tragic fate was not yet finished with the Morgan family, as Eleanor passed away shortly afterwards.

Laura and William Simmons became the parents of two daughters during the first four years of their marriage, and over the next eight years it may very well have seemed that their family was complete. However, when William signed on to the *Titanic* as a passage cook, a third daughter was on her way. Theresa was born during the last quarter of 1912, and Laura lovingly raised all three girls on her own, never remarrying.

Elizabeth and William Small were married in 1905 and definitely had two daughters of their own, one born in 1904 and the other in 1911. Confusingly, the 1911 census listing shows them as having been married for 16 years and having given birth to eight children, of whom three survived. While it is difficult to fully account for this disparity, it is pertinent to note that Elizabeth was a widow from an earlier marriage that took place in 1896 and was the mother of a son from that union. William lost his life as a leading fireman when he was aboard the *Titanic*. He became the father of William Jr. late in 1912, whom Elizabeth named in memory of her beloved husband.

Rosina Thomas had two loved ones aboard the *Titanic,* her husband Joseph Thomas and her brother Charles Barrow. It is unlikely that the two men spent much, if any, time together on the ship as Joseph was a fireman and Charles was an assistant butcher. Both Joseph and Charles perished when the *Titanic* went down, a tragic blow to Rosina. She was left behind in

Southampton, raising her son who was born in 1910 and awaiting the birth of another child late in the year, naming him William Charles Thomas. She raised both boys on her own, not remarrying until 1930, after which she had at least one more child.

## Other 1912 Births

During the first seven years after May and Henry Ashe were married they added two sons and a daughter to their family. May had grown accustomed to Henry being away at sea during that time, working on a variety of White Star liners as a waiter. He boarded the *Titanic* as the third class glory hole steward. Widowed as a result of the *Titanic* disaster, May gave birth to a daughter later in the year and named her Gladys May. The girl passed away in 1917, and both the father and the daughter he never met were remembered together on the family tombstone. The other three children were raised to adulthood by their caring mother, who never remarried in the years that followed.

When Harriet Heather married Albert Coleman in 1910, he was already a seasoned victualing crew member, having first gone to sea half his lifetime ago when he was only 13, working in a variety of positions. He served as the first class saloon steward on the *Titanic,* and with his death when the ship went down he left behind his wife, a son born in 1911, and another on the way whom the mother would name George. Harriet remained unmarried afterwards.

A son was born to Ada and Alan Franklin in June of 1911, the same year in which the couple married. Alan was aboard the *Titanic* as a second class saloon steward and became a posthumous father to a daughter named Blanche by year's end. Little is known about Ada's life afterwards, although some evidence suggests she married once again in 1913.

Bridget Delia McGillicuddy married Henry Hart in July of 1911. At the time they were both living in Massachusetts, a popular state for Irish emigrants to settle when they left the Emerald Isle. Eleven days later on August 10 they boarded the *Cymric* and headed to Killorglin in County Kerry, where Delia still had family. Income was tight, so Henry decided to head back to Massachusetts and seek a position as a general laborer. His plans to travel across the Atlantic on the *Celtic* were stalled by the coal strike, so he boarded the *Titanic* instead. Delia remained behind, and gave birth to a boy later in the year, naming him after his deceased father. It is generally believed that she and her son remained in County Kerry afterwards.

Janet "Jennie" Hamilton Latimer had grown accustomed to the responsibilities of raising her three sons while her husband was away at sea. When she married Andrew Latimer in 1902, he had been a widower of three years and already had three other children, ranging in age from fourteen to twenty. He and Jennie started raising a new round of children after 1905. Boarding the *Titanic* as chief steward, a well-paid position, he would never return, nor would Jennie's younger brother, assistant smoke steward Ernest Hamilton. With Andrew's death, Jennie was on her own as she awaited the birth of her fourth child and first daughter. She named the girl Janet Hamilton, which had been her own maiden name. Janet Latimer remained unmarried, raised her children, and dealt with the hardship of the death of her youngest son in 1921 when he was only ten years old.

Both Constance and Alfred Rowe were English, although Alfred was actually born in Peru, the son of English citizens. Constance and Alfred married rather late in life. At the time of their 1901 wedding, she was 36 and he was 48, which made blessings of a growing family particularly special. While one son died while still an infant, their daughter and two other sons were in good health. Because Alfred's parents had left Peru and settled in Texas where they purchased extensive ranchland, he and Constance settled there for some time. Then in 1910 they returned to the United Kingdom and made their home in Crabwall, Cheshire. Alfred lost his life on the *Titanic*, which he had boarded for a trip back to Texas to meet with the manager of his land holdings. Later in the year Constance gave birth to another son, Alfred Kingsley, raising their four children to adulthood on her own.

Georgina Beatrice Ryan was in a family way when her husband, Thomas, boarded the *Titanic* as a third class steward. She gave birth to a daughter, Gladys, in the months that followed, but the young girl would pass away by year's end. Beatrice continued raising their other two daughters, who were then aged four and two, and she remarried in 1916.

# Sources

## Introduction

Behe, George M. *The Carpathia and the Titanic: Rescue at Sea.* Self-published: www.lulu.com, 2011.

"Carpathia's Role in Titanic's Rescue." *The Maritime Executive,* May 31, 2015. https://www.maritime-executive.com/article/carpathias-role-in-titanic-rescue.

"Master Philip Aks." *Encyclopedia Titanica,* 2018. https://www.encyclopedia-titanica.org/titanic-survivor/frank-philip-aks.html.

"Miss Elizabeth Gladys Millvina Dean." *Encyclopedia Titanica,* 2018. https://www.encyclopedia-titanica.org/titanic-survivor/millvina-dean.html.

"Miss Ruth Elizabeth Becker." *Encyclopedia Titanica,* 2018. https://www.encyclopedia-titanica.org/titanic-survivor/ruth-elizabeth-becker.html.

"Mr. John Borland Thayer." *Encyclopedia Titanica,* 2018. https://www.encyclopedia-titanica.org/titanic-survivor/john-borland-thayer-jr.html.

"Mrs. Madeleine Talmadge Astor." *Encyclopedia Titanica,* 2018. https://www.encyclopedia-titanica.org/titanic-survivor/madeleine-talmage-astor.html.

"Mrs. Weisz on the Titanic." *Encyclopedia Titanica,* 2018. https://www.encyclopedia-titanica.org/mrs-weisz-carpathia.html.

"On Board the Carpathia." *The Times,* April 20, 1912. Quoted in https://www.encyclopedia-titanica.org/on-board-carpathia.html, July 4, 2007.

"Ruth Elizabeth Becker Blanchard." *Angelfire,* n.d. http://www.angelfire.com/biz6/RuthBeckerBlanchard/story.html.

Stringer, Craig. "RMS Carpathia: Out of the Dark of the Dawn." *Encyclopedia Titanica,* 2012. https://www.encyclopedia-titanica.org/out-of-the-dark-of-the-dawn-rms-carpathia-craig-stringer.html.

## The Birth of the *Titanic*

"Arrol Gantry." Titanic Fandom, 2017. https://titanic.fandom.com/wiki/Arrol_Gantry.

Beveridge, Bruce, Scott Andrews, Steve Hall, and Daniel Klistorner. *Titanic: The Ship Magnificent,* Volume One: Design & Construction. Edited by Art Braunschweiger. Chalford, Stroud, Gloucestershire: The History Press Limited, 2008.

Cox, Frank. "The Titanic's First Victim." Encyclopedia Titanica, May 15, 1912. https://www.encyclopedia-titanica.org/the-titanics-first-victim.html.

Cox, Frank. "The Untimely Death of James Dobbin: Shipwright." Encyclopedia Titanic, May 23, 1912. https://www.encyclopedia-titanica.org/the-untimely-death-of-james-dobbin-shipwright.html.

"Deaths of Shipyard Workers." *Encyclopedia Titanica*, 2019. https://www.encyclopedia-titanica.org/deaths-of-shipyard-workers.html.

Eaton, John P. and Charles A. Haas. *Titanic: Triumph and Tragedy*, 2nd ed. New York: W. W. Norton & Company, 1994.

Fowler, David. "Titanic Launch." *Titanic Facts,* 2019. https://titanicfacts.net/titanic-launch/.

Green, Rod. *Building the Titanic.* London: Carlton Books Limited, 2005.

"Launch of the Titanic." *The Belfast Newsletter*, June 1, 1911. http://www.irelandseye.com/titanic/launch.htm.

Louden-Brown, Paul. "The Man Who Launched the Titanic." Titanic Belfast, 2019. https://titanicbelfast.com/discover/titanic-stories/who-launched-titanic/.

Louden-Brown, Paul. "Who Really Designed Titanic?" Titanic Belfast, 2019. https://titanicbelfast.com/discover/titanic-stories/who-really-designed-titanic.aspx.

McCaughan, Michael. *The Birth of the Titanic.* Montreal: McGill – Queen's University Press, 1998.

McCluskie, Tom. *Harland & Wolff: Designs from the Shipbuilding Empire.* London: PRC Publishing, Ltd., 1998.

"Mr. William Henry Marsh Parr." *Encyclopedia Titanica,* 2019. https://www.encyclopedia-titanica.org/titanic-victim/william-henry-marsh-parr.html.

"Preparing Titanic's Slipway." National Museums Northern Ireland, 2019. http://test.nmni.com/Design-Build/Drawing-Office-to-Slipway/Preparing-Titanics-slipway-(2).html.

"RMS Titanic – Coal Bunkers." Super Ships World, 2019. http://www.supershipsworld.com/white-star-line/rms-titanic/orlopdeck/coal-bunkers.

"RMS Titanic – Ship of Dreams." Titanic and Company, 2006. http://www.titanicandco.com/index.html.

"Testimony of Alexander Carlisle." *Titanic Inquiry Project,* as taken from the British Wreck Commissioner's Inquiry, June 10, 1912. https://www.titanicinquiry.org/BOTInq/BOTInq20Carlisle01.php.

"Titanic: Building the Largest Moving Object in History." Ultimate Titanic, 2019. https://www.ultimatetitanic.com/construction/.

## Conception

### Ada Julia Elizabeth Bone Doling

Hamilton, Keith. "Titanic's News: One Family's Loss at Sea." *Southern Daily Echo,* September 30, 2009. Quoted in http://www2.newsquest.co.uk/hampshire/southampton/titanic/SOTON_TITANIC_NEWS52.html.

"Miss Elsie Doling." *Encyclopedia Titanica,* 2018. https://www.encyclopedia-titanica.org/titanic-survivor/elsie-doling.html.

"Mr. Edwin Charles Wheeler." *Encyclopedia Titanica,* 2018. https://www.encyclopedia-titanica.org/titanic-victim/edwin-charles-fred-wheeler.html.

"Mr. Henry Price Hodges." *Encyclopedia Titanica,* 2018. https://www.encyclopedia-titanica.org/titanic-victim/henry-price-hodges.html.

"Mrs. Ada Julia Elizabeth Doling." *Encyclopedia Titanica,* 2018. https://www.encyclopedia-titanica.org/titanic-survivor/ada-doling.html.

"Second Class Passengers." *Signature Theater, 2018.* https://www.sigtheatre.org/titanicticket/second-class#MrsAdaJuliaElizabethDoling.

"Titanic Passengers Promenading on the Boat Deck." *Encyclopedia Titanica,* January 10, 2012. https://www.encyclopedia-titanica.org/titanic-passengers-promenading-on-the-boat-deck-20047.html.

## Ethel Louisa Clarke Beane

"Ethel Beane, Who Survived Titanic Sinking, Dead at 90." *New York Times,* September 20, 1983. Quoted in https://www.encyclopedia-titanica.org/ethel-beane-who-survived-titanic-sinking-dead-at-90.html, July 30, 2004.

Frawley, Margaret. "Sinking of Titanic Still Horror to Couple Honeymooning on Ship." *Rochester Democrat and Chronicle,* April 15, 1931. Quoted in https://www.encyclopedia-titanica.org/sinking-titanic-still-horror-couple-honeymooning-ship.html, August 28, 2013.

"Mr. Edward Beane." *Encyclopedia Titanica,* 2018. https://www.encyclopedia-titanica.org/titanic-survivor/edward-beane.html.

"Mrs. Ethel Louisa Beane." *Encyclopedia Titanica,* 2018. https://www.encyclopedia-titanica.org/titanic-survivor/ethel-beane.html.

Paul, Gill. *Titanic Love Stories.* Lewes, East Sussex, United Kingdom: Ivy Press, 2011.

"Titanic Survivor Ethel Beane Dies in Nursing Home." *Rochester Democrat and Chronicle,* September 17, 1983. Quoted in https://www.encyclopedia-titanica.org/titanic-survivor/ethel-beane.html, August 28, 2003.

Wirgau, Peggy. "Mysterious Rescue – Titanic Honeymoons, Part X," May 26, 2015. https://peggywirgau.com/2015/05/06/mysterious-rescue-titanic-honeymoons-part-x/.

"Women Work Hard for Rescued Folk." *New York Times,* April 21, 1912. Quoted in https://www.encyclopedia-titanica.org/women-work-hard-for-rescued-folk.html, July 30, 2004.

## Kate Florence Phillips

Bracken, Robert and Michael Findlay. "Titanic's Very Youngest Survivors." *Voyage* 27, (Winter 1998): 155.

"Former Residents of Worcester Drown." *Berrow's Journal,* April 20, 1912. Quoted in P. B. Lound, *RMS Titanic: Made in the Midlands,* Stroud, Gloucester, UK: The History Press, 2017.

Lound, P. B. *RMS Titanic: Made in the Midlands.* Stroud, Gloucester, UK: The History Press, 2017.

"Miss Kate Florence Phillips." *Encyclopedia Titanica,* 2018. https://www.encyclopedia-titanica.org/titanic-survivor/kate-phillips.html.

"Mr. Henry Samuel Morely." *Encyclopedia Titanica,* 2018. https://www.encyclopedia-titanica.org/titanic-victim/henry-samuel-morley.html.

Walker, Ellen Marie. Foreword. *Titanic,* by John Hodges, New York: Vantage Press, Inc., 1999.

## First Trimester

## Juliette Marie Louise Lafargue Laroche

"French Passengers Embarking in Cherbourg." *La Cité de la Mer*, n.d. https://cherbourg-titanic.com/en/2011/11/les-francais-embarques-a-cherbourg/.

Geller, Judith B. *Titanic: Women and Children First.* New York: W. W. Norton, 1998.

"Joseph Laroche – The Only Black Man to Die on the Titanic." *Kreol*, November 26, 2015. https://kreolmagazine.com/culture/history-and-culture/joseph-laroche-the-only-black-man-to-die-on-the-titanic-2/#.XBAXDmhKjQB.

Laroche, Juliette. Letter to her father, April 11,1912. Quoted in George Behe, *On Board RMS Titanic: Memories of the Maiden Voyage*, Raleigh, North Carolina: Lulu.com Press, 2011.

"Le Chicago a Ramané Hier au Havre des Survivants du Titanic." *Excelsior*, May 2, 1912. Quoted in https://www.encyclopedia-titanica.org/le-chicago-ramene-hier-au-havre-des-survivants-du-titanic.html.

"Miss Louise Laroche." *Titanic Historical Society*, n.d. https://titanichistoricalsociety.org/miss-louise-laroche/.

"Mr. Joseph Philippe Lemercier Laroche." *Encyclopedia Titanica*, 2018. https://www.encyclopedia-titanica.org/titanic-victim/joseph-laroche.html.

"Mrs. Juliette Marie Louise Laroche." *Encyclopedia Titanica*, 2018. https://www.encyclopedia-titanica.org/titanic-survivor/juliette-laroche.html.

"Mrs. Weisz on the Carpathia." *Encyclopedia Titanica*, 2018. https://www.encyclopedia-titanica.org/mrs-weisz-carpathia.html.

"Titanic's Black Passenger: Creating Historical Fiction from Historical Fact." *Blackpast*, 2017. https://blackpast.org/perspectives/titanic-s-black-passenger-creating-historical-fiction-historical-fact.

"Une Rescapée du Titanic." *Le Matin*, May 3, 1912. Quoted in https://www.encyclopedia-titanica.org/une-rescapee-du-titanic.html.

## Adele Hakim Nasser (Adāl Hakīm Naṣr Allāh)

Elias, Leila Salloum. *The Dream and Then the Nightmare: The Syrians Who Boarded the Titanic*. Damascus, Syria: Atlas for Publishing and Distribution, 2010.

Moses, John G. *From Mt. Lebanon to the 'Sea of Darkness.* Self-Published, T. C. Peteres Printing Company, 2000.

"Mr. Niqūlā Khalīl Naṣr Allāh." *Encyclopedia Titanica,* 2018. https://www.encyclopedia-titanica.org/titanic-victim/nicholas-nasser.html.

"Mrs. Adāl Naṣr Allāh." *Encyclopedia Titanica,* 2018. https://www.encyclopedia-titanica.org/titanic-survivor/adele-nasser.html.

Nasser, Adele. Letter to Madeleine Astor, 1912 . Quoted from "Mrs. Nasrallah Writes to Mrs. Astor," *Fort Wayne News,* April 19, 1912 (date doubtful), as recorded in *Encyclopedia Titanica,* January 22, 2015, https://www.encyclopedia-titanica.org/mrs-nasrallah-writes-to-mrs-astor.html.

Pierce, Nicola. *Titanic: True Stories of Her Passengers, Crew and Legacy.* Dublin: The O'Brien Press Ltd., 2018.

## Helen Margaret Walton Bishop

"Bishops Arrive Home and Relate Many Things about Titanic Not Told Before." *Dowagiac Daily News,* May 10, 1912. https://www.encyclopedia-titanica.org/bishops-arrive-home-and-relate-titanic-not-before-told.html.

"Bishops Go Before Senate Board of Inquiry to Give Story of Titanic Disaster." *Dowagiac Daily News,* April 26, 1912. https://www.encyclopedia-titanica.org/bishops-go-senate-board-inquiry-give-story-titanic-disaster.html.

"Carpathia Lands in New York City and the Bishops Wire They're Safe." *Dowagiac Daily News,* April 19, 1912. https://www.encyclopedia-titanica.org/carpathia-lands-new-york-city-and-bishops-wire-theyre-safe.html.

Geller, Judith B. *Titanic: Women and Children First.* New York: W. W. Norton, 1998.

"Mr. and Mrs. Bishop Give First Authentic Interview Concerning Titantic [sic] Disaster. *Dowagiac Daily News,* April 20, 1912. https://www.encyclopedia-titanica.org/bishop-interview-concerning-titanic-disaster.html.

"Mr. Dickinson H. Bishop." *Encyclopedia Titanica,* 2018. https://www.encyclopedia-titanica.org/titanic-survivor/dickinson-bishop.html.

"Mrs. Helen Margaret Bishop." *Encyclopedia Titanica,* 2018. https://www.encyclopedia-titanica.org/titanic-survivor/helen-bishop.html.

*Titanic Disaster: Hearings.* Washington, D.C.: Government Printing Office, 1912.

Young, Matt. "The Tragic Story of Helen Bishop." *News.com.au,* April 15, 2018. https://www.news.com.au/lifestyle/real-life/news-life/the-tragic-story-of-helen-bishop/news-story/24df0be3367fcdfae3cb9834e186f5ca.

## Mary Eloise Hughes Smith

Bracken, Robert and Michael Findlay. "Titanic's Very Youngest Survivors." *Voyage* 27, (Winter 1998): 154.

"Daughter of Representative Hughes Weds." *Washington Post,* February 9, 1912. https://www.encyclopedia-titanica.org/daughter-of-representative-hughes-weds.html.

"Debutante, Bride, Widow, Mother and All in the Course of One Short Year." *Waterloo Times-Tribune,* November 22, 1912. https://www.encyclopedia-titanica.org/debutante-bride-widow-mother-and-all-in-course-of-one-short-year.html.

"Father of Mrs. Smith's Boy Went Down with the Ship." *New York Tribune,* December 1, 1912. https://www.encyclopedia-titanica.org/father-of-mrs-smiths-boy-went-down-with-ship.html.

Geller, Judith B. *Titanic: Women and Children First.* New York: W. W. Norton, 1998.

"Ismay Condemned for Taking Boat." *Washington Times,* April 19, 1912. https://www.encyclopedia-titanica.org/ismay-condemned-for-taking-boat.html.

"Mr. Lucian P. Smith." *Encyclopedia Titanica,* 2018. https://www.encyclopedia-titanica.org/titanic-victim/lucian-philip-smith.html.

"Mrs. Eloise Hughes Smith and Her Son." *New York Tribune,* April 15, 1913. https://www.encyclopedia-titanica.org/titanic-survivor-eloise-hughes-smith-and-her-son-lucien.html.

"Mrs. Mary Eloise Smith." *Encyclopedia Titanica,* 2018. https://www.encyclopedia-titanica.org/titanic-survivor/mary-eloise-smith.html.

"Second Titanic Baby Born." *Chicago Examiner,* December1, 1912. https://www.encyclopedia-titanica.org/second-titanic-baby-born.html.

*Titanic Disaster: Hearings.* Washington, D.C.: Government Printing Office, 1912.

Whited, Brandon. "The Trials of Mary Eloise Smith." *Encyclopedia Titania,* August 7, 2015. https://www.encyclopedia-titanica.org/trials-eloise-hughes-smith.html.

## Catherine McHugh Bourke

"Loss of the Titanic." *Connught Telegraph,* May 25, 1912. https://www.encyclopedia-titanica.org/loss-titanic.html.

"Miss Catherine McGowan." *Encyclopedia Titanica,* 2019. https://www.encyclopedia-titanica.org/titanic-victim/catherine-mcgowan.html.

Molony, Senan. *The Irish Aboard Titanic.* Dublin, Ireland: Wolfhound Press, 2000.

"Mr. John Bourke." *Encyclopedia Titanica,* 2018. https://www.encyclopedia-titanica.org/titanic-victim/john-bourke.html.

"Mrs. Catherine Bourke." *Encyclopedia Titanica,* 2018. https://www.encyclopedia-titanica.org/titanic-victim/catherine-bourke.html.

Rainey, Sarah. "The Village Still Haunted by Its Titanic Loss." *The Telegraph,* April 11, 1912. https://www.telegraph.co.uk/history/titanic-anniversary/9195690/The-village-still-haunted-by-its-Titanic-loss.html.

"Titanic - Mayo Connection." *Addergoole Titanic Society,* 2019. http://addergoole-titanic.com/contentPage/164855/mayo_connection.

"Titanic – The Addergoole 14." *Geni.com,* 2019. https://www.geni.com/projects/Titanic-The-Addergoole-14/11057.

## Argene Genevesi del Carlo

"Argene del Carlo." *Geni,* 2019. https://www.geni.com/people/Argene-del-Carlo/6000000015882327347.

"Bride Walks Beside Casket of Husband." Unidentified newspaper, 1912. https://www.encyclopedia-titanica.org/bride-walks-beside-casket-of-husband.html.

"Bride Who Was Rescued from Death Finds She Is a Destitute Widow." *New York Herald,* April 22, 1912. https://www.encyclopedia-titanica.org/bride-rescued-from-death-finds-she-is-destitute-widow.html.

"Certificato di Nascita (Birth Certificate of Salvata del Carlo)." *Encyclopedia Titanica,* 2018. https://www.encyclopedia-titanica.org/certificato-di-nascita-birth-certificate-salvata-del-carlo.html.

"È Morta l'Ultima Superstite del Titanic." *Il Tirreno, Edizione Lucca,* October 31, 2008. http://iltirreno.gelocal.it/lucca/cronaca/2008/10/31/news/e-morta-l-ultima-superstite-del-titanic-1.1714952?refresh_ce.

"Mr. Philip Aks." *Encyclopedia Titanica,* 2018. https://www.encyclopedia-titanica.org/titanic-survivor/frank-philip-aks.html.

"Mr. Sebastiano Del Carlo." *Encyclopedia Titanica,* 2018. https://www.encyclopedia-titanica.org/titanic-victim/sebastiano-del-carlo.html.

"Mrs. Argene Del Carlo." *Encyclopedia Titanica,* 2018. https://www.encyclopedia-titanica.org/titanic-survivor/argene-del-carlo.html.

## Second Trimester

### Mary Graham Carmichael Farquharson Marvin

Bracken, Robert and Michael Findlay. "Titanic's Very Youngest Survivors." *Voyage* 27, (Winter 1998): 154.

Herbert, Stephen. "Henry Norton ('Harry') Marvin." *Who's Who of the Victorian Cinema,* 2019. http://www.victorian-cinema.net/harrymarvin.

"Marriage of Daniel Marvin and Mary Farquharson." *New York Times,* March 17, 1912. https://www.encyclopedia-titanica.org/marriage-daniel-marvin-and-mary-farquharson.html.

"Mr. Daniel Warner Marvin." *Encyclopedia Titanica,* 2018. https://www.encyclopedia-titanica.org/titanic-victim/daniel-warner-marvin.html.

"Mrs. Mary Graham Carmichael Marvin." *Encyclopedia Titanica,* 2018. https://www.encyclopedia-titanica.org/titanic-survivor/mary-marvin.html.

"Mrs. W. D. Marvin." *The Times,* April 20, 1912. https://www.encyclopedia-titanica.org/marvin-prostrated.html.

Paul, Gill. *Titanic Love Stories.* Lewes, East Sussex, United Kingdom: Ivy Press, 2011.

"Young Couple Wed Twice." *Newspaper unknown,* April 5, 1912.

### Ada Mary Worth West

Jones, Laetitia Latham. "The Titanic's Cornish Connection," 2019. https://laetitialathamjones.com/2018/08/03/the-titanics-cornish-connection/.

"Mr. Edwy Arthur West." *Encyclopedia Titanica,* 2018. https://www.encyclopedia-titanica.org/titanic-victim/edwy-arthur-west.html.

"Mrs. Ada Mary West." *Encyclopedia Titanica,* 2018. https://www.encyclopedia-titanica.org/titanic-survivor/ada-mary-west.html.

Trewhela, Lee. *Cornwall Live,* March 14, 2018. *https://www.cornwalllive.com/whats-on/heroic-tragic-cowardly-tales-58-1339399.*

Wardrop, Murray. "Father Brought Family Hot Milk before Perishing on Titanic." *The Telegraph,* March 26, 2009. https://www.telegraph.co.uk/news/5052221/Father-brought-family-hot-milk-before-perishing-on-Titanic.html.

## Johanna "Hannah" Godfrey O'Brien

Devlin, Martina. "My Family's Dark Secret and the Legend of the Titanic." *Belfast Telegraph Digital,* September 5, 2007. https://www.belfasttelegraph.co.uk/life/my-familys-dark-secret-and-the-legend-of-titanic-28062520.html.

Molony, Senan. *The Irish Aboard Titanic*. Dublin, Ireland: Wolfhound Press, 2000.

"Mr. Thomas O'Brien." *Encyclopedia Titanica,* 2018. https://www.encyclopedia-titanica.org/titanic-victim/thomas-obrien.html.

"Mrs. Hannah O'Brien." *Encyclopedia Titanica,* 2018. https://www.encyclopedia-titanica.org/titanic-survivor/johanna-hannah-obrien.html.

"Thomas and Hannah O'Brien." *Titanic Experience Cobh,* January 31, 2018. http://www.titanicexperiencecobh.ie/2018/01/31/thomas-hannah-obrien/.

## Madeleine Talmage Force Astor

"Americans in Rome." *New York Times,* April 7, 1912. https://www.encyclopedia-titanica.org/rome-society.html.

"Astor Gave up Lifeboat Seat." *Brooklyn Daily Eagle,* April 19, 1912. https://www.encyclopedia-titanica.org/astor-gave-up-lifeboat-seat.html.

"Astor Offers $1000 as Wedding Fee." *New York Times,* September 7, 1911. https://www.encyclopedia-titanica.org/astor-offers-1000-as-marriage-fee.html.

"Astors Sail for Egypt." *New York Tribune,* January 25, 1912. https://www.encyclopedia-titanica.org/astors-sail-for-egypt-15461.html.

"Astor Wedding Date Not Set." *New York Times,* September 1, 1911. https://www.encyclopedia-titanica.org/astor-wedding-day-not-set.html.

"Astor Widows, Now Said to Be on Edge of Social Duel." *The Washington Times,* n.d. https://www.encyclopedia-titanica.org/astor-widows-now-said-to-be-on-edge-of-social-duel-18615.html.

Behe, George. *Titanic: The Return Voyage*. Morrisville, NC: Lulu Press, 2019.

"Capt. Rostron Guest of Mrs. J. J. Astor." *New York Times,* June 1,1912. https://www.encyclopedia-titanica.org/capt-rostron-guest-mrs-j-j-astor.html.

"Clerical Carpenter to Marry Col. Astor." *New York Times,* September 9, 1911. https://www.encyclopedia-titanica.org/clerical-carpenter-marry-col-astor.html.

"Col. Astor Buried in Grave beside Mother." *New York Times,* May 4, 1912. https://www.encyclopedia-titanica.org/col-astor-buried-grave-beside-mother.html.

"Col. Astor May Wed Any Day." *New York Times,* September 2, 1911. https://www.encyclopedia-titanica.org/col-astor-may-wed-any-day.html.

"Colonel Astor's Will." *The Times*, July 27, 1912. https://www.encyclopedia-titanica.org/colonel-astors-will-18207.html.

"Col. Astor to Wed Madeleine Force." *New York Times*, August 2, 1911. https://www.encyclopedia-titanica.org/col-astor-wed-madeleine-force.html.

"Col. Astor Weds Madeleine Force." *New York Times*, September 10, 1911. https://www.encyclopedia-titanica.org/col-astor-weds-madeleine-force.html.

"Colonel John Jacob Astor." *Encyclopedia Titanica*, February 3, 2019. https://www.encyclopedia-titanica.org/titanic-victim/john-jacob-astor.html.

"Criticise Pastor Who Married Astor." *New York Times*, September 11, 1911. https://www.encyclopedia-titanica.org/criticise-pastor-who-married-astor.html.

Geller, Judith B. *Titanic: Women and Children First*. New York: W. W. Norton, 1998.

Halpern, Samuel. "Keeping Track of a Maiden Voyage." *Encyclopedia Titanica*, 2019. First published in *The White Star Journal*, Titanic Historical Society, 2006. https://www.encyclopedia-titanica.org/keeping-track.html.

"Home News Gave City First News of Carpathia's Landing." *Daily Home News*, April 19, 1912. https://www.encyclopedia-titanica.org/home-news-gave-city-first-news-carpathias-landing.html.

Kaplan, Justin. *When the Astors Owned New York*. New York: Penguin Press, 2006.

Kavaler, Lucy. *The Astors: A Family Chronicle of Pomp and Power*. New York: Dodd, Mead, & Company, 1966.

"Meets Carpathia." *Oak Leaves*, April 27. 1912. https://www.encyclopedia-titanica.org/meets-carpathia.html.

"Met by Stepson." *The Daily Banner*, April 19, 1912. https://www.encyclopedia-titanica.org/met-stepson.html.

"Minister Who Wed Astor Quits Church." *New York Times*, November 8, 1911.https://www.encyclopedia-titanica.org/minister-who-wed-astor-quits-church.html.

"Mrs. Astor." *New York Times*, April 17, 1912. https://www.encyclopedia-titanica.org/mrs-astor.html.

"Mrs. Astor in No Danger." *New York Times*, April 21, 1912. https://www.encyclopedia-titanica.org/mrs-astor-ill.html.

"Mrs. Astor Is Ill, But Not Critically." *New York Times*, April 20, 1912. https://www.encyclopedia-titanica.org/mrs-astor-ill.html.

"Mrs. Astor Near Collapse at Pier." *Washington Herald*, April 19, 1912. https://www.encyclopedia-titanica.org/mrs-astor-near-collapse-at-pier.html.

"Mrs. Madeleine Talmage Astor." *Encyclopedia Titanica*, February 3, 2019. https://www.encyclopedia-titanica.org/titanic-survivor/madeleine-talmage-astor.html.

"Mrs. Nasrallah Writes to Mrs. Astor." *Fort Wayne News*, April 19, 1912. https://www.encyclopedia-titanica.org/mrs-nasrallah-writes-to-mrs-astor.html.

"Pastor is Congratulated." *New York Times*, September 8, 1911. https://www.encyclopedia-titanica.org/pastor-is-congratulated.html.

"Say Astor Wedding Is Near at Hand." *New York Times*, September 7, 1911. https://www.encyclopedia-titanica.org/say-astor-wedding-is-near-at-hand.html.

"Son for Mrs. Astor; Named for Father." *New York Times*, August 15, 1912. https://www.encyclopedia-titanica.org/son-for-mrs-astor-named-for-father.html.

"Titanic Passenger Sues." *New-York Tribune*, August 3, 1912. https://www.encyclopedia-titanica.org/titanic-passenger-sues-19141.html.

"Will Appeal to Mrs. Astor." *The Sun Times*, July 29, 1912. https://www.encyclopedia-titanica.org/will-appeal-to-mrs-astor-19135.html.

Wilson, Derek. *The Astors: The Life and Times of the Astor Dynasty 1763 – 1992*. London: Weidenfield and Nicholson, 1993.

## Third Trimester

**Marion Estelle Stauffer Kenyon**


Bracken, Robert and Michael Findlay. "Titanic's Very Youngest Survivors." *Voyage* 27, (Winter 1998): 154.

"Chicagoans Seek Kin." *Chicago Daily Journal,* April 17, 1912. https://www.encyclopedia-titanica.org/chicagoans-seeking-kin.html.

"Dr. Alice May Leader." *Encyclopedia Titanica,* 2019. https://www.encyclopedia-titanica.org/titanic-survivor/alice-leader.html.

Holman, Hannah. *Titanic Voices.* The Hill, Stroud, Gloucestershire, UK: Amberley Publishing, 2011.

Leader, Alice. Letter to Sarah Babcock, April 16,1912. Quoted in George Behe, *On Board RMS Titanic: Memories of the Maiden Voyage,* Raleigh, North Carolina: Lulu.com Press, 2011.

"Meets Carpathia." *Oak Park Oak Leaves,* April 27, 1912. https://www.encyclopedia-titanica.org/meets-carpathia.html.

"Mr. Frederick Roland Kenyon." *Encyclopedia Titanica,* 2018. https://www.encyclopedia-titanica.org/titanic-victim/frederick-kenyon.html.

"Mrs. Kenyon's Account." *Oak Park Oak Leaves,* April 27, 1912. https://www.encyclopedia-titanica.org/mrs-kenyon-account-titanic-sinking.html.

"Mrs. Margaret Welles Swift." *Encyclopedia Titanica,* 2019. https://www.encyclopedia-titanica.org/titanic-survivor/margaret-welles-swift.html.

"Mrs. Marion Estelle Kenyon." *Encyclopedia Titanica,* 2018. https://www.encyclopedia-titanica.org/titanic-survivor/marion-kenyon.html.

"Oak Park Titanic Survivor." *Chicago Daily Tribune,* April 21, 1912. https://www.encyclopedia-titanica.org/oak-park-titanic-survivor.html.

"Titanic Survivor Writes of Horror to Friend Here." *Evening Bulletin,* April 20, 1912. https://www.encyclopedia-titanica.org/titanic-survivor-writes-horror-friend-here.html.

### Mary Emma Miller Corey and Claire Bennett Karnes

Engberg, Peter. "Lost Ladies." *Encyclopedia Titanica,* January 6, 2018. https://www.encyclopedia-titanica.org/lost-ladies.html.

"Joy and Sadness Comes with News." *Cleveland Plain Dealer,* April 20, 1912. https://www.encyclopedia-titanica.org/joy-and-sadness-come-with-news.html.

Miller, Michael. "Pittsburgh Family Reveals Titanic Secret." *Pittsburgh Business Times,* June 28, 1999. https://www.bizjournals.com/pittsburgh/stories/1999/06/28/editorial2.html.

"Mrs. Claire Karnes." *Encyclopedia Titanica,* 2018. https://www.encyclopedia-titanica.org/titanic-victim/claire-karnes.html.

"Mrs. Frank Karnes Believed on Titanic." *Pittsburgh Post-Gazette,* April 18, 1912. https://www.newspapers.com/clip/10083278/mrs_frank_karnes_believed_on_titanic/.

"Mrs. Mary Emma Corey." *Encyclopedia Titanica,* 2018. https://www.encyclopedia-titanica.org/titanic-victim/mary-phyllis-elizabeth-corey.html.

### Maria Mathilda Gustafsson Backström

Björkfors, Peter. "The Finns on the Titanic." *Siirtolasiuus Institute Migration,* 1998.

Ljusglimtar, Annaevas. "Sommarstuge," August 10, 2016. https://annaevaa.wordpress.com/2012/04/14/titanic-100-ar/

"Maria Backstrom's Account." *Uusi Aura,* n.d. https://www.encyclopedia-titanica.org/maria-backstroms-account.html.

"Miss Erna Alexandria Andersson." *Encyclopedia Titanica,* 2019. https://www.encyclopedia-titanica.org/titanic-survivor/erna-andersson.html.

"Mr. Anders Vilhelm Gustafsson." *Encyclopedia Titanica,* 2019. https://www.encyclopedia-titanica.org/titanic-victim/anders-vilhelm-gustafsson.html.

"Mr. Johan Birger Gustafsson." *Encyclopedia Titanica,* 2018. https://www.encyclopedia-titanica.org/titanic-victim/johan-birger-gustafsson.html.

"Mr. Karl Backström." *Encyclopedia Titanica,* 2018. https://www.encyclopedia-titanica.org/titanic-victim/karl-alfred-backstrom.html.

"Mrs. Maria Mathilda Backström." *Encyclopedia Titanica,* 2018. https://www.encyclopedia-titanica.org/titanic-survivor/maria-mathilda-backstrom.html.

## Babies

### The *Titanic*'s Youngest Survivors

"Achievements in Public Health, 1900-1999: Healthier Mothers and Babies." *MMWR Weekly,* October 1, 1999. https://www.cdc.gov/mmwr/preview/mmwrhtml/mm4838a2.htm.

Battle, Bella. "My Grandma Was Conceived on Board the Titanic." Encyclopedia Titanica, *The Sun,* April 12, 2012. https://www.thesun.co.uk/archives/news/525797/my-grandma-was-conceived-on-board-the-titanic/.

"Certificato di Nascita (Birth Certificate of Salvata Del Carlo." Birth Certificate, 1912. https://www.encyclopedia-titanica.org/certificato-di-nascita-birth-certificate-salvata-del-carlo.html.

Crowe, Kenneth C. II. "St. Agnes Cemetery Discovers Link to Titanic." *Times Union,* June 11, 2018. https://www.timesunion.com/news/article/St-Agnes-Cemetery-discovers-its-link-to-the-12979662.php?fbclid=IwAR3QU8PtyIOlslHEyqL6Yeask1HgXjQOnb0WXzK8LJCiyY0QYqp2FAJ_0Dc.

Devlin, Martina. "My Family's Dark Secret and the Legend of the Titanic." *Belfast Telegraph*, September 5, 2007. https://www.belfasttelegraph.co.uk/life/my-familys-dark-secret-and-the-legend-of-titanic-28062520.html.

Eligon, John. "Fight for Astor Estate Mirrors Battle 50 Years Ago." *New York Times,* April 25, 2009. https://www.nytimes.com/2009/04/26/nyregion/26astor.html.

"Immigrant Ships Transcribers Guild: SS Titanic from SS Carpathia." Manifest, June 18, 1912. https://immigrantships.net/v6/1900v6/titanic19120418_14.html.

"John Jacob Astor VI." *Wikipedia,* April 5, 2019. https://en.wikipedia.org/wiki/John_Jacob_Astor_VI.

"John Jacob Astor Weds Ellen French." *New York Times,* July 1, 1934. https://www.encyclopedia-titanica.org/john-jacob-astor-weds-ellen-french.html.

Kavaler, Lucy. *The Astors: A Family Chronicle of Pomp and Power*. New York: Dodd, Mead, & Company, 1966.

"Lucian Philip Smith, II." Find a Grave, 2019. https://www.findagrave.com/memorial/181909870/lucian-philip-smith.

"Lucien P. Smith Jr Inheritance 1919." *Evening Public Ledger,* April 23, 1919. https://www.newspapers.com/clip/12014796/lucien_p_smith_jr_inheritance_1919/.

"Mrs. John J. Astor 3rd Gives Birth to Son." *New York Times,* July 20, 1935. https://www.encyclopedia-titanica.org/mrs-john-j-astor-gives-birth-son.html.

"Mrs. Latīfah al-Ba'qlīnī." Encyclopedia Titanica, 2019. https://www.encyclopedia-titanica.org/titanic-survivor/latifa-baclini.html.

Phillips, Ellen. Recollections, n.d. Quoted in "Kate Phillips' Daughter's Story (Conceived on Titanic Claim)." Encyclopedia Titanica, November 12, 2005, https://www.encyclopedia-titanica.org/ellen-phillips-story.html. Submitted by Senan Molony, assisted by the *Daily Mail* ,for article in *White Star Journal*, September 2002.

"The Rich Boy Nobody Wants." Original article posted to Encyclopedia Titanica Facebook page, March 31, 2019, by Jim Kalafus.

"Second Titanic Baby Born." *Chicago Examiner,* December 1, 1912. https://www.encyclopedia-titanica.org/second-titanic-baby-born.html.

"Son for Mrs. Astor; Named for Father." *New York Times,* August 15, 1912. https://www.encyclopedia-titanica.org/son-for-mrs-astor-named-for-father.html.

"Third Widow, Due to Titanic Wreck, Becomes a Mother." *The Washington Herald,* November 30, 1912. https://www.encyclopedia-titanica.org/-third-widow-due-to-titanic-wreck-becomes-a-mother-19202.html.

"Titanic Babies." Oocities, October 2009. http://www.oocities.org/thetitanicstop/Babies.html.

Walker, Ellen Mary. Foreword for Hodges, John Richard, *Titanic – The Story of a Maritime Tragedy, 1998. Quoted* by "Titanic – The Story of a Maritime Tragedy," *johnrichard.fast-page.org,* 2018, http://www.johnrichard.fast-page.org/titanic.html?i=2.

Whited, Brandon. "The Trials of Mary Eloise Smith." *Encyclopedia Titania,* August 7, 2015. https://www.encyclopedia-titanica.org/trials-eloise-hughes-smith.html.

"William Dick Dies; An Industrialist." *New York Times,* September 6, 1953. https://www.encyclopedia-titanica.org/william-dick-dies-an-industrialist.html.

Wilson, Derek. *The Astors: The Life and Times of the Astor Dynasty 1763 – 1992.* London: Weidenfield and Nicholson, 1993.

## Epilogue

### The Mothers' Lives after the *Titanic*

"Argene del Carlo." Geni, January 22, 2019. https://www.geni.com/people/Argene-del-Carlo/6000000015882327347, including an account originally published in *Il Tirreno,* February 19, 1998, and reprinted/translated

from
http://www.titanicdiclaudiobossi.com/Html/Biografie%20italiani_179.htm.

"Bravery of Bournemouth Husband Who Went Back to Die on Titanic." *Daily Echo,* March 26, 2009. https://www.bournemouthecho.co.uk/news/4234379.bravery-of-bournemouth-husband-who-went-back-to-die-on-titanic/.

Devlin, Martina. "My Family's Dark Secret and the Legend of the Titanic." *Belfast Telegraph Digital,* September 5, 2007. https://www.belfasttelegraph.co.uk/life/my-familys-dark-secret-and-the-legend-of-titanic-28062520.html.

Elias, Leila Salloum. *The Dream and Then the Nightmare: The Syrians Who Boarded the Titanic*. Damascus, Syria: Atlas for Publishing and Distribution, 2010.

"Eloise H. Smith Dies in Cincinnati." *Charleston Gazette,* May 4, 1940. https://www.encyclopedia-titanica.org/eloise-h-smith-dies-in-cincinnati.html.

Encyclopedia Titanica. *Encyclopedia-titanica.org,* 1996-2019. (Specific entries consulted for each of the individual survivors under consideration.)

"Ethel Beane, Who Survived the Titanic, Dead at 90." *New York Times, September 20, 1983.* https://www.encyclopedia-titanica.org/ethel-beane-who-survived-titanic-sinking-dead-at-90.html.

"Haiti History 101: The Haitian Family on the Titanic." Kreyolicious, n.d. http://kreyolicious.com/haitian-titanic-family/1290.

"Helen Bishop – Titanic First Class Passenger." Titanic Pages, 2012. https://www.titanicpages.com/1stclass/helenbishop.

"Hughes and Wright Wedding Announced." *Charleston Daily Mail,* January 12, 1930. https://www.encyclopedia-titanica.org/hughes-and-wright-wedding-announced.html.

Phillips, Ellen. Recollections, n.d. Quoted in "Kate Phillips' Daughter's Story (Conceived on Titanic Claim)." Encyclopedia Titanica, November 12, 2005, https://www.encyclopedia-titanica.org/ellen-phillips-story.html. Submitted by Senan Molony, assisted by the *Daily Mail* ,for article in *White Star Journal,* September 2002.

Kavaler, Lucy. *The Astors: A Family Chronicle of Pomp and Power*. New York: Dodd, Mead, & Company, 1966.

Ljusglimtar, Annaevas. "Sommarstuge," August 10, 2016. https://annaevaa.wordpress.com/2012/04/14/titanic-100-ar/.

"Michigan Wife Gets $100,000 Alimony." *Chicago Examiner*, January 18, 1916. https://www.encyclopedia-titanica.org/michigan-wife-gets-100000-alimony.html.

"Miss Louise Laroche." Titanic Historical Society, originally published as "A Haitian French Family Which Traveled in Second Class Aboard the Titanic," *Titanic Commutator*, 1995. https://titanichistoricalsociety.org/miss-louise-laroche/.

"Mrs. Dick Married to Fiermonte, Boxer, in Civil Ceremony in Hospital Room Here." *New York Times*, November 28, 1933. https://www.encyclopedia-titanica.org/mrs-dick-married-fiermonte-boxer-civil-ceremony-hospital-room.html.

"Mrs. Eloise Hughes Smith Reweds." *New York Times*, April 11, 1923. https://www.encyclopedia-titanica.org/mrs-eloise-hughes-smith-reweds.html.

"Mrs. John J. Astor to Marry W. K. Dick." *New York Times*, June 18, 1916. https://www.encyclopedia-titanica.org/mrs-john-j-astor-marry-w-k-dick.html.

"Mrs. Shamaley Funeral Rights Set for Friday." Unidentified El Paso Newspaper, January 21, 1970. https://www.encyclopedia-titanica.org/item-341.html.

"Revealed: How Hero Father Died on Titanic after Leaving Lifeboat to Fetch of Milk for Wife and Children." *Daily Mail Reporter*, March 25, 2009. https://www.dailymail.co.uk/news/article-164731/Revealed-How-hero-father-died-Titanic-leaving-lifeboat-fetch-flask-milk-wife-children.html.

"Smith Funeral Plans Delayed: Prominent Huntington Woman Dies; Survivor of Titanic." *Huntington Herald Dispatch*, May 9, 1940. https://www.encyclopedia-titanica.org/smititanic-survivor-smith-funeral-plans-delayed.html.

"Titanic Survivor Dying." *New York Times*, November 6, 1914. https://www.encyclopedia-titanica.org/titanic-survivor-dying.html.

"Titanic Survivor Ethel Beane Died in Nursing Home." *Rochester Democrat and Chronicle*, September 17, 1983. https://www.encyclopedia-titanica.org/titanic-survivor-ethel-beane-died-nursing-home.html.

Whited, Brandon. "The Trials of Mary Eloise Smith." *Encyclopedia Titania*, August 7, 2015. https://www.encyclopedia-titanica.org/trials-eloise-hughes-smith.html.

Wilson, Derek. *The Astors: The Life and Times of the Astor Dynasty 1763 – 1992*. London: Weidenfield and Nicholson, 1993.

Wirgau, Peggy. "Titanic's Haitian Passenger." Peggywirgau.com, March 16, 2017. https://peggywirgau.com/2017/03/16/29412/.

## Widowed Mothers and Posthumous Fathers

"Alfred G. Rowe." *Geni*, 2019. https://www.geni.com/people/Alfred-G-Rowe/6000000016197454471.

Encyclopedia Titanica. *Encyclopedia-titanica.org*, 1996-2019. (Specific entries consulted for each of the individual *Titanic* victims who became posthumous fathers.)

"Johann Law Hume Costin." *Geni*, 2019. https://www.geni.com/people/Johann-Law-Hume-Costin/6000000015997428189.

"The Unborn Babies of the Titanic." Encyclopedia Titanica, September 12, 2013. https://www.encyclopedia-titanica.org/the-unborn-babies-of-the-titanic.html.

Witter, James. Letter to Walter Lord. July 9, 1955. https://collections.rmg.co.uk/collections/objects/486186.html.

# Index

# Other Books by the Authors

The following works of juvenile fiction were co-authored by Ned W. Schillow and Dru T. Schillow:

*Titanic Hearts: Collecting Coins for a Titanic Cause*. Xlibris Corporation, 2007.

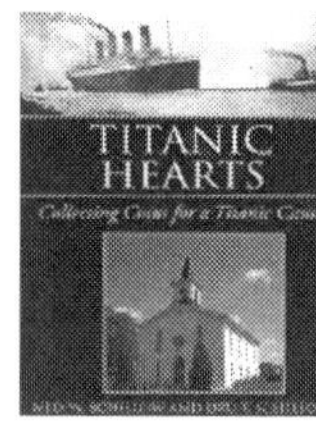

*Titanic Tears: Leaving Ireland*. Xlibris Corporation, 2007.

---

The following non-fiction books were written by Ned W. Schillow

*Lifeboats Adrift: Surviving the Titanic*. Printed by CreateSpace, 2017.

*The Titanic and Pennsylvania: The Keystone State Connection*, Volume 1. Printed by CreateSpace, 2015.

*The Titanic and Pennsylvania: Links to the Keystone State*, Volume 2. Printed by CreateSpace, 2015.

*Titanic Officers and a Gentleman.* Printed by KDP, 2018.

Printed in Great Britain
by Amazon

54494507R00160